THE
PACIFIC CREST TRAIL
EXPLORING AMERICA'S WILDERNESS TRAIL

By **MARK LARABEE** and **BARNEY SCOUT MANN**

Foreword by **CHERYL STRAYED**

RIZZOLI
NEW YORK

PACIFIC CREST TRAIL
ASSOCIATION

TO THE VISIONARIES—THE TIRELESS VOLUNTEERS, AGENCY PARTNERS,

ADVOCATES, AND DONORS—WHO TURNED THE

PACIFIC CREST TRAIL DREAM INTO REALITY AND TO ALL THOSE

TODAY WHO CHAMPION AND PROTECT IT.

CONTENTS

FOREWORD

I FIRST HEARD OF THE PACIFIC CREST TRAIL IN DECEMBER OF 1994, after a guidebook to the California section of the trail at an REI outside of Minneapolis caught my eye. I was waiting in line to pay for my purchase when I picked up the book and scanned its cover. I was only killing time. I wasn't trying to change my life. At approximately 2,650 miles long, the paragraph on the back of the book informed me, the PCT is a wilderness trail that runs the entire length of California, Oregon, and Washington, along the spine of the Sierra Nevada and Cascade mountain ranges.

Imagine that, I thought in astonishment before setting the book back onto the shelf and leaving the store.

Within days I returned and bought the book. Once I'd learned of the PCT's existence, I simply could not stop imagining it. I felt compelled to take a long walk on the trail by what can only be described as a calling. The truest voice that speaks to each of us on occasion told me I had to go. The trail would come to mean a lot of important things to me in the years that followed but, from the very first moment I held that guidebook in my hands, I understood about it perhaps the most important thing, which has remained at the core of my passionate love for the trail in the decades since that day at the REI: that the PCT was magnificent and grand and I, in all of my ordinary smallness, had only to set foot on it to be part of it.

I wasn't the first or the last person to be dazzled by the notion of a wilderness trail on which one can start *here* and end up all the way *there* only by taking one humble step at a time. In 1926, a teacher in Bellingham, Washington, named Catherine Montgomery came up with the idea of the PCT when she articulated her vision of a border-to-border trail and encouraged Joseph Hazard and his fellow mountaineers to "do something big for western America" by forging it. A few years later, Clinton C. Clarke took up the cause and spent the rest of his life working to create the trail. In the years since, as the PCT was finally granted official status as a national scenic trail in 1968 and completed in 1993, countless people—many organized under the leadership of what is now the Pacific Crest Trail Association—have advocated for and labored on the PCT.

I can't speak for any of those people and articulate what they were thinking when they decided to do what they did to make the PCT what it is today, but I imagine a good part of what drove them was that same sense of wonder I had when I first learned of the trail. My wonder deepened over the course of the 94 days I spent hiking solo on the PCT in the summer of 1995—during which I trekked approximately 1,100 miles in what turned out to be a snow-plagued, hopscotching journey from the Mojave Desert to the Columbia River— and it deepens more every time I return to the trail now. Whether one hikes an hour or several months on the PCT, it's impossible not to feel the power of the enormous possibility and also to be profoundly humbled by it.

It's a wonder, of course, that's rooted explicitly in our essential connection to nature—there are plenty of long highways that don't inspire the same awe, after all. The PCT passes through some of the most astounding landscapes in the world, from unspoiled deserts to snowy mountains, from pristine lakes to towering rocky crags, from verdant river valleys to lush rain forests. The highest peak in the continental

OPPOSITE: Tiger swallowtail butterfly on a thistle along Deep Creek, Southern California (left); wild sweet peas near Warner Springs, 100 miles north of the Mexican border (middle); a pasque flower seedpod and grasshopper near Chinook Pass, William O. Douglas Wilderness, Washington (right).

THE PACIFIC CREST TRAIL

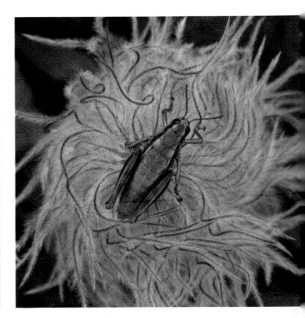

United States is just off the PCT, as is the deepest lake. The only way one can access all those landscapes and features is at foot (or hoof) speed. The PCT can't be experienced out the window of an automobile. The wildflowers growing along the way don't stream past in a blur. They are one flower and then another. The PCT demands that you know It step by step, breath by breath, sunset by sunrise by sunset by sunrise again. Which ends up mattering.

By the time I'd finished my long hike, I'd lost six toenails and gained everything that mattered. I felt the potent, accumulative force of all those sunsets and flowers in me. The great naturalist John Muir wrote of one of his many treks in the Sierra Nevada, "We are now in the mountains and the mountains are in us." When I read that line I knew he was right: the mountains will not leave us if we enter them. The PCT became—and will always be—a kind of home to me.

In an era during which we are un-wilding the planet at an astonishing pace, it's useful to remember that my experience is not singular. The reason Muir's words resonate is because they are still true. Throughout time humans have found the natural world to be a perspective-shifter, a soul re-balancer, a mind calmer, a place that reminds us that we are only one species among a vast and diverse array of them. On my long hike, I often went days without seeing another person, but I've never felt more connected to other people than I did on the PCT. Because of my time on the PCT, never again will I forget the quiet power of my own—and your own—resilience. Always I'll know that nature's redemptive beauty is present and available to all of us.

Us. When I speak of the trail that's whom I say it belongs to. But what I really mean is it exists because people who came before us decided not to ruin it and now it's our job to protect it so we, and the generations that follow us, can experience it. The PCT belongs to no one, which is of course the astounding glory of it. The PCT belongs only to its vast, beautiful, harsh, mysterious, diverse, unexpected, indifferent, tender, ever-changing, ancient self. It's wild. Like us.

INTRODUCTION

"THIS LAND IS YOUR LAND . . . " WE SANG THE SONG AS CHILDREN but it forever rings true: this land *was* made for you and me.

Out in the great landscape of western America, the Pacific Crest Trail (PCT) climbs and descends, rambles along, dives into canyons and forests, and crosses rugged mountains and arid deserts. Like life, the trail ebbs and flows. Why do we go out there? Is it the place? Is it a state of mind? What are we searching for? Are we searching at all?

Out there, along the path from Mexico to Canada, you're immersed in beauty. That's a reason to go, but you can also find beauty at the seashore. At a backcountry lake around a campfire with a tight group of friends, the day becomes a celebration. But you also can make personal connections in the city. Those reasons may fit into your narrative of why you travel the trail. They may not. They may only be part of your reason.

Some would say the answer to the eternal question—"Why?"—is simple. For others, it's more complex. Why? It doesn't really matter. You know why you go. It's personal.

Being out in nature, walking or riding your horse on the PCT, certainly is a state of mind. It's special. Iconic. You go out there and lose yourself, and, as soon as you do, you find yourself—in that perfect moment—when the clicking clock seems to pause and you forget about the often empty grind that weighs you down and you just breathe. You live.

We will talk about the creation of the path in these pages. We'll focus not on the step-by-step journey, but on the many people who have contributed to the grand idea to make and champion the great PCT. This book is largely about them and their struggle, past and ongoing. Through their stories, you'll discover why what they've done is important and why their legacy matters. It's their history and the history of a great trail.

But for now, for a brief moment, think about being there, experiencing it. It's in that context that their contributions matter most.

There's something truly liberating about carrying everything you need to survive in a backpack or a saddlebag. Spending days this way strips away so much. The sweat and dust cling to your legs, the funk embeds itself in your clothing, and yet you feel cleansed. All of life is consolidated to the basics.

You wander. You meander. Minutes are meaningless. You marvel at a tiny flower squeezing existence from desert sand. You stop to enjoy the beauty of moss-covered rocks next to a bubbling stream and understand why a Japanese gardener continues to strive for perfection that will never come. You stand at the base of a tall conifer and look up, or stare at the stars in the night sky. And you feel small, even insignificant, while at the same time, perfectly at peace.

The longer you stay out there, the more at home you feel, the more yourself you become. Perhaps because it's temporary, it's more precious. Realities are what they are, even despite our greatest wishes. You can come back. You must. You will.

The Pacific Crest Trail

2,650 miles from Mexico to Canada

The Pacific Crest Trail

Interstate Highway

US Highway

N

In the 21st century, does true adventure remain? Street-crossing signs tell you how many seconds are left before the light will change. Animals live in zoos behind bars. You can "run" through the Swiss Alps on a gym treadmill while watching the scenery go by on a glowing screen. But on the PCT, the mere act of walking or riding carries you through a looking glass that is the trail. Anything can happen: a bear appears out of nowhere; a bald eagle glides past within arm's reach while you walk a high pass; a waterfall fills the air with a roaring din, pulsing endlessly, like blood pumping through your veins.

These experiences and feelings bind us. For those who have never set foot on the trail, the possibility is electrifying. Either way, we all share the secret of the PCT, that sense of wonder. And that explains why it's here, why so many have added a verse to its grand poem.

The PCT speaks to what is best about the United States. Its story is one of men and women who moved mountains, at least the mountain of bureaucracy. With tenacity and cunning, lots of ink, will, and a little luck, Congress and President Lyndon B. Johnson officially designated the PCT as a national scenic trail with the signing of the National Trails System Act of 1968.

It was a time of great change and upheaval in America. Stewart Udall, the secretary of the interior under Presidents John F. Kennedy and Johnson, wrote about the alarm people were feeling over population growth and development, forces with the potential to permanently alter the country's relationship with the land. Udall supervised the writing of the *Trails for America* report, precursor to the National Trails System Act. The PCT is part of his legacy.

The Pacific Crest and Appalachian Trails were the country's first two national scenic trails. They are forever linked as sister trails. The PCT has nearly always been seen as the younger sibling, perhaps because the AT was so close and therefore more tangible to the folks in Washington, DC. Its progress was certainly further along. No matter. Today, there are 11 national scenic trails, part of a nationwide system that offers the best of the best in unique outdoor experiences, scenic beauty, and wilderness.

That's another of the country's great gifts to the world. The Pacific Crest Trail runs through 48 wilderness areas and six national parks. It is often called the "Wilderness Trail" because about half of its 2,650 miles runs through congressionally designated wilderness, land set aside under the powers of the 1964 Wilderness Act.

In the 1930s and 1940s, a relentless groundswell of support for the environmental movement pushed those in power to create this wilderness-saving law. Think Sierra Club, National Resources Defense Council, and the Wilderness Society. These organizations were created by people who understood that while setting aside roadless areas and national parks was all well and good, such preservation could just as easily vanish with the stroke of a pen in Washington, DC. In the face of much opposition, they acted. The Wilderness Act created the National Wilderness Preservation System and immediately set aside more than nine million acres. In the last five decades, Congress has added more than 100 million acres to this amazing land bank.

Early PCT visionaries such as Catherine Montgomery, Clinton C. Clarke, Warren Rogers, and many others pushed the idea of this long trail through California, Oregon, and Washington and never let it go, prodding the government to be its best self, to go one better than it likely would have on its own. While Clarke is considered the father of the trail, it's clear he was also the trail's first volunteer. After diving into the endless stream of letters he wrote, ideas he pitched, and maps he sent to the United States Forest Service and National Park Service in search of a federal commitment to the cause, one could conclude nothing less.

So we dedicate this book to all PCT supporters—anyone who has given time, attention, or money; anyone who has championed the cause by sticking a tool in the earth or picking up a pen; anyone who has sat through a seemingly endless meeting, pushed back against powered opposition, or made countless phone calls; any members of Congress who carried the flag or government employees who kept the trail on the front burner; and anyone who has loaded a horse with supplies, sharpened an old crosscut saw, or cooked a bottomless pot of stew for a trail crew.

You are the history of the Pacific Crest Trail and the Pacific Crest Trail Association.

It's true that most people want to do something in life to leave a mark on the world. And our culture and society seems hell-bent on recognizing those who become famous, even for the trivial, while often forgetting the world's true champions. Know this: your effort on behalf of the trail is worthy of recognition. You are likely not famous but you have left your mark. You have helped protect one of the best places on earth, one that helps define who we are and shapes our soul as a country.

The Pacific Crest Trail is, after all, a trail of the people. We can only name a few of the army of contributors in these pages. But their stories are your stories. We celebrate everyone who has helped along the way. And, most of all, we thank you.

OPPOSITE: South of Pinchot Pass in the Woods Creek drainage, Central Sierra Nevada, California.

CHAPTER ONE

ORIGINS

The Saga of the Pacific Crest Trail

Over the course of a million years, four great ice sheets invaded the North American landmass. The last retreated 10,000 years ago, laying bare a magnificent crest on the continent's west rim. Once the land was released from the icy grip, wild game returned; soft paws and sharp hooves carved faint trails up mountain flanks, uncounted threads leading toward saddles and passes. Native American tribes established themselves in the ensuing millennia, blazing paths from their villages. The Klamaths crossed the Cascades to exchange goods with the Molalas. The Paiutes breached the Sierra Nevada, thrusting through five separate gaps in the jagged teeth of the range to trade balls of salt, pine nuts, and woven baskets with the Miwoks and Yokuts, who provided shell beads, berries, acorns, and arrow shafts.

All along the western North American mountain rim, First Nation bands probed and found the navigable passes, parsing the rifts with light footprints. But these paths shared one trait: they ran east–west; they *crossed* the mountains. In *Pathway in the Sky*, Hal Roth's book about the John Muir Trail, he wrote of these early trekkers: "The object was to get across the range quickly." After all, what practical reason existed for a north–south path along saw-toothed ridges?

In 1805, near today's Bridge of the Gods, where the Pacific Crest Trail (PCT) crosses the Columbia River, the Corps of Discovery led by Meriwether Lewis and William Clark encountered bands of Klickitats and Multnomahs, two more tribes who engaged in trans-Cascade trade. This iconic PCT place name came from their joint legend—the god Sahale built a land bridge damming the Columbia. It's not hard to imagine a Multnomah or a Klickitat brave, sated on deer and huckleberries, peering south from the flank of Mount Hood toward Mount Jefferson, Three Fingered Jack, and Mount Washington and, for a moment, musing, "What if I headed south past those three giants and beyond?"

Lewis and Clark's great foray west sprang the door for American migration. In the ensuing decades, their small band turned to hundreds and then thousands in a prairie-crossing torrent. Crude canoes and foot traffic gave way to riders on horseback, then waves of emigrant prairie schooners, and finally the smoke-belching trains of the iron horse. As Manifest Destiny played out, throngs entered and exited the Cascades and the Sierra Nevada. But just as for the Klamaths and Paiutes, it was about crossing a barrier, about moving as quickly as possible through mountains on an east-to-west line. Wilderness Press, in its venerable PCT guidebook series, glibly summed up the 1800s viewpoint: "The idea of a recreational trail along the crest of these ranges probably never entered anyone's mind."

The first record of someone thinking differently was in 1884. It happened in the lowlands, a pastoral field outside Fresno, California. Theodore Solomons sat bareback on his horse, watching his uncle's Holstein cattle graze on alfalfa. Glancing over the peaceful bovine backs, Solomons saw the white-capped Sierra Nevada arrayed on the valley's east rim like an immense tapestry. At that moment he saw himself traveling it end to end, north to south. "The idea of a crest-parallel trail through the High Sierra came to me one day while herding my uncle's cattle . . . I made up my mind that somehow soon I would make that journey," he wrote in a February 1933 letter, as quoted by Roth in *Pathway in the Sky*.

Solomons was all of 13 years old. But without that youthful vow, there might not have been a Pacific Crest Trail, and quite possibly this book would never have been written. A youth's dreams began the PCT's great story.

PREVIOUS SPREAD: Bighorn Plateau, the classic gateway to Mount Whitney and the Sierra in California.
OPPOSITE: The view from the Bridge of the Gods overlooks the mighty Columbia River, which separates Oregon and Washington.

Every Native American tribe that crossed these mountain barriers had a creation story. Around countless campfires, the Shastan people told their story, *How Old Man Above Created the World*. Over glowing coals, the Chinooks told their *Origin of the Tribes*, which featured cunning Coyote and Wishpoosh, the Great Beaver.

But what is the creation story of the Pacific Crest Trail? How many times has the PCT saga been told before? Do hikers regale each other with PCT creation stories, voices rising over the campfire sparks, like the Native Americans of yore? In 1988, there was a slim 10-page pamphlet written by Larry Cash and aptly titled *A Brief History*. Five hundred copies were printed. In 1998, a doctoral dissertation covered the development of western trails through 1940. Four copies exist. The Wilderness Press guidebooks crammed the entire history of the PCT into a few pages. For a short while, the Pacific Crest Trail Association (PCTA) had an official historian—past president Larry Cash. But when Cash stepped down in 2002, he did so with two requests: first, update *A Brief History*, and second, appoint a new PCTA historian. The trail has had so many other needs and, despite good intentions, neither of Cash's requests was fulfilled. But here, in these pages, the PCTA answers Cash's call.

The Pacific Crest Trail's story is not one of gods or great beavers. Coyote tricks no one. The PCT creation story features people. And the story is this: at every juncture when the trail was threatened, every time the trail's bright light might have been snuffed out, one person, one small group, rose up and stepped into the breach. Always. A trail can only fail once. Then it is nevermore. The PCT's creation story is the story of one person, then another; of one small group and then another still; all repeated over and over.

Two Men, a Knockdown Blow, and the Big Burn

In 1899, two men sparred in a boxing ring set inside a great mansion the likes of which only existed in the Gilded Age. One was 33 and the other 41. The younger man had a six-inch height advantage, but the older packed 35 more muscled pounds on his short frame. Stripped to the waist, they traded blows. Smack! A roundhouse punch knocked the elder to the canvas. Yet they became fast friends. Much later, in his book *Breaking New Ground*, the 33-year-old wrote of that day, "I had the honor of knocking the future President of the United States off his very solid pins." Gifford Pinchot, slim as a barber's pole and more than six feet tall, was six years shy of becoming the first chief of the United States Forest Service on the day of the sparring match. Pinchot's punch had flattened his future boss, a squat fireplug of a man named Theodore Roosevelt.

One year later, 1900, Roosevelt was elected vice president and there matters might have rested. But in September 1901, President William McKinley was assassinated and Roosevelt was sworn in to the top spot. The ardent outdoor lover and his former sparring partner rolled up their sleeves and went to work.

The Forest Service was created in 1905 and Roosevelt appointed Pinchot its first chief. During the next half decade, 1905 to 1910, the landmass of designated national forests more than doubled, rising from 75 million to 172 million acres. But the agency was cash starved. Many people reviled the newfangled goal of "conservation." Indeed, Speaker of the House Joseph Cannon roared out his attitude toward the Roosevelt and Pinchot agenda: "Not one cent for scenery!" Ironically, today, when Pacific Crest Trail Association volunteers successfully lobby Congress on their annual Hike the Hill trip in February, they pass Cannon's dusty plaque in the rotunda of a congressional office building bearing his name.

In 1908, administrations changed. Pinchot had thrived under Roosevelt, but under the 300-pound William Taft, both Pinchot and the Forest Service withered. It was an open question whether the Forest Service would survive at all. Then came a potentially lethal blow. Early in 1910—10 months after taking office—Taft fired Pinchot.

That summer, in the northern Rocky Mountains, a deadly combination smoldered. The timber was drought dry and a series of thunderstorms lit 3,000 small lightning fires. On August 20, hurricane-force winds blew in from the north. The resulting firestorm leveled whole towns, leaving nothing but ashes. Eighty-seven people died and three million acres, an area the size of Connecticut, was charred. It was the largest forest fire in US history. They called it the "Big Burn."

With the ashes still warm, Pinchot rose from forced obscurity. He mounted a media onslaught. "For the want of a trail, the finest white pine forests in the United States were laid waste and scores of lives lost," he said. Pinchot gave this interview in the then-popular *Everybody's Magazine* and he gave many others. Ten months hadn't passed since the Big Burn when, at Pinchot's urging, Congress doubled the Forest Service's budget so the agency could build fire lookout stations and trails.

And so, in the second decade of the 1900s, in California, Oregon, and Washington, Forest Service crews started to connect one mountain peak to the next, beginning a network of trails—some of which, defying previous logic, ran north to south.

OPPOSITE: President Theodore Roosevelt and Forest Service Chief Gifford Pinchot stand on the deck of the river steamer *Mississippi*, October 1907.
ABOVE: The PCT through lodgepole pines in Diamond Peak Wilderness, Oregon.

Theodore Solomons and the John Muir Trail

The story of the John Muir Trail (JMT), one might suppose, is about John Muir. But it's not. As great as he was, as much as Muir's name is synonymous with the Sierra Nevada, his tie to the eponymous trail is a quirk of timing. To tell the tale of the JMT, we must return to Theodore Solomons. The one obscure book about him— Shirley Sargent's *Solomons of the Sierra*—calls him the "Lost Trailblazer of the Sierra."

So many 13-year-olds' dreams are passing flights of fancy, but not his. Upon returning to San Francisco after his summer in the Fresno fields, Solomons held tight to his vision—blazing a path over and through the crests of the High Sierra. In high school, he lit out on his first climbs. The summit register of Mount Tamalpais, a 2,572-foot Bay Area landmark, shows his first ascent in 1886. Not long after that, Solomons and a classmate made a three-day round trip to Mount Diablo, one of the region's highest peaks at 3,848 feet. But these paled before the High Sierra.

Solomons's older brother became a lawyer and his younger brother aspired to attend the University of California, Berkeley, but when Solomons graduated high school in 1888, much to his family's consternation, he threw a blanket roll over his back and set out to walk. For three months, he trekked from Fresno to Lake Tahoe over the High Sierra.

"When I was eighteen [I] took a long vacation trip from the lower Fresno mountains to Lake Tahoe . . . I got my first feel of the High Sierra under my foot. This initial journey through a mildly contoured, well-mapped region yielded only the personal result of whetting the urge to a full-length crest-wise journey. It

took four years of working and saving and some six months of preparation before I was both able and ready for the plunge," he wrote in a 1940 *Sierra Club Bulletin*.

From 1892 to 1895, Solomons mounted three historic expeditions. During the first, his mule, Whitney, carried his bulky camera and photographic glass plates. He took the first photographs of Banner and Ritter Peaks, the iconic mountains towering over Thousand Island Lake, a mandatory camera stop for every PCT hiker. At times, Solomons pulled others along, including Joseph Le Conte and William Colby, whose names grace Le Conte Canyon and Colby Pass. At times, Solomons pressed on alone. Always, he meticulously kept notes and mapped the terrain. At the end of one expedition, when he returned days late to Yosemite Valley, he was told they were "organizing a relief expedition to rescue me or kill the bear."

During his third and last expedition in 1895, Solomons came to a particularly spectacular hanging valley surrounded by striking peaks. They were all unnamed and he referred to them as "a fraternity of Titans." Then he named them after the great evolutionists: Mounts Darwin, Huxley, Wallace, Haeckel, Fiske, and Spencer. He named the icy body of water at their feet Evolution Lake. Today many swear that Evolution Valley and these Solomons-named peaks compose the finest landscape the Sierra has to offer.

The chapter title in Shirley Sargent's book about these expeditions is "Terra Incognita." But by the time Solomons finished, these broad blanks in the Sierra maps were completed. In February 1896, Solomons sent the four-year-old Sierra Club a 125-page typewritten report, a large-scale detailed map, and 139 photographs. Many of his photos were of areas never photographed before. The Sierra Club published a letter Solomons wrote accompanying his detailed report: "I have described a possible continuous route through the High Sierra from Yosemite to King's River Canyon . . . This journey would be of surpassing interest to the scenery-loving public and will eventually become as renowned as the Grand Tour of Switzerland." It ran nearly 200 miles and Solomons had fulfilled his vow; he'd laid out the trail he'd imagined when he was 13 years old.

Taking Solomons's trail south the final 30 miles to Mount Whitney was left to others. Chief among them were Joseph Le Conte and Bolton Brown, who did so over the next few years.

In 1914, there was a happy coincidence. Meyer Lissner, chief political lieutenant of Hiram Johnson, California's governor, went on the Sierra Club's annual High Sierra outing. By its end, he was suggesting that the Sierra Club seek legislation for High Sierra trails. He pledged his own and Governor Johnson's support. The Sierra Club quickly set to work drawing up a bill.

State Senator William Carr introduced the legislation on January 28, 1915. But four weeks before, at age 76, the indefatigable defender of the Sierra, John Muir, had died. Soon after, one of the Sierra Club drafters, Solomons's hiking companion William Colby, inserted one change, so that as submitted the bill was titled "An ACT: Appropriating Money for the Construction of a Trail in the Sierra Nevada Mountains to be known as the 'John Muir Trail.'"

The bill passed and by the end of the 1920s the John Muir Trail was largely complete. The final sections required backbreaking rockwork and the liberal use of blasting powder—thus were completed the almost-vertical Golden Staircase north of Mather Pass and the southern approach to the 13,117-foot Forester Pass. The work was dangerous. Below Forester Pass one trail worker died. Fifty-four years after young Solomons made his pledge, the JMT was complete. So when the idea of a Mexico-to-Canada trail first struggled to take root, it did so on ground partially plowed; 200 miles of the hardest-to-build trail was already in place.

OPPOSITE: Diamond Mesa, as seen from the John Muir Trail portion of the PCT in California.
ABOVE: Theodore Solomons, in 1895, on his third expedition scouting what would become the John Muir Trail.

Trailblazer: Fred Cleator

Fred Cleator had just finished his third day working in an Oregon logging camp. The 25-year-old Minneapolis native contemplated his blisters. What had he gotten himself into? This wasn't why he'd come west. But at the end of this June day in 1908, he got word by telegram. There's no record of who signed it, but most likely it was Gifford Pinchot himself. Cleator was reprieved; he had been hired as a ranger. So began a 35-year Forest Service career.

Cleator was posted to Republic, a rough-and-tumble gold-mining town in northeastern Washington. For nine years, he conducted timber sales in saloons. He rose to assistant forest supervisor and in late 1918 transferred to Portland, Oregon, the Forest Service Region 6 headquarters for all of Oregon and Washington.

World War I had just ended, and the world was gripped by a massive flu pandemic that killed far more people than the Great War. But in Oregon, the brand-new Columbia River Highway had opened and there were more and more of Henry Ford's new cars running through the beauty of the gorge. Appetite whetted, the driving public wanted more. A road along the Cascade Crest was proposed that would go all the way from Mount Hood to Crater Lake, Oregon, some 270 miles. Cleator was put in charge of surveying the route.

Cleator set out in July 1920, head of a six-man Forest Service survey crew. Its assignment was to lay out the Cascade Highway route. Beforehand, it was arranged that 500 diamond-shaped metal signs would be delivered to Cleator for posting. They attached them to trees, like so many Hansel and Gretel breadcrumbs, but these signs were long lasting. The enameled-metal signs read "Oregon Skyline Trail." Cleator spent three months in the woods dutifully surveying a road, but what he'd actually done was blaze a hiking trail. Money never was allocated for the road. No matter. Oregonians fell in love with their trail.

Fifteen years later, in 1935, Cleator revealed his crew's true feelings in a report he wrote about the trip: "The entire party, including the road engineer, [felt] it would be sacrilege to spoil such country with a highway." Trail maps were published in the 1920s. Another 270 miles of the crest trail now lay ready and waiting.

In 2014, two researchers, Rod Farlee of Sequim, Washington, and Stuart Barker of Canterbury, England, independently located Cleator's field diary in Forest Service archives. Baker was at University of Kent working on his American Studies master's degree and chose as his thesis topic the Oregon Skyline Trail. Farlee was also interested in Cleator. Cleator wrote with a firm hand in pencil. Naming lakes and other geographic features, he jotted each down. He described how when their cook's tooth went bad, road engineer Lenzie used a pair of pliers and "put his knee on the cook's breast, got a good grip on the tooth and yanked it out." The diary also noted how they reported to headquarters by homing pigeon. But on Sunday, August 1, 1920, before leaving to summit Diamond Peak, a 14-mile round trip, Cleator paused to write this:

> *I am beginning to think that a Skyline Trail the full length of the Cascades in Washington and Oregon, joining a similar trail in the Sierras of California, would be a great tourist advertisement. For that matter it might be continued thru [sic] British Columbia and up the Alaska highlands. This is a future work but it would be fine to plan upon.*

This is the first written record of the idea of the Pacific Crest Trail. This mention precedes "Mother of the Trail" Catherine Montgomery's suggestion by six years. It precedes the work of "Father of the Trail" Clinton

OPPOSITE: Mount Rainier looms over Fred Cleator and a Forest Service team on the Packwood Glacier in Washington's Goat Rocks Wilderness. Today the Packwood Glacier is a fraction of the size shown in this mid-1930s photo.

"The Freedom of Trousers": Women's Hiking Attire

In 1921 in Seattle, neither fashion nor rule required women to wear ankle-length bloomers into the wild. But just barely. Witness this October 25, 1921, unsigned correspondence to Professor Edmond Meany, president of the Seattle Mountaineers for 27 years:

> *I was once more confronted by one of the rules of your organization—that woman shall wear skirts until the actual hike begins, somewhere away from the city limits. Professor Meany, may I enquire if the thought back of this ruling is protection of the modesty of women Mountaineers, or of the morals of the remainder of the inhabitants of Seattle? If the former, we can lose our modesty just as surely and easily in trousers beyond the city limits as in the same trousers within city limits. . . . My dear Professor Meany, for the love of purity and sound, wholesome, uncommon sense, let the Mountaineers get away from this artificial modesty, clear their minds of this foggy doubt and permit its women to know, as its men do, the freedom of trousers, all the way from their front doors, over the trail and back again.*

C. Clarke by 12 years. Most interestingly, this written record of the PCT precedes by eight months the first written record of the idea of the Appalachian Trail. Which raises this question: Which trail was proposed first, anyway?

For the rest of his career, Cleator worked out of the Region 6 headquarters in Portland. There is no indication that he ever discussed that Sunday's long trail dream with anyone. But in the late 1920s, when Catherine Montgomery's Mexico-to-Canada trail idea was catching fire, Cleator was the supervisor of recreation for Region 6 and he sprang into action. Joseph Hazard described it in his 1946 book *Pacific Crest Trails from Alaska to Cape Horn*: "In 1928 came reality and results! . . . Mr. Cleator named, announced, and developed the Cascade Crest Trail."

Hazard makes short work of a much longer story, for it took nearly a decade. But by the mid-1930s, along the crest of Washington State's Cascades, 450 more miles of trail were largely mapped and being built. One more great foundation block in place.

Like Solomons, Cleator named many geographic features. And like Solomons, Cleator named none for himself. In the summer of 1968, a 13,034-foot peak near Muir Pass, directly above the PCT, was formally named Mount Solomons. And eight miles east of the PCT in the Glacier Peak Wilderness is 7,725-foot Mount Cleator. But unlike Mount Solomons, the name isn't on government maps. Mount Cleator's designation is only informal.

No matter. He's remembered here as one of the many government champions who made the PCT a reality.

Mother of the Trail: Catherine Montgomery

Single women were *spinsters* and newspapers might identify a woman as Mrs. *John* Doe, not by her given name, Josephine. That's how it was in 1899, when 32-year-old Catherine Montgomery came to Bellingham, Washington. She'd accepted a top-end position, $70 a month, as one of the founding faculty members of what would become Western Washington University. Montgomery was tall, with her dark hair tied in a frizzy bun. Her accent declared her parents' heritage as Scotch. And she was single.

The noun *spinster* has disappeared from the lexicon, and so too the verb for Montgomery's great love, *tramping*. On days she wasn't training the state's future elementary school teachers, Montgomery could be seen tramping in the surrounding forests, hills, and mountains. She was a dauntless outdoorswoman, no matter the de rigueur ankle-length bloomers women were expected to wear into the wilderness.

Montgomery found a fellow tramper in Ida Baker, another of the founding faculty. Baker was Montgomery's best friend, and one of the very few who ever called the stern Montgomery "Kate." When Baker died in 1921, Montgomery wrote a eulogy for *The Normal Messenger*, the Whatcom Normal School newspaper, titled "Tramping Together." "Memories of financial struggle, of trans-continental trips, of farming together, come to me as I recall the locking of Ida Baker's life with mine, but above all comes the memory of tramping together," she wrote.

Four years before that, Baker published an article in *American Forestry*, a national monthly journal. It described her 10-day tramp around Mount Baker with another unnamed woman. And after Baker died, Montgomery kept on reading the journal. In April 1924, a three-page feature article caught her attention: "The Appalachian Trail: From Maine to Georgia by Foot Trail—A Little Hike of 2,000 Miles—Along the Skyline of the Appalachian Ranges."

Montgomery's tramping and the Appalachian Trail article stirred like a primordial soup. The result was the "birth" of the Pacific Crest Trail. Joseph Hazard recorded the moment as if he'd had a video camera. Hazard was a famed Seattle mountaineer. The night of January 13, 1926, he was the featured speaker at Bellingham's Mount Baker Club. But Hazard's day job was selling textbooks, and so in the morning he met with Supervising Teacher Catherine Montgomery. Hazard described it in his 1946 book *Pacific Crest Trails from Alaska to Cape Horn*:

> *The first official action toward the promotion of a Pacific Crest Trail was taken in the year 1926. The suggestion came from Miss Catherine Montgomery at the close of a business interview of an hour's duration:*
>
> *"Do you know what I've been thinking about, Mr. Hazard, for the last twenty minutes?"*
>
> *"I had hoped you were considering the merits of my presentation of certain English texts for adoption!"*
>
> *"Oh that! Before your call I had considered them the best—I still do! But why do not you Mountaineers do something big for Western America?"*
>
> *"Just what have you in mind, Miss Montgomery?"*
>
> *"A high winding trail down the heights of our western mountains with mile markers and shelter huts—like these pictures I'll show you of the 'Long Trail of the Appalachians'—from the Canadian Border to the Mexican Boundary Line!"*

Hazard continued: "That very evening I carried the plan to the Mount Baker Club of Bellingham. Favorable action was taken. The rest of the mountain clubs of the Pacific Northwest promptly contacted all other outdoor organizations. All adopted the project with enthusiasm and organized to promote it."

Montgomery was born on Prince Edward Island. Her parents sailed from Scotland on a masted schooner in the same 1840s transatlantic wave that brought John Muir across the pond to Wisconsin. When she was three, her family moved to tiny Schuyler, Nebraska, and at 20 she moved west to Chehalis, Washington, where she began her teaching career.

"Mother of the Trail"
Catherine Montgomery
circa 1910.

Montgomery lived 90 years, from 1867 to 1957. The Civil War and Sputnik bracketed her life. Her obituary noted she was a "militant crusader." But to her student teachers she must have shown a gentler side, for in 1908 the college newspaper summed her up in one line: "Miss Montgomery—To know her is to love her, so we say, for just and true and kind of heart is she." The obituary described accomplishments—suffragette, founding faculty, 1920 Democratic candidate for state superintendent, founder of women's clubs, and more. But there was no mention of the Pacific Crest Trail.

When she retired in 1926, her annual salary was $3,200, but when she died in 1957 she left an estate of $100,079, the equivalent of nearly $850,000 in 2015. She bequeathed her fortune to a Washington State Forest preserve and with it they built the Catherine Montgomery Interpretive Center. Thousands of school-children in buses visit each year. Not long ago, a center ranger was asked if he knew of a connection between Montgomery and the PCT. His answer was, "No." That has been rectified. And though no mountain bears her name, on March 21, 2010, Catherine Montgomery was inducted into the Northwest Women's Hall of Fame. In a packed hall in Bellingham, attendees heard about her life and then the induction citation was read verbatim. This is the final paragraph:

> *Of her many legacies, perhaps the most enduring is her vision of a hiking trail along the ridges of the Pacific Coast that she began to champion starting in 1926. Others took up the cause and, today, that 2,650-mile-long trail that runs from Canada to Mexico attracts thousands of hikers. She is justly called "the Mother of the Pacific Crest Trail."*

Father of the Trail: Clinton C. Clarke

According to the first edition (1973) of the Wilderness Press's PCT guidebook series, "The idea of the PCT originated in the early 1930s in the mind of Clinton C. Clarke." Not so. Little is known about Clarke and much of what has been published is unsupported. There is no evidence Clarke was a successful oilman and assertions that he "never hiked the trail" and was an "arm-chair hiker" are not true. Former PCTA Board President and Historian Larry Cash's *A Brief History* got it right: "Clarke was a man of metropolitan tastes who studied literature at Harvard and co-founded the famous Pasadena Playhouse. He was active for more than 35 years in Boy Scouting. He was also an active amateur photographer."

Born in 1873, Clarke attended Williams College as an undergraduate and Harvard for his master's. Clinton C. Clarke—that's how he nearly always wrote his name—moved west to Southern California, to foothills backed against the PCT's San Gabriel Range, to a new mansion on Millionaire's Row. It was 1906 and he and his new bride, Margaret, had just returned from their honeymoon—a 10-month, around-the-world cruise. Margaret's diary of the "20,771-mile" journey first lists pages of wedding gifts. "Salad fork and spoon—Uncle Tom." The 1910 census stated Clarke's occupation as "own income." In the 1920 census, at age 46, Clarke listed "retired." He was born and married with a silver spoon in his mouth.

A PhD dissertation noted in 1998, "It is virtually impossible to find biographical materials on Clarke, who for all of his activities was a very private individual."

OPPOSITE: Palisade Creek tumbles just below the Golden Staircase, the last portion of the John Muir Trail to be completed.
ABOVE: Attending a two-week Sierra Club expedition, "Father of the Trail" Clinton C. Clarke stands atop Glen Pass above Rae Lakes Basin in 1911. With his bedroll on his back and a spoon tucked in his hatband, the indefatigable Clarke was ever at the ready.

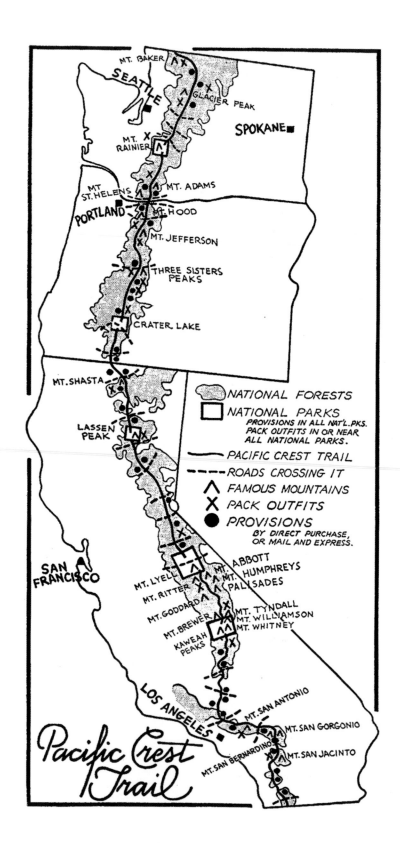

While at Harvard from 1898 to 1900, Clarke wasn't the only one there who'd make a mark on the nation's trails. Benton MacKaye was an undergraduate. MacKaye was the future "Father of the Appalachian Trail." Did the two men cross paths? If so, what did they say to each other?

During 1910 and 1911, Clarke went each summer on the Sierra Club's weeks-long expeditions. Each trek brought a horde of 200 that moved every few days from one High Sierra base camp to the next. An amateur photographer, Clarke took photos, two of which were published in the *Sierra Club Bulletin*, and two of his tattered albums lay un-indexed in the University of California, Berkeley's Bancroft Library. One of the albums offered photo enlargements for sale for 50 cents each. There's one photo of 38-year-old Clarke atop the PCT's Glen Pass. There's a bedroll tied to his back, a compass in his hand, and a spoon tucked into his hatband. One of Clarke's expeditions tramped through an achingly beautiful valley. Clarke strolled Hetch Hetchy before it was dammed.

With that trail background and his active interest in the Boy Scouts, Clarke was fertile ground when, in the early 1930s, Montgomery's trail idea migrated south. By then, Clarke and his wife had exchanged their Millionaire's Row house for the resort-like Green Hotel in downtown Pasadena, California. In 1932, Clarke picked up the long-trail baton with a vengeance.

Clarke often wrote about his advocacy work in the third person. In his 1945 book, *The Pacific Crest Trailway*, he wrote: "In March 1932, Mr. Clinton C. Clarke of Pasadena, California, proposed to the United States Forest and National Park Services the project of a continuous wilderness trail across the United States from Canada to Mexico, passing through the states of Washington, Oregon and California. . . . The project was approved and adopted, and Mr. Clarke was placed in charge."

Dan White described Clarke in his book *The Cactus Eaters* as "One part John Muir, five parts General Patton." Like Patton, Clarke excelled at mechanized assault, but instead of tanks, Clarke's weapon was a typewriter. In his meticulous files there must be a thousand hand-typed letters.

Clarke wrote to the heads of the Forest Service, National Park Service, Sierra Club, and other outdoor clubs. He spent hours upon hours studying maps, piecing together his trail, slowly tracing a pencil line from Mexico to Canada. He'd latched onto a name. He was going to call his supertrail the John Muir Trail. Clarke was surprised at the objections.

Horace Albright, director of the National Park Service, was genuinely enthusiastic. "Your letter of November 12 brings welcome news that you are planning to continue promoting the John Muir Trail," he wrote back. Albright instructed the superintendents of each national park through which the trail passed to map where the trail would run and send it to Clarke. But Albright could offer no funds. Nor could anyone; it was the Great Depression. Clarke's own money flowed out at an equal speed to his typing.

By 1933, Clarke had stitched together a first set of maps. They were 25 pages long. The next year he wrote Albright that he'd finished a refined set of "five maps 65 feet long." As 1934 began to close, Clarke had a modicum of support and a long line on a map. He'd built upon Solomons's and Cleator's trails and filled the gaps on existing paths, roads, and hope. But he was a man with two problems. The negative response to his proposed name was rising to a crescendo, and for all the behind-the-scenes interest he'd raised, Clarke knew he needed some great spark to spur the general public's interest.

How the Trail Got Its Name

In 10 years, nothing like it had happened at a Seattle Mountaineers board meeting. In September 1932, Clinton C. Clarke wrote to the Mountaineers proposing that they rename the Cascade Crest Trail to the John Muir Trail as a part of his trail from Mexico to Canada. Heatedly, the Mountaineers board first passed one motion—send Clarke's idea packing—and then reversed itself, referring the question instead to the Federation of Western Outdoor Clubs. When Clarke wrote to the Mazamas outdoor club in Portland, Oregon, they weren't any more receptive to changing the name of their Oregon Skyline Trail.

"We are for you heart and soul in regard to the thing as a whole . . . The name 'John Muir Trail,' however, is one that we feel very strongly should be used only for the High Sierra trail . . . We must stand firmly in our objection," wrote the Sierra Club. Even the National Park Service, Clarke's ardent supporter, bluntly wrote, "[S]ome other name must be found to placate the feeling around in the States of Washington and Oregon."

The crossfire threatened to bring down the trail. At the peak of the imbroglio, Dr. Harold C. Bryant, acting director of the National Park Service, wrote to Clarke: "Would it not be wise to hit upon some such name as the 'Cascade Sierra Trail,' the 'Pacific Crest Trail,' or the 'High Pacific Trail?'" Clarke grasped the "Pacific Crest Trail" with the enthusiasm of a man lost in the desert who'd been offered a cold drink. Within a week, Clarke's typewriter keys generated a string of letters, all with something similar to what he wrote to the Sierra Club: "I believe I have a solution to naming the Canada–Mexico trail. Let us call it—'THE PACIFIC CREST TRAIL.'"

The National Park Service lauded Bryant for establishing the NPS nature interpretive program. Bryant's last posting was as superintendent of Grand Canyon National Park. In 1954, when he retired, he received the Department of the Interior Distinguished Service Award. But to the PCTA's knowledge, never before has Bryant been publicly acknowledged for his role in naming the Pacific Crest Trail.

OPPOSITE: Early PCT map from *Sunset Magazine*, July 1936.

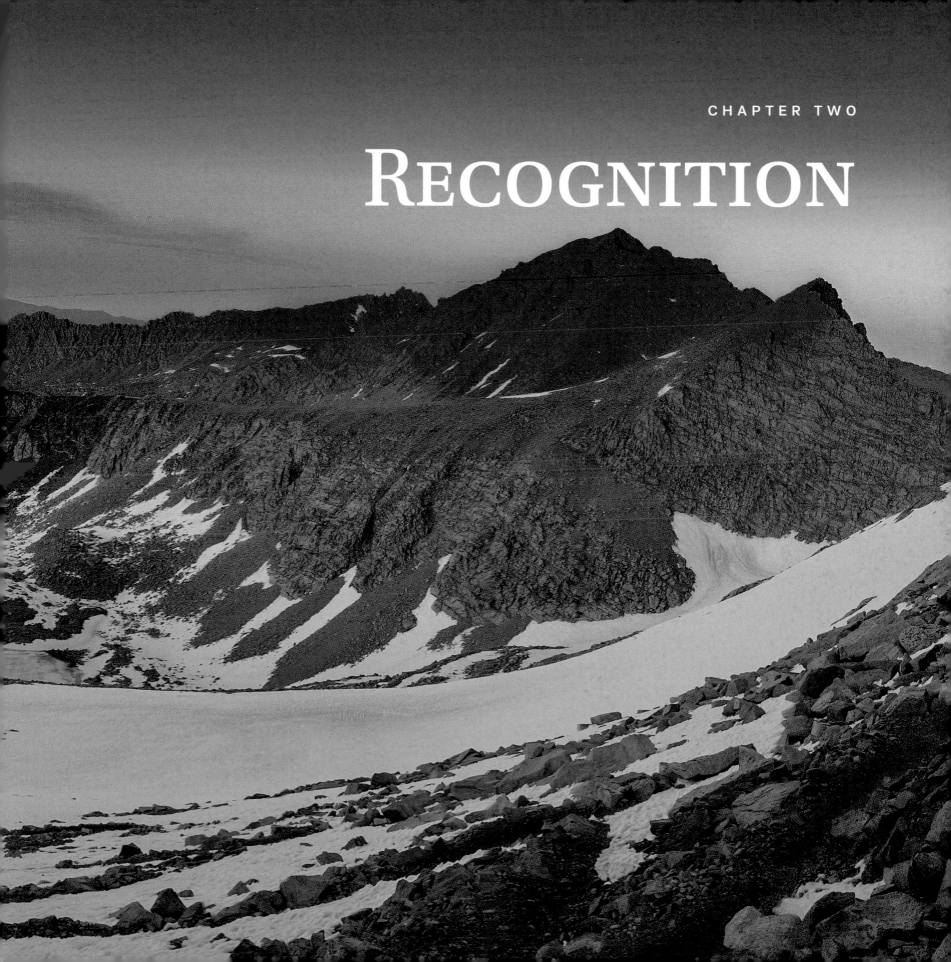

CHAPTER TWO

RECOGNITION

The Death of Donald Downs

Big, handsome, and blond, Donald I. Downs was simply "Buck" to his fellow trail workers. It was 1930 and he was only 18. Part of a National Park Service crew of six, Downs helped carve the way up Forester Pass's steep face, laying a path passable to stock, yet so vertical that today it still makes Pacific Crest Trail hikers dizzy.

Stripped to his waist, sweating above tree line, Downs swung a sledgehammer and crowbarred granite, knowing that what he did was important. One of his crewmates, Donald Griffin, 21, put it into words: "This trail was meant to last through the ages. It was part of the John Muir Trail."

PREVIOUS SPREAD: Looking north from Forester Pass, the high point of the PCT at 13,117 feet.
BELOW: PCT pioneer Warren Rogers (right) with one of the YMCA relay boys.
OPPOSITE: The trail twists its way to the top of Forester Pass in California.

"Fire in the hole! Fire in the hole!" Their "powder man" George Carey always hollered twice before blowing the charges. They would take cover as another granite boulder blew into rock chips.

After three weeks of work, Downs had acquired what Griffin called an "enviable tan." And, Griffin said, "This particular day apparently was just like any other."

"Fire in the hole! Fire in the hole!" Downs took cover and squeezed in with a crewmate in the overhang of a massive boulder. At 175 pounds per cubic foot, this granite beast topped 40 tons. Immovable. The dynamite blew, rock shards rifled the air, and Downs heard a deep rumble beneath him. A mountain god cleared its throat. Forty tons shifted, crushing Downs's arm above the elbow and snapping his collarbone. Pinned. Frantic sledgehammer blows freed his arm, but as his crewmates carried him down to camp, Downs already knew he was going to lose it.

There were no antibiotics, no helicopters, and no satellite phones. It took three days before word got out and a doctor reached camp. Under a hissing gasoline lantern, Dr. Frazer amputated Downs's gangrenous arm. The news reached his mother, a widow, and she reached Downs in camp two days after the operation.

The *Fresno Morning Republican* wrote, "The anxious mother had to admit defeat when death stepped in at midnight." It would be nice to think that Downs died in her arms. We don't know.

There is a plaque set next to the trail on the south side of Forester Pass. It's actually on the rock that killed him. It does not reveal the circumstances of Downs's untimely death or the depth of his suffering. Few hikers probably even notice it, but it reads: While Engaged in Trail Construction an Accident / at This Point Resulted in the Death of / Donald I. Downs / Born September 29, 1911 / Died September 2, 1930 / His Fellow Workers Place This Tablet to His Memory.

Warren Rogers and the YMCA Relay

In a time of flagpole sitters and dance marathons, Clinton C. Clarke realized his trail needed an attention-grabbing hook. Never one to start at a lower rung, Clarke wrote directly to James E. West, chief Boy Scout executive, in April 1935. Clarke proposed a Boy Scout relay from Mexico to Canada. Hiking between 25 and 100 miles each leg, each Scout troop would hand a parchment scroll off to the next. This would be "the first exploration of the Pacific Crest Trail." Each boy's name would be engraved on the parchment. West found the idea "most interesting and intriguing," but in the end took a pass—the Boy Scouts were focused on their first National Jamboree that summer.

PCT Stowaway

The first transit of the entire PCT wasn't by a person. It was by an object—the logbook. It has been nearly 80 years since the logbook reached Monument 78, but it still exists. It's in a fireproof safe, lovingly cared for by Warren Rogers's son, Donald. The leather is stippled with wear and age and the gold letters "Relay Log" have lost their gloss, but the stories inside still gleam with tales of the first exploration. But one story isn't told. The relay had a secret stowaway.

In year three, 1937, Rogers reported to Clarke, "As the fellows were getting the log book stamped and signed by the postmaster of Campo the customs agents gave the boys a package of Mexican cigarettes and told them to give them to the customs agents on the Canadian line. The cigarettes have been carried OK but not much publicity given this item—you understand."

On May 18, 1939, nearly a year after the relay finish, Olias Norman of the Seattle "Y" wrote to Rogers. He sent him a map carried for most of the relay and added, "I also discovered in our store room this morning a little package which on investigation I found to be a package of cigarettes which was given by a customs official at Mexico to be delivered to a customs official at Canada. Somewhere, somehow, we slipped up on this. What do you think we ought to do, or shall we forget it?"

And there the record of the stowaway cigarettes ends.

Around the same time, the Sierra Club—now happy with Clarke—offered to cosponsor the first-ever Pacific Crest Trail System Conference. It would be in Yosemite Valley, scheduled at the same time as two other Sierra Club conferences. Ansel Adams was in charge and the famed photographer helped Clarke make the arrangements and send out invitations.

At the early June conference, Clarke found himself with the heads of three YMCAs. Never shy, Clarke pitched his relay concept. Blanchard R. "Chard" Evarts of San Diego, Paul W. Somers of Pasadena, and Charles G. Norman of Seattle liked it and ran with it. A scant week later, on June 15, 1935, the first YMCA relay team stood before a crowd of 3,500 as four Native American chiefs blessed them at the California Pacific International Exposition in San Diego's Balboa Park. Carrying a letter from the head of the San Diego "Y" to his counterpart in Vancouver, Canada, the relay team was driven to Campo, a sleepy border crossing 60 miles east of San Diego where the trail started. Clarke, who wasn't present, sent along a black leather-bound logbook embossed with "Pacific Crest Relay Log 1935–36—YMCA." At 10:50 a.m., with the ink barely dry on a Campo postmark, the seven-member team, including Evarts, started hiking north.

Not two hours had passed before the first mishap. The team forgot the logbook on the trail and had to backtrack two miles in 100-degree heat. A more serious threat surfaced on June 20, just before Team 3 took over. The YMCA teams of three to six boys were to cover 50-mile legs and then hand off the logbook to the next in line. No one was prepared for the difficulty of traveling on the ground the line Clarke had drawn on his maps.

F. P. Knapp of the San Francisco "Y" was in charge and he sent out a cry for help. "This Mexico to Canada Hike has been wished on me," he wrote in a letter to a young YMCA camping leader, Warren Rogers.

Two years before, Rogers, a leader at the "Y" in Alhambra, California, read about Clarke's long trail idea in the *Alhambra Post Advocate*. He immediately drove to Pasadena to meet Clarke. The 27-year-old Rogers became a PCT apostle and by the time of Knapp's letter, Rogers was the PCT System Conference executive secretary. Rogers answered Knapp's call by pulling on his boots. Rogers guided Teams 3 through 14 over the rest of the summer.

ABOVE: The first YMCA relay team crosses the Mexican border at the Campo customs house. This is the first of 40 teams, each one hiking a minimum of 50 miles as they pass a leather logbook from one team to the next (left); Warren Rogers kneels on the far left with one of the final YMCA relay boy teams in Washington State. After four years, Team 40 reached the Canadian border on August 5, 1938 (right).

Rogers was scarecrow thin, but had a determination gained under fire—he'd been a polio-limping youth who by dint of will became an outdoorsman and mountain climber. The schoolyard taunts and the cruel nickname "Step-and-a-Half" became "Cactus" to his hiking friends. And he was "Cactus" to the Depression-era teens that made up the YMCA relay boys. Without Rogers, Clarke's lofty relay would have likely fallen flat. With Rogers, for four summers, with 40 teams in total, the logbook worked its way north. Newspapers and national magazines picked up the story. On August 5, 1938, Team 40 carried the logbook to Monument 78 on the Canadian border.

Forever after, Clarke wrote that the PCT was passable, continuous, and existing. The YMCA relay literally put the PCT on the map. The year after the relay, the National Park Service put the Pacific Crest Trail on its national recreation map for the first time.

Rogers's response to Knapp's call in 1935 would be the first of two times he saved the trail.

Relay Boys: Gordon Petrie and Marcus Moschetto

They must be in their late 80s or 90s. The logbook recorded every relay boy's name and address, but that contact information was more than 70 years old. In total, there were 144 YMCA relay boys. They came from 28 different "Y"s, from San Diego to Seattle. The Portland YMCA sent out the most—eight teams. They were teens then. How many might still be alive? Did they recall the trek or had the memory faded to a dying will-o'-the-wisp? Was there a chance any had photos? The logbook contained so few. Did these relay boys have any inkling of the future import of their trek?

Names listed in the Social Security Death Index were crossed out. When investigation yielded a modern phone number, a young voice answered, "Uncle Steve died four years ago." So many brick walls. On October 6, 2009, at 8:40 p.m., another hopeful phone call was made. The phone listing was for Gordon Petrie, Team 31, summer 1937. In Sisters, Oregon, a woman's voice answered. She sounded young. Her response: "Gordon is sleeping upstairs. He still talks about that trip. He has a photo album." Shirley Petrie was his bride of 67 years.

Petrie was interviewed and his photos preserved. He was feted in newspaper and magazine articles. Gordon and Shirley attended a dinner with the PCTA Board of Directors and they thanked him for his role in exploring and proving the concept of the PCT. Petrie died at age 92 in 2014.

After Petrie, four more relay boys surfaced. Blake Bevill, Team 2, was age 96 when interviewed. Eugene Farnham was age 91 when he told his stories. John Power was on Team 40, the one that reached the monument, but when he was found he was in a rest home, his memory gone.

Marcus Moschetto, a member of Team 38, had hiked deep in the northern Washington Cascades. Like Petrie, Moschetto's memory was sharp and he, too, had kept photos. There were wonderful images; in one, he is seen using the logbook as a pillow.

BELOW: Relay Team 31 from the Portland YMCA totes Trapper Nelson wooden pack frames between Oregon's Big Lake and Olallie Lake. Gordon Petrie leads, followed by Norman Rupp, Bud Moran, and Lloyd Craft (left); Relay Team 38, with 15-year-old Marcus Moschetto on the left, poses in the North Cascades in Washington (right).

Publicity

The media has played a role in the Pacific Crest Trail from the beginning. Headlines generate interest and marshal public opinion. Clarke apparently was wise to this.

September 5, 1936, Portland, *The Oregonian*: "Father of Border-to-Border Project Arrives Here: If there is any danger of the human race forgetting how to walk there is a 2,260-mile trail from the Canadian to the Mexican border now open exclusively to pedestrian travel which will put mankind on its feet again. Since the Pacific Crest Trail system is new, Clarke admitted yesterday, it is a challenge for some venturesome hiker to travel the entire distance in one continuous walk. Clarke believes it can't be done, that to get through in two years would be a feat."

September 10, 1936, Portland, *The Oregonian*: Daniel Wyatt responded to Clarke's challenge. "I am sure that I could hike the complete distance in eight months at most, barring sickness or accidents . . . I mean business and would like to have Mr. Clarke read this." But there is no record of Wyatt setting out on his hike.

So it's no surprise that the YMCA relay generated dozens of newspaper articles. Typical headlines were: "Trail Will Join Two Nations," "Pacific Trail Challenges Hikers," and "Relay Hikers Return."

But the Facebook of that era was radio. Warren Rogers aired hundreds of radio talks and interviews about the PCT. A few scripts still survive as part of the Warren Lee Rogers Collection at the Huntington Research Library near Los Angeles.

KOIN, Portland, Oregon, June 14, 1937: "Just beneath the summit crests of the great walls of the Cascade range in Washington and Oregon and the Sierra Nevada in California lies the Pacific Crest Trail. It is a true wilderness pathway across the United States from Canada to Mexico . . . This afternoon, Mr. Rogers is here in the studio of KOIN and Mr. Church is going to interview him concerning the development of the trail system . . ."

Since the relay ended, there's no record of a relay boy speaking before a hiker crowd and there's no record of a relay boy holding the logbook again. In April 2013, 90-year-old Moschetto traveled cross-country from Maine, and he spoke before a standing-room-only crowd at the Annual Day Zero Pacific Crest Trail Kick Off. He wasn't an experienced public speaker, but beforehand he said, "Don't worry, I'm talking about something I love." He told of canned corned beef and Ry-Krisps, of bears, and of getting lost. He spoke before 200 people who knew how important the relay had been and, if not for the likes of Moschetto and his brethren, there might be no Kick Off or no PCT. Just before the end, Moschetto was asked what would it mean to him to hold the logbook again. "It would be amazing," he said. And the logbook was placed in Moschetto's hands.

The crowd rose and gave him a standing ovation. He said it was the first time in his life he'd had people stand and clap for him like that. Afterward, they stood in line for half an hour to get his autograph.

Ten days later, a note came from Moschetto's son: "I can't tell you how much this meant to my family and especially my father. . . . For a brief time he was 15 again."

Clarke Fights for the Trail's Survival

Clarke wrote that the relay covered "the 2,300 miles in four summers without mishap or sickness. This is the first traverse of the entire trail and no difficulty or trouble was encountered." But the relay logbook described plenty of trouble following Clarke's proposed path:

> **June 20, 1935, Team 2:** *"Off the trail for four miles."*
>
> **August 8, 1936, Team 23:** *"As usual, we went around trying to find the trail."*
>
> **July 20, 1938, Team 38:** *"We spent three grueling hours fighting brush up the mountain only to be finally turned back by sheer rock walls and an 80-foot waterfall. Finally decided to fight our way back to trail up White River which we reached at 7 pm very tired and discouraged. By mutual agreement the first thing we did was to pray."*
>
> **July 21, 1938, Team 38:** *"We lost what little trail there was and spent 1½ hours before we got back on right trail."*

The saving graces of the route were the foundation-block trails: the John Muir, Oregon Skyline, and Cascade Crest Trails. Those miles were nearly rock solid. But for so many of the miles, the boys slogged north on a mapped route more an expression of hope than reality. Passable, continuous, and existing—it was Clarke's determination and will that made it so. The logbook kept its secret.

The relay was over. In Oregon and Washington, Forest Service Region 6 was posting new Pacific Crest Trail signs all along the trail. In 1937, the Forest Service approved the first official trail marker. W. J. Pollock designed the iconic diamond-shaped sign that identified the Pacific Crest Trail System. The agency required the signs to be 7½ inches tall and 4¾ inches wide. The sign was to be constructed of "stamped 24 gauge rustproof steel," with the tall tree and letters enameled green on a white background. The Forest Service printed a 10-page pamphlet in spring 1937 showing exact dimensions, letter style, and sample text for the stamped metal and constructed wood signs.

Eighty years later, a few diamond signs still exist on the trail. You should be so lucky as to see one. They are often half-swallowed by tree bark, the enamel rusted and chipped, stolen, or, worse, maimed to the point of worthlessness by target shooters.

The signs were going up and Clarke was printing and selling thousands of PCT bulletins, maps, and pamphlets. "Only 250 miles of the 2,265 miles would be outside the National Forests and National Parks"— he wrote variations of this sentence in almost every bulletin as well as in his book. This quotation was from his 1942 bulletin.

He was so proud that his trail was almost entirely on government land, unlike its eastern counterpart. In his June 1940 bulletin, the numbers were 2,225 and 260. In his 1945 PCT book, with no real change on the ground, he wrote the trail was "2,156 miles long and only 160 are in private hands."

The National Park Service also waxed enthusiastic. Arno Cammerer, National Park Service director, wrote to Clarke, "We are anxious to join you in your efforts to develop this enterprise."

By 1940, after eight years of dauntless effort, Clarke was in a consolidating mode, riding success. It was almost a moment when he could rest on his laurels. Then Clarke got a stunning letter from Stuart Bevier Show.

ABOVE: Original blueprint of the diamond-shaped Pacific Crest Trail System trail marker from a 1937 Forest Service pamphlet.

OPPOSITE: Likely at least 70 years old, a weathered trail symbol marks the PCT near Mount Thielsen, Oregon.

S. B. Show, as he signed his letters, was head of Forest Service Region 5, which includes most of California. On March 14, 1940, Show wrote Clarke, "The situation here is entirely different from that found in the National Forests of Washington and Oregon. We regret that a more thorough investigation of the whole project was not undertaken when it was first proposed by you, but we feel that it is better to recognize our mistake than to continue leading the public to believe that there is such a thing as the Pacific Crest Trail, when actually no such trail exists, nor is it feasible to construct such a trail in the National Forests of California."

The PCT was a mistake? No such trail exists? Clarke was flabbergasted and blazed with righteous indignation. Clarke accused Show of calling him a "liar," which he said no one had done since he first came to California 40 years earlier. Clarke wrote back, "To say of the Pacific Crest Trail in California 'actually no such trail exists, nor is it feasible to construct such a trail' is like announcing that the 'Southern Pacific R.R. between San Francisco and Los Angeles does not exist and can not be built.'" But, as Clarke pointed out, the railroad did exist and, he said, so did the trail.

Clarke wrote to Show's boss, Assistant Secretary of Agriculture James Camy, "For over four years now the Pacific Crest Trail from Mexico to Canada has been covered in parts by many explorers; it's an approved fact."

Clarke and Show engaged in more pointed correspondence, but Show didn't budge—in Region 5 the Forest Service would not support the trail. But Show had left Clarke a few crumbs and he made the most of them. "I was seriously disturbed at the danger of my eight years work being jeopardized and the splendid progress of the P.C.T. project being checked," he wrote. "I understand from your letter that the Forest Service will not speak of the P.C.T. in California as not 'feasible' or 'practicable' or not in 'existence.' So let us consider the question closed."

But even after "closing" the question Clarke couldn't resist this dig: "I think you will deeply regret if you drop out now. In the near future when this great Pacific Crest Trail is world known and universally beloved, people everywhere will ask why the Forest Service in California lost courage, and what they hoped to accomplish by quitting just when the prize is won."

Of course we see today that Clarke was right.

Genesis of the British National Trail System

The Mother Country, the United Kingdom, has a 2,500-mile system of 15 national trails. Were the Pacific Crest Trail and the Appalachian Trail following the Old World's footsteps? No, just the opposite.

On June 22, 1935, journalist Tom Stephenson published an article with a provocative headline in London's *Daily Herald*: "Wanted: A Long Green Trail."

Stephenson bemoaned the public's lack of access to the wild, open moors and then he took his homeland to task. He asked, "Why should not we press for something akin to the Appalachian Trail?" And on the heels of that he held the PCT (under its old John Muir Trail moniker) as a shining example to emulate. "The John Muir Trail . . . reaches from the Canadian border through Washington, Oregon and California to Mexico. For 2,500 miles without any slogging on hard roads, one may follow this track over lofty peaks, by deep-cleft canyons and through great National Parks and reserves saved for all time from spoliation by unplanned and irresponsible building. After allowing for the difference in geographical scale, what can we in England offer to compare with these enterprises?"

It took 30 years. Stephenson and so many never let up and, in 1965, Pennine Way opened, the first British national trail.

OPPOSITE: In the North Cascades, the Murray family nears the Canadian border as they complete their two-year thru-ride of the PCT. *Life* magazine featured the Murrays' trek in a September 3, 1971, article.

CHAPTER THREE

IT'S OFFICIAL

World War II Brings Hard Times for the PCT

For eight years, the Pacific Crest Trail bucked the current of the Great Depression, riding the zeal of Clinton C. Clarke, Warren "Cactus" Rogers, and the Relay Boys.

Rogers was already thinking ahead to the 1941 winter holiday season. It was a December Sunday and he was writing a friend for work advice. At the top of the page Rogers made a note: "I just heard over the radio about Japan bombing Pearl Harbor."

World War II swept in like a tsunami; nothing swam against that roaring tide. Squared up against the war effort, trail promotion efforts were doomed. The PCT dream flickered and dimmed.

The Forest Service was decimated, losing 2,000 employees to the armed services. Recreation and conservation were sacrificial lambs. Trees became a commodity as prized as steel. America's forests were cut and machined into PT boats, gunstocks, fighter planes, truck beds, boat docks, barracks, and

an avalanche of wood crates to box up all the supplies. The Forest Service estimated it took three trees to equip each American soldier.

There was no money for trails and there was little interest. The momentum built during a half decade of annual Pacific Crest Trail System conferences ended. Clarke's typewriter was largely silent.

When the war ended, great celebrations erupted across the country. Ten million shed their uniforms as the soldiers, sailors, and airmen returned home. They wanted jobs. They wanted families. They wanted new cars, not hiking paths. They'd had their fill of marching with loads on their backs.

In 1932, Clarke had been an indefatigable 59. But as the 1940s turned into the 1950s, Clarke was near 80. His stiffened fingers no longer clattered away producing new crops of letters. The PCT System annual conferences never started up again after the war.

Rogers married in 1945 and in 1948, at 40, he was ready to start a family. That year he not only worked full time, but also built his own home. Rogers picked out each redwood board for the siding. He was so proud—there wasn't a single knot to mar the wood. Three children quickly followed. Rogers had little bandwidth for the trail, and with his mentor Clarke lagging as far as the PCT was concerned, Rogers felt rudderless.

The PCT concept hung in the balance. Trees blew down, rain fell, and bridges washed away. Avalanches roared and in their plunge they erased another stretch of trail. Untended trails do not disappear in a generation. Untended trails disappear all but overnight.

But a few bright lights kept the trail idea alive.

The First Proposals to Hike and Ride the PCT

JOSEPH WAMPLER

In December 1948, the newsletter of the Trails Club of Oregon ran this notice:

> *Mexico to Canada Expedition: The United States has been crisscrossed literally by thousands of exploring parties since Columbus first discovered the new world. Yet, the fact is amazing but true that no party has ever made a continuous trip along the entire length of the Sierra Nevada/Cascade mountain crest from one border of the United States to the other. Such a hiking trip is now being planned by Joseph C. Wampler, archaeologist-mountaineer.*

The start date was set for April 1, 1949. In the same newsletter, Wampler wrote, "The group of scientist-adventurers will need six months to complete their 2,200-mile journey."

Wampler said his fellow travelers should be historians, botanists, ornithologists, geologists, foresters, and other scientists. "The party will be small, probably ten to fifteen persons. Participants must be in excellent health, preferably with experience in mountaineering or field work, and will be expected to perform the usual camp chores," he wrote.

Wampler's notice was the expedition's high-water mark. In 1965, Hal Roth's *Pathway in the Sky* reported that Wampler "tried to promote a trip along the Pacific Crest Trail from Mexico to Canada but found few takers. Shortening his trip to the John Muir Trail in 1950 he began his present schedule of summer outings."

PREVIOUS SPREAD: Mount Shasta is visible from the PCT for nearly 450 miles. Here the volcano lords over the PCT near Squaw Valley Creek, Northern California. OPPOSITE: South of Ebbetts Pass in California, a rainbow crowns a Sierra Nevada crest.

In the 1950s and 1960s, at a rate of 12 to 25 at a time, Wampler exposed several thousand people to the John Muir Trail. It was a civilized exposure. "Joe had a cook, a second cook, and a college-age helper or two," Roth wrote. They also had a toilet and bath tents. Before the phrase "Leave No Trace" was coined, Wampler prided himself on placing his backcountry kitchen "near a stream." And every morning before 6:00 a.m., Wampler did one thing all his clients remember; he roused "the camp with a series of tremendous yodels."

In 1960, Wampler coauthored *High Sierra: Mountain Wonderland*. The book made one reference to the Pacific Crest Trail. Under "Selected Readings," it listed: Clarke, Clinton J. [*sic*], *The Pacific Crest Trailway*, Pasadena, 1945.

MARTIN PAPENDICK

In his open-collared sailor's uniform, Martin Papendick had a medium build with an all-American face. No wanderlust showed in his World War II US Navy photo. At the war's end, he was one minnow in the returning school 10 million strong. But in 1950, quite alone, Papendick set out to tackle the Pacific Crest Trail.

Papendick served on the USS *Kalinin Bay* in the Pacific. He survived kamikaze attacks in the Philippines. His ship was one of Admiral Ziggy Sprague's mini-carriers that saved the day for General Douglas MacArthur at Leyte Gulf. Once home, Papendick attended college and graduated from Michigan State in 1950 with a bachelor's degree in geology. Well before graduating, Papendick set his sights on making the "first all-the-way walk" on the Appalachian Trail. But another service vet beat him. In 1948, army veteran Earl Shaffer finished the AT while Papendick was in his junior year.

After learning about Shaffer, Papendick wrote in *Appalachia* in 1951, "I decided to be the first to traverse . . . the Pacific Crest Trail." In mid-June 1950, he began at Manning Park, Canada. "The terrain from that point southward is just about as rugged mountain country as one could find in the West. Two weeks without seeing another person made me wonder why I had not tried a more populated area." On that first PCT outing, Papendick lasted two weeks.

A year later, Papendick changed course and set out on the Appalachian Trail. This time he was successful, hiking from the northern terminus, Mount Katahdin, to Mount Oglethorpe, Georgia, then the southern end of the AT. Papendick wrote, "I had no guidebook" and I "hiked countless alternate routes." In 1952, he returned to tackle his nemesis, the PCT. He began his second attempt on July 4, again starting from Manning Park. He finished at Campo on December 1, 1952—149 days later. Papendick wrote a three-page article that appeared in the 1953 issue of *Appalachia*, America's oldest mountaineering journal. He was as open about hiking substantial off-route sections on the PCT as he had been on the AT:

> On December 1, 1952, I reached the Mexican Border near Campo, California, after five months of backpacking over Pacific crests from British Columbia. Forest trails, mountain roads, alpine cattle paths, and stretches without trails were encountered in the 2,275-mile trip.

Papendick generated a small splash of press, doing his part to keep the PCT alive. Then he disappeared from the trail's story. His name wasn't in the Wilderness Press PCT guidebooks. It wasn't in *A Brief History*. His name didn't surface again until the late 1990s. Papendick was already suffering from dementia when someone tried to record his story. Some credit Papendick with being the first PCT thru-hiker.

OPPOSITE: A portion of the 119 Boy Scouts and their 14 leaders march through the Three Sisters area as part of the 1954 Boy Scout Trail Log Expedition (left); two Boy Scouts release homing pigeons carrying the day's news to Portland, Oregon, for the evening newspaper (right).

RALPH ELLE AND THE 1954 BOY SCOUT PCT RELAY

Twenty years after Clarke suggested a relay to the Boy Scouts, the seed finally took root. In 1954, the Boy Scouts staged a full-scale PCT relay. Starting simultaneously at four different locations and carrying four different logbooks, they planned to cover the entire trail in one season. Each logbook would be passed on from one group of scouts to the next. A similar set of treks was planned for the Appalachian Trail.

Deep in the Yosemite Valley Library archives there is still a training manual for the "1954 Pacific Crest Trail Log Expedition." Some sample tips for scout leaders:

- *Don't smoke while walking on trails, wait until you rest.*
- *Burn tin cans out—a burnt can disintegrates in 4 months, an unburned tin can will last 3 and a half years to 4. Bury them.*
- *Take particular care not to allow bacon to soak through its container and stain other articles in the pack.*

The manual unabashedly used capital letters for one instruction: "The Log Book MUST BE KEPT MOVING over the Trail, no emergency should stop its progress. THE LOG BOOK—MUST GO ON!"

News reports followed the relay progress. Like a searchlight piercing the night, this spotlight on the PCT helped keep the dream alive.

There were daily reports on some legs and they reached the city via a unique courier. From the Portland, Oregon, *Daily Journal*: "The gray early morning mist that hung over the Cascade mountain peaks

was just beginning to glow a bright orange as Ralph Elle released two homing pigeons and watched them flap into the crisp air."

Sixty years later, Elle still recalls the cardboard box strapped atop his pack. It held two homing pigeons. Elle hiked an 80-mile leg in Oregon from Gold Lake to McKenzie Pass. His large group was a throwback to an earlier age, to the early 1900s when the Sierra Club thought nothing of taking 200 into the wilderness. Elle hiked with 119 boys and 14 leaders. They formed a quarter-mile-long line against the backdrop of the snowcapped Three Sisters. Every morning, Elle and his patrol squeezed duplicate copies of the latest news into two tiny capsules. Clipped to the birds' feet, they sent their feathered charges winging toward Portland for the evening paper. From the *Daily Journal*: "Two of the birds will be released daily with the hope that at least one will get through avoiding falcons."

News wasn't the only thing delivered by air. From the *Daily Journal*: "It rained food from the skies Wednesday in the rugged Three Sisters area." US Air Force bombers resupplied the boys. Some 1,200 pounds of food descended swinging on parachutes. Elle has photos of the rose-colored smoke bomb marking the drop zone. One parachute didn't fully open and the pallet landed with a thump. There was a great cloud of yellow powdered eggs. "We lost a lot of powdered eggs. But none of us were sorry about that," Elle said.

"THE LOG BOOK—MUST GO ON!" And so the four logbooks did. But so often poor trail conditions were overwhelming. Instead of hiking the entire length, the expedition covered just three-quarters of the PCT.

One year after the hike, in June 1955, the Boy Scouts' national magazine *Boys' Life* carried a five-page article about the relay. The magazine's circulation topped one million. That coverage stoked the PCT's fire. It was one lone beacon in an otherwise dark time.

DON AND JUNE MULFORD

Not long after Clarke and Catherine Montgomery died in 1958, a northwest ranching couple, Don and June Mulford, sold their herd of prize-winning polled shorthorns. Rangers said what they planned to do was crazy.

In 1959, Alaska and Hawaii were still territories. The PCT was an oft-broken track. The only thing predictable was its regular disappearance from maps and the ground. On April 19, 1959, the Mulfords saddled up. They took everyone's refrain—"Can't be done"—and threw it to the wind. Starting at the Mexican border, the Mulfords and four horses set off to thru-ride the Pacific Crest Trail.

"And Don's horse, Traveller, a big strawberry roan, he liked to chase bears. He would tree 'em. Just like a dog, he'd go after 'em," June said in a 2009 interview.

Starting in the late 1940s, the Mulfords had ranched for a decade along the Cowlitz River in Washington. Don had heard of the Pacific Crest Trail in 1937 while still a teen. Two decades later, he sold the idea to his wife. With the $10,000 from their cattle sale, they bought horses, tackle, saddlebags, and a wind-up 16 mm Bell & Howell movie camera. What was left would finance their ride. On their first night out, Don did what he'd do every night. He wrote in his journal. One time, when a thundershower wouldn't let up, he sought out the only dry place to write—an outhouse. The two of them loved being asked, "Where are you going?" They'd answer "Canada" and grin. "It takes about five minutes before some of them believe us," said Don.

Pushing steadily north, they bought, sold, or traded horses depending on their needs. In all, nine horses participated in the trek. Two died—one from lockjaw and the other put down after breaking a leg.

OPPOSITE: Don and June Mulford and their pack animals skirt the edge of California's Big Bear Lake on their first thru-ride of the PCT in 1959.

In the Sierra, the snow blocked their way. They had to retreat south. For three days they scraped the bottoms of their saddlebags. "Pancakes and coffee," June said, "Three times a day."

From Don's journal:

Many are the hours that we have ridden in silent awe, as we look out on nature's wonders. No sound breaks the stillness, except the dull thud of the horses' feet, an occasional bridle chain tinkling and the creak of saddle leather.

The wind was blowing so hard that it would almost lift you out of the saddle.

As luck would have it we got our shoes fixed today, the same as the horses.

When they rode through a town, reporters stopped them for an interview. The big-city newspapers sent a reporter and photographer into the field. The *Seattle Post-Intelligencer* did a two-page Sunday spread. By that point, Don, a strapping 41-year-old, had dropped 30 pounds, and June, nine years his junior, had lost more than 20. At Leech Lake near White Pass, Washington, the *Post-Intelligencer* reporter drew this out of Don: "If we can encourage even one other couple to take to the trail, we will have done them a favor they'll never forget."

In the heart of Washington, with days short and gear giving out, cold rain became the norm and then snow. On September 6, Don wrote, "After feeding the horses I brushed the new fallen snow from my jacket and entered the tent. June looked up from trying to patch the air mattresses. 'It is no use.' This was our third set of air mattresses. It was June's birthday."

After five months and a week, under skies anxious to release another layer of fat flakes, Don wrote, "We reached the Canadian border at 10:30 on this day, September 25, 1959."

June had sewed her own vest for the ride. Two pockets were specially cut to hold the 16 mm movie film. They shot 50 rolls. The Mulfords made a 90-minute movie and for a while they rented movie theaters to show it throughout the Northwest. They shined one more bright light on the PCT for a short while.

Soon after returning to their Cowlitz ranch house, Don, like Clarke, set to work typing. He transcribed his journal, finishing 180 pages later. He condensed it into an article for *National Geographic*. It was rejected. Don then tucked his journal in a manila envelope and laid it on a closet shelf.

The August 5, 1963, edition of *Sports Illustrated* magazine included stories about heavyweight boxer Sony Liston's defeat of Floyd Patterson in Las Vegas and the New York Yankees' lock on the pennant with a month left in the baseball season. Near the magazine's end, there was a six-page article on the Pacific Crest Trail. It called the PCT "a national treasure," and asked the critical question, "Why, then, is the Pacific Crest Trail so little known?"

Don's journal carried these prescient lines: "These trails will all be abandoned, one by one, if more people don't use them."

Don Mulford died in 1991. In 2000, the sixth edition of the PCT guidebook series said, "In 1988, Jim McCrea became the first 'thru-equestrian.'" Don and June Mulford had been forgotten.

In June 2009, June Mulford answered a phone call and found herself talking about her historic trek. It was the first time in years. She'd been in the process of a big housecleaning. The PCT movie reels were on the list to be thrown out.

OPPOSITE: Don Mulford at the 13,600-foot Trail Crest near Mount Whitney's summit in California. Mulford contemplated the route ahead before turning back in the face of heavy June snow.

The Mulfords' 16 mm footage has been saved. You can buy a DVD copy in the Pacific Crest Trail Association online store. Don Mulford's voice narrates the journey. Don's trail journal has been dusted off and finally shared with the world. On the 50th anniversary of their finish, *The Oregonian* ran a full-page article on their trek. And in 2012, Oregon Public Broadcasting did a half-hour TV special. The special runs at least four times a year and each time June gets phone calls.

Warren Rogers and the Clinton C. Clarke Papers

In 1958, within a span of eight months, both Clinton C. Clarke and Catherine Montgomery died. Both had a hand in the birth of a national treasure, yet neither would see their dream come to fruition.

The Bellingham Herald ran an extensive obituary about Montgomery—founding faculty of Western Washington University, founder of a children's library on Prince Edward Island, Canada, but there was no mention of the Pacific Crest Trail. As for the "Father of the PCT," his obituary was headlined, "Cotton Mather Descendant Dies Here."

What was going to happen to the PCT records that Clarke had so meticulously kept? There were boxes and boxes of them. Like Montgomery, Clarke was childless. There was no one to decide the fate of these records except Clarke's attorney, Vern Brydolf. The records were tagged for the dustbin.

Clarke left equal parts of his estate to the Pasadena Playhouse, the Pasadena Home for the Aged, and the Boy Scouts. Near the end of his life had Clarke given up hope? Had the father of the PCT given up on his dream?

Warren Rogers was living in the snug 800-square-foot, two-bedroom bungalow he'd built in south Los Angeles for himself and his wife, Mary. But as they added their three kids—Don, Paul, and Candace—the house became as crammed as a hiker's pack with a 10-day load. That was the state of affairs when Rogers got word that Clarke had died. Ignoring the practical objections, Rogers decided he'd save Clarke's files and bring them to his house.

Unlike in 1935, when Rogers had been asked to lend a hand, this time he had to pry his way in. Clarke hadn't mentioned Rogers in his handwritten will, so Rogers was an interloper, a gate-crasher. He was forced to beg, cajole, and prove his bona fides. "Look in the papers," he pleaded with Brydolf. "You will find my name on the letterhead among Mr. Clarke's effects."

Persistence. Often while hiking or riding on the PCT or battling on its behalf, persistence is everything. Rogers wore down Brydolf as sure as John Muir's glaciers ground smooth the hard Sierra granite. Rogers brought carload after carload of Clarke's records to his house. From that point, PCT correspondence was routed to Rogers. Rogers became the face of the trail.

The beloved bungalow nearly burst its seams. Rogers built a shed, but it only helped a bit. Clarke's boxes were going to stay under his roof. And on top of that, Rogers bought a printing press to further his trail efforts. His eldest son Don said, "The press filled the garage." Warren and Mary slept in the living room, the only place left.

Setting lead type in old-fashioned plates, Rogers launched a half dozen camping magazines. Each included the PCT, but each in turn sputtered out. Rogers was working sporadically. His PCT efforts were easily the equivalent of a full-time job—if only they paid the bills. Just as in the 1930s, Rogers was on radio

ABOVE: Warren Rogers on the PCT during the years of the YMCA relay.
OPPOSITE: The PCT heads toward Sourdough Gap in Washington's William O. Douglas Wilderness.

shows again touting the PCT. Twice he appeared on national TV—Art Linkletter's *House Party*. All the while Rogers's money dissipated. His kids' childhood memories were filled with cranking the big press and setting lead type. They loved their dad, but they resented the long hours he spent on the PCT.

As the 1960s headed toward its midpoint, Rogers's trail expenditures threatened to overwhelm his wages. To what length was Rogers willing to go? His debts piled and his son Don still recalls the strain in his dad's voice talking with bill collectors.

But there was a glimmer of hope from the opposite coast. In Washington, DC, for the first time in 20 years, there was serious talk of a national trails bill. Rogers should have focused on shoring up his family's finances. Instead, Don said, "Dad redoubled his trail efforts."

Surely Rogers knew what was on the line. Every year his family stained and oiled that handpicked redwood siding. Was Rogers willing to bet the house?

Legislation

The first national trails bill was introduced in Congress in 1945. It called for a nationwide system of trails 10,000 miles long. The Appalachian Trail was specifically included. The Pacific Crest Trail was not. Representative Daniel Hoch of Pennsylvania submitted the bill on February 13, 1945. After one perfunctory committee hearing, the bill died. One official, US Army Major General Philip Fleming, administrator of the long-defunct Federal Works Agency, said this about the bill: "The extension and improvement of public highways which have taken place throughout the States would seem definitely to make any such system of trails unnecessary."

The next time he ran, Hoch was voted out of office. In 1948, at Hoch's urging, a near-identical trails bill was introduced. It was ignored, deemed not worthy of even a short hearing. Hoch died in 1960, and in all that time no further trails bill was introduced in Congress.

"Ask not what your country can do for you, ask what you can do for your country." Eight inches of fresh snow lay on the ground but the day was sunny in 1961 when President John F. Kennedy was inaugurated. His young shoulders bore a nation's hopes. Pundits began calling his administration "Camelot." Did this mean a new day for trails? A wry quip of Supreme Court Justice William O. Douglas revealed a crystal-clear answer. Douglas, who was an ardent conservationist, remonstrated his friend, the new president: "The trouble is, Jack, you've never slept on the ground." One journalist wrote that the closest Kennedy "came to nature was to peer through binoculars at a moose from his lodge window."

President Kennedy appointed Stewart Udall as secretary of the interior. Udall was certainly inclined to pursue a trail agenda. But the end result was as predictable as the response on the day Udall suggested Kennedy join him for a hike. In September 1963, Udall and Kennedy were in Wyoming staying at the Rockefellers' Grand Teton lodge. It was an incomparable setting. Udall suggested that he and Kennedy get up for an early nature walk. Kennedy's staffers looked at Udall and laughed.

Two months later, Kennedy was assassinated.

While Kennedy had been a Boston Brahmin, the next man in the Oval Office was a Texas rancher. Under President Lyndon B. Johnson, would trails fare better? If it had been left solely to Johnson, most likely not.

Sunday, August 16, 1964, might well be one of the most important days for national trails legislation. President Johnson was alone at the White House. His wife, Claudia Alta Taylor Johnson, affectionately known as Lady Bird, was away. What was on his mind? The man was preoccupied with his prize bulls—how well would they place at the Blanco County Fair? The Secret Service finally delivered the wired report after 11:00 p.m., and Johnson must have slapped a thigh and smiled. The ranch walked away with six first-place ribbons and the reserve champion bull. So reported Johnson's daily diary.

When the administrations had changed, Udall stayed on as secretary of the interior. Trails were still one of his goals and he also wanted to protect the country's threatened wild rivers. But how do you get the attention of a rancher focused on trophy cattle? Udall made an end run instead. He courted the first lady.

In 1960, Daniel Ogden had worked for the Kennedy campaign and after the election, secured a position in the Department of the Interior. In 1962, the Bureau of Recreation was created and Udall appointed Ogden the assistant director of planning and research. Two years later, Udall approached Ogden and said, "I need your help to plan a trip." Udall wanted to take Lady Bird Johnson rafting down the Snake River. All

First Lady Claudia "Lady Bird" Johnson floats the Snake River near the Teton Range with Secretary of the Interior Stewart Udall. This 1964 raft trip helped influence President Lyndon Johnson's decision two years later to push legislation establishing the PCT as one of the first two national scenic trails.

the planning revolved around a special lunch at a spot reachable only by water. With the Grand Tetons as a backdrop, Udall planned to pitch Lady Bird his plans to protect the nation's rivers and to build a nationwide system of trails.

Ogden was the advance man for the float trip. Working closely with the National Park Service, Ogden knew how much might be riding on Udall's lunch with Lady Bird. Everything was arranged. Big inflatable rafts were set to deliver them to a particular spot on the banks of the Snake River. The report came to Ogden the night before: "The river is too low. There isn't enough water coming down the Snake River to float to the picnic site." The rafts couldn't make it. Ogden huddled with Udall and then, he said, "We called the Bureau of Reclamation and told them to open up the dam." There are benefits to being the secretary of the interior. Upstream, the big valves turned and water flowed in a surge.

The LBJ Presidential Library archives preserved the moment in a photo. Lady Bird looks up and she's beaming as Udall points out the sights using his full arm. The two are side by side sitting on the thick walls of a gray raft. The Grand Tetons slice the sky, cheering Udall in his efforts. Udall got his lunch. No record has surfaced recording what they said. But Johnson's diary shows that he spoke to his wife that night at 11:05 p.m., just before he got word about his showstopping bulls.

Not even six months later, on February 8, 1965, Johnson delivered a special message to Congress. At the last minute he hesitated. Vietnam, the Achilles' heel that would bring Johnson down, was much on his mind. But he signed the message and by noon it left the White House, crossing the grassy expanse of the National Mall to be delivered within the great white Capitol Dome. This text is referred to as Johnson's American Beauty Message. Like a musical's overture, it led with the main theme; the composer's muse was Lady Bird.

> *For centuries Americans have drawn strength and inspiration from the beauty of our country. It would be a neglectful generation indeed . . . which failed to preserve and extend such a heritage for its descendants.*

William O. Douglas

It was a close call at the 1944 Democratic Convention— many thought Supreme Court Justice William O. Douglas would get the nod to be Franklin Roosevelt's vice president. If so, Douglas would have become president nine months later when Roosevelt died. Instead, the convention went with the quiet senator from Missouri, Harry Truman.

On Sunday, October 2, 1949, Douglas squeezed in one last trail ride before the opening of the Supreme Court's fall term. Mounted on a spirited stallion, Douglas climbed out of Chinook Pass in the Cascades, rising on switchbacks on the Pacific Crest Trail. Later that night he'd take a red-eye flight from Seattle to Washington, DC, to make the 10:00 a.m. Monday start of the court's next term. But then his horse spooked, reared, and . . .

From *The Seattle Times*, October 3, 1949: "Justice William O. Douglas, one of the leading liberals of the US Supreme Court, was injured gravely yesterday in the Cascade Mountains he loved as a boy. He suffered 13 rib fractures and a punctured lung when his frightened horse fell and rolled on him. 'He rolled over me and I could hear all my bones break,' said Douglas."

"Douglas Rallies from Injuries" was the headline days later. After recovering, Douglas served on the Supreme Court until 1975. Today, just south of Chinook Pass, PCT hikers walk through the William O. Douglas Wilderness.

There were five full paragraphs devoted to trails. Ogden drafted them. The written text carried an all-caps heading: "TRAILS." After citing "the forgotten outdoorsmen" who liked to walk and hike, Johnson threw down the gauntlet: "We must have trails." The tall Texan proposed:

> We need to copy the great Appalachian Trail in all parts of America. I am requesting, therefore, that the Secretary of the Interior work with his colleagues in the federal government and with state and local leaders and recommend to me a cooperative program to encourage a national system of trails.

Such was the result of a lunch on the Snake River, made possible by a timely release of water from a dam and a conversation with an influential wife of a president, all as requested by Ogden, advance man. On such matters a trail's fate may turn. Johnson leaned his broad shoulders into this trail proposal and put the full weight of his administration behind seeking legislation for trails.

Ogden chaired the effort to write the report for Johnson's trail bill. Ogden's steering committee consisted of himself and three others: Theodore Swem, National Park Service; Hamilton Pyles, Forest Service; and Eldon Holmes, Bureau of Land Management.

The seminal *Trails for America* report was issued in September 1966. Senate and House bills were drafted and promptly introduced to effect the report's recommendations. The bill proposed three categories of trails: national scenic trails, recreational trails, and metropolitan area trails. The report recommended that the Appalachian Trail be designated the first national scenic trail. The PCT and other trails were relegated to a study category for possible future consideration.

The phrase "possible future consideration" was like a sentence to purgatory for the PCT. Consider the Continental Divide Trail. The CDT runs from Mexico to Canada along the spine of the Rockies. For the CDT, "future consideration" means that today it is still unfinished, lightly traveled, and little known. More than a decade passed, not until 1978, before the CDT was designated a national scenic trail. But that decade setback left the CDT immeasurably behind.

Warren Rogers's Legacy

In 1966, Warren Rogers's financial lifeblood was hemorrhaging. A major magazine backer deserted. Significant advertisers disappeared. Caught up in his monetary pressure cooker, the liens and notices on Rogers's house threatened to boil over.

His son Don said, "I remember Dad constantly writing letters, constantly on the phone, just pushing as hard as he could to get Mr. Clarke's dream fulfilled." To that end, one could hardly look back on history and dwell on Rogers's personal failure. Posterity would see only his success.

The *Trails for America* report was issued and bills were introduced in the House and the Senate. Would the PCT be an official scenic trail or would it merely be *studied*?

Rogers spent his time promoting the PCT, not on rounding up more advertisers. Hearings were set on the bills early in 1967. Rogers redoubled his efforts but as 1966 closed, he lost one battle: Rogers and his family were forced to move out of the beloved house that he had built.

OPPOSITE: The steep North Cascades dwarf the Murray family and their pack string as they pass alongside Washington's Mica Lake in 1970.

The committee hearing in the House of Representatives began on March 6, 1967. This time it wasn't perfunctory; the hearing lasted two full days. The transcript was 206 pages. Forest Service Chief Ed Cliff testified that the PCT existed along almost its entire proposed length and it had been passable for hiking since 1937. Representative Roy Taylor of North Carolina, who had introduced Johnson's bill, reiterated that stance. He told the committee that much of the Pacific Crest Trail currently exists. The state of affairs on the Continental Divide Trail, Taylor said, was just the opposite. The sad fact, Taylor conceded, was that there were so few existing trails along the Divide.

Not even two weeks later, on March 15, 1967, the Senate began its committee hearing on the National Trails System. It also devoted two days. On July 1, 1968, the Senate passed a National Trails System Act. In its version, the Appalachian Trail, the Pacific Crest Trail, and the northern half of the Continental Divide Trail would be the first designated national scenic trails. The PCT was in. On July 15, 1968, the House passed its version. It was far narrower. The Appalachian Trail was the only designated national scenic trail. The PCT and 13 other trails were designated for future study. The PCT was out.

Members of the House and Senate conferred on the final language of the bill. Which would it be? The Joint Conference Report was issued on September 12, 1968. The House and the Senate quickly agreed to the recommended changes.

Late morning on October 2, 1968, President Johnson greeted François Tombalbaye, the president of Chad. That night Johnson held a formal state dinner. The day was chock-full and hectic. But the effect of one 39-minute interval still reverberates today.

The setting was the East Room of the White House. A large map was hung and there were so many conservation dignitaries present that President Johnson ran out of pens. Starting at 1:17 p.m., the president signed acts creating Redwood National Park and North Cascades National Park, he signed the National Wild and Scenic Rivers Act, and he signed the National Trails System Act.

The National Trails System Act designated two trails as the nation's first national scenic trails. One was the Appalachian Trail. The other was the Pacific Crest Trail.

What factors tipped the scales in the PCT's favor? It's impossible to state for certain, but the foundation for the trail bill, Ogden's *Trails for America* report, stated one thing clear as rain: since 1937 the PCT was "continuously passable" and "in existence." It said that the CDT and its fellows "are only ideas."

"If hundreds of years from now American boys and girls can tramp along the Pacific Crest Trail and bless us for all that we have done to save this great wilderness pathway, all our effort, all our striving, and all our work will have been worth it," Ogden wrote. "No greater monument to our concern for our fellow human beings could be our legacy to the future."

The 1968 National Trails System Act affected Rogers deeply. It vindicated his efforts. For the rest of his life Rogers worked tirelessly to make the PCT a reality on the ground and to see it completed. Rogers suffered a stroke in his late 70s, but he kept typing letters, often writing that he was typing it all with one finger. He died in 1992 at age 83.

After Rogers's death, Louise Marshall, then president of the Pacific Crest Trail Association, said, "I think it's due to Warren's efforts that the whole idea of the Pacific Crest Trail remained alive." Warren Rogers saved the PCT one last time.

OPPOSITE: Mount Rainier is the backdrop for a September sunset in Washington's Goat Rocks Wilderness.

Today on a quiet street in Santa Ana, California, there is a neat, trim, white-painted house. It sits proud and in good repair. No visual evidence shows that it was once clad in handpicked redwood siding. When Rogers built it in 1948, certainly he must have thought he was building an enduring family legacy. That was not to be. Today another family lives there.

But there is something today that is as proud and in good repair. It is Rogers's legacy: the Pacific Crest Trail.

CHAPTER FOUR

LITERATURE

The First Pacific Crest Trail Best Seller: Eric Ryback

Just as with knighthood, the National Trails System Act bestowed an honorific on the Pacific Crest Trail. With the flourish of President Lyndon Johnson's pen, the PCT was dubbed the Pacific Crest National Scenic Trail. It might still be the PCT to its friends, but when cocktail attire was required, it was the PCNST.

Much change was afoot. No more would the likes of Clinton C. Clarke have to shuffle their feet standing hat in hand. No more begging the United States Forest Service for a sliver of attention. With the full force of the law, Congress directed the secretary of agriculture to take charge. The Forest Service was the lead agency responsible for the PCT.

National Trails System Act, Public Law 90-543 stated, "The Secretary of Agriculture shall establish an advisory council for the Pacific Crest National Scenic Trail."

The Pacific Crest National Scenic Trail Advisory Council first met in San Francisco on November 19, 1970. At lunch, there was a highly anticipated guest speaker. Less than a month before, the speaker received a telegram from the chief of the Forest Service:

> On behalf of the Forest Service, United States Department of Agriculture: Congratulations, Eric for your 2,300 mile hike from Canada to the Mexican border along the newly designated Pacific Crest Trail. . . . E. P. Cliff, CHIEF

Eric Ryback remains the only thru-hiker to receive a telegram of congratulations from the chief of the Forest Service. Ryback was 18 years old. He was the youngest person in the room.

In Michigan, five months before, on June 10, 1970, members of the Belleview High Class of 1970 walked one by one to receive their diplomas—but one was missing. That AWOL classmate was walking, too. That same day, Ryback set out from Canada's Manning Park bearing an 80-pound pack, heading south on the PCT.

Kon-Tiki was what cast Ryback adrift from his Michigan moorings. His mother gave him the book. Ryback had been a high school varsity long-distance swimmer who by happenstance saw an Appalachian Trail sign on a family camping trip. Then he read Thor Heyerdahl's *Kon-Tiki*. That was "the force that solidified my adventurous drive," he said in a 2008 interview. Ryback quit the swim team to focus on hiking the Appalachian Trail. In a bitter pique, Ryback's swim coach said he'd be a failure and his teammates shunned him.

In 1969—the summer of Woodstock and Neil Armstrong's walk on the moon—Ryback hiked the Appalachian Trail, becoming the 41st person to thru-hike it. When Ernest and Patricia Ryback met their son at the end, his first words were, "Next summer I'm hiking the Pacific Crest Trail."

He spent his senior year earning money for the trip, writing letters to the Forest Service for PCT maps— such as they were—and writing *First Step*, his book about his AT adventure. He submitted *First Step* to Wilderness Press. Thomas Winnett, the publisher, rejected it.

Before his PCT trek, Ryback sewed the flags of Mexico, Canada, and the United States on the back of his Kelty pack. He mailed five food drops. The distance between each resupply would be 375 miles.

Leaving Manning Park at 6:00 a.m., Ryback arrived at Monument 78 at the Canadian border in time for lunch. The chest-high metal obelisk stood as it had since 1905. It would be 18 more years before the modern monument, a cluster of five fir pillars of varying heights, would be flown by helicopter to the site.

PREVIOUS SPREAD: A rare storm looms over Joshua trees in Southern California's Kelso Valley. OPPOSITE: Author and thru-hiker Eric Ryback soaks up the sun in Tuolumne Meadows, Yosemite National Park, California, in 1970.

The North Cascades harbor massive ice fields that last through June and into July. On a steep slope high above Hopkins Lake, Ryback's boots broke free on a traverse. He flipped on his back and flew downward. Scared. Out of control. His external-frame backpack saved him. One metal corner dug in, spraying snow, and he leaned hard into it. He ground to a stop. That night, while his high school classmates sat down to family celebratory dinners, Ryback dined alone.

Moving south, two weeks later he was at Stevens Pass brushing civilization—a gas station candy machine. Ryback converted eight dimes into as many candy bars and ravenously devoured them.

He reached the Oregon border two days after Independence Day, and on July 30 crossed into California. In Northern California, not far from Old Station, he came off the trail to re-sole his boots. Darlene Young was car camping, but when she saw the huge backpack she took Ryback into her campsite for dinner. "He seemed so lonesome, so starved for human contact," she said.

Ryback ate a whole loaf of bread. He rolled the slices into chunks and then dipped each one into a jar of jam. Young had bought a half gallon of milk that day. Ryback drank it. She wasn't that much older than Ryback, but he brought out her maternal instincts. She walked him back to the trail and what she still clearly recalls was his strong need to finish. "It wasn't about disappointing family or friends. He didn't want to disappoint himself," she said in a 2008 interview.

Like a boat entering a foreign port, Ryback received an escort for the final leg. Forest Service Lands Officer John Caragozian met Ryback at Warner Springs. They hiked an alternate 65-mile route due to a recent wildfire.

Ryback finished on October 16 with television and newspaper reporters present. *The San Diego Union-Tribune* reported, "Ryback's father, Ernest . . . who has not seen his son since June 8, ran across several hundred yards of plowed fields to welcome him." Soon afterward, Ryback received the invitation to speak at the first meeting of the PCNST Advisory Council.

At that meeting Ryback met Winnett of Wilderness Press, the man who'd rejected his AT manuscript. Before this PCT hike, Ryback told his hometown newspaper that he planned to write a book about his PCT hike. Winnett said that Ryback offered his yet-to-be-written PCT book, but Winnett wasn't interested.

Ryback remembers it differently. He said Winnett was interested, along with other publishers. But he went with Chronicle Books, which published *The High Adventure of Eric Ryback* in 1971. The book was a runaway hit. It was translated into Japanese and Norwegian. After two editions in hardcover and four in paperback, it sold more than 300,000 copies. Ryback was suddenly in demand as a speaker and writer. He was the subject of the first feature article in the inaugural issue of *Backpacker* magazine.

After his 1970 PCT hike, Ryback attended the University of Denver. In 1972, at age 20, he hiked the Continental Divide Trail (CDT) with his 18-year-old brother, Tim Ryback. They wrote a book about the hike, *The Ultimate Journey*, which Chronicle Books published in 1973.

Today, it's still not uncommon to hear someone say, "I first heard about the PCT from Eric Ryback's book." Ryback set loose a wave of interest in the PCT. His book's success also provided the impetus for the PCT's bible—Wilderness Press's PCT guidebook series.

But while Ryback was hiking the CDT, the bullet train that was his newly found success was about to be derailed.

OPPOSITE: Wilderness Press publisher Thomas Winnett scouts the trail for the PCT guidebook series in the 1970s (left); before digital printing, guidebook maps were made by hand by painstakingly assembling layers of paper and clear plastic strips. This topographic map was razor cut to show the underlying blue paper layer for Little Grass Valley Reservoir. This is an original used for the first edition of the PCT guidebook series (right).

Thomas Winnett and the PCT Guidebook Series

In the 1950s and 1960s, Fybate Notes were a popular crutch for students cramming for finals at the University of California, Berkeley. The publisher was Thomas Winnett, a lean, bodysurfing, World War II vet. His business thrived—students were always looking for a leg up—but the advent of Xerox copiers in the 1960s left him ill at ease. Students could buy one copy of Fybate Notes and copy more for their friends.

This was the setting in 1966 when Winnett met an old friend for lunch. Winnett and Karl Schwenke were sitting in a booth in Berkeley's La Fiesta restaurant. "We got to talking about the Sierra Nevada . . . We decided that there was probably a market for trail guides. So we decided to make one," said Winnett. In May 1967 they published *Sierra North: 100 Back-Country Trips*. It sold out. So did the second printing. In quick succession the new Wilderness Press printed *Trails of the Angeles*, *Sierra South*, and other titles. Winnett created the pocket-sized High Sierra Hiking Guide series, the popular 96-page booklets that covered one 15-minute quadrangle map. They fit in a shirt or blue jeans pocket. Many hikers sported that recognizable snug bulge.

In 1971, Winnett saw Ryback's PCT best seller fly out of bookstores. Did he feel a tinge of jealousy?

Jeff Schaffer, one of the Wilderness Press guidebook authors, recalled, "Eric Ryback really was very important getting things started . . . Tom seized on it and said 'Well hey . . . I got a guide to the John Muir Trail. I got one to the Yosemite Trail. I might as well have one to the Pacific Crest Trail.'"

In the summer of 1972, Winnett and four others set out to scout the PCT in California. John Robinson covered from the Mexican border to Tehachapi. Jim Jenkins pushed a surveyor's wheel all through the

A Family Ride

The Pacific Crest Trail was featured in *Life* magazine's "Special Issue on Americans Outdoors," September 3, 1971. The article ran under the title "A family clip-clops all the way from Mexico to Canada." Over the course of two summers, 1969 and 1970, Barry Murray, his wife Bernice, and their three young children, Barry Jr., Bernadette, and Colette, rode the length of the PCT on horseback.

Murray opened his article this way: "My wife Bernice, in her model agency wardrobe, and me, typecast in my vested suit as an ad agency photographer in San Francisco, were both very depressed with our lives. We now know why, but it took us 2,500 miles of travel on horseback to find out."

In April 1969, the Murrays and James Miller, a teenage family friend, left from Campo, California, at the Mexican border with six horses to ride and six as their pack train. "We had thrown together a slapdash collection of packs, saddles, and gear for about $1,000 and allotted ourselves $40 a week for food," Murray wrote. Their canvas pack covers bore a freshly painted message that made their goal clear: "Mexico to Canada."

The first summer was a high snow year, but the family still made it 1,360 miles, nearly reaching Mount Lassen before winter drifts forced them to retreat. They began their second season minus Miller, but along the way they gained one other—one of their horses, Daisy, gave birth. They named the foal Tagalong.

When they crossed the Columbia River from Oregon to Washington, the Bridge of the Gods posed a particular challenge. First, there was the official permission hurdle. When Murray wrote ahead for clearance to take their pack train across the 150-foot-high, quarter-mile-long open-metal-grate span, the response he got back wasn't confidence building. The reply: "If you can do it, go ahead."

OPPOSITE: The Murray family pack train north of California's Tuolumne Meadows. ABOVE: The Murray family below the Packwood Glacier in Washington's Goat Rocks Wilderness.

When the family and horses reached the other side, Murray said "it was like crossing a quarter-mile of cattle guard in the sky."

In ever increasing bad weather and with snow falling throughout their final week, they "struggled over a nearly impassable trail. We were not sure we would make it until we were within two miles of our goal." But after nine months of traveling over two summers, make it they did.

The once-bright message was now faded and the paint was chipped, but the prophecy on their pack covers had come true: "Mexico to Canada."

Some years later Murray wrote, "The saddest day of my life was ending our sojourn of nine months far, far too soon. I have been quoted many times for saying—'Part of my life has been lived, and nothing will ever be the same again.'"

southern Sierra. Winnett took on from Crabtree Meadow to Interstate 80. Schaffer covered the longest segment, working his way from Interstate 80 to Castle Crags. Andrew Husari followed the trail from there to the Oregon border. It was a wild rush to get it all done in one season.

On May 10, 1973, *Pacific Crest Trail: Volume I: California* was released. Over time, the California guide was split into two volumes; today they are both in their sixth editions. In 1974, the Oregon and Washington guidebook was released. It is now in its seventh edition. In 2008, the PCT guidebook series won the National Outdoor Book Award in the classic category. In recent years, hikers have turned to free online maps such as the *Halfmile* series, but Winnett and his guides ruled the trail scene for four decades.

When Winnett died in 2011 at age 89, the Pacific Crest Trail Association published an article titled "Remembering Thomas Winnett." It read, in part:

> *Winnett gave thousands the confidence to explore the high country and set them on the path toward protecting the outdoors. The phrase "We held him close to our hearts" often marks someone's passing. Thousands in the hiking community did exactly that for years preceding Winnett's death. Tucked in so many chest pockets were Wilderness Press Pocket Guides or the torn-out pages from PCT guidebooks. Roslyn Bullas, who recently sat at the editorial helm of Wilderness Press, called Winnett's death "the passing of an era."*

The Winnett Caper

Earl Shaffer was the first thru-hiker on the Appalachian Trail and, just like Ryback, Shaffer's 1948 accomplishment made the national news. Shaffer waited 30 years, but, like Ryback, he also published a book about his trek: *Walking with Spring*. Even as late as the 1990s, Shaffer held court before standing-room-only crowds. Shaffer died in 2002. Not long afterward *Walking with Spring* went into its fourth printing.

Shaffer's trail diary and other records reside in the Smithsonian. In 2011, a West Virginian lawyer meticulously retraced Shaffer's steps. He became convinced that Shaffer had "skipped ten percent or more." The report didn't seem to dent Shaffer's reputation.

In the AT world, Shaffer, Benton MacKaye, and Myron Avery stand as giants. MacKaye is considered the "Father of the Appalachian Trail." In 1921 he published an article proposing the AT. Ten years later, Avery became chairman of the Appalachian Trail Conference and his reign lasted 21 years. But from the mid-1930s onward, Avery and MacKaye had an all-too-public acrimonious feud.

It would be nice if no disputes marred the PCT's history. It would be nice if the tale of Winnett and Ryback ended with what was written above. But to do that would leave a gap in the saga of the trail.

In the whirlwind summer of 1972, while the Ryback brothers were hiking the Continental Divide Trail (CDT), Winnett and his crew were scouting for the PCT guidebooks.

Winnett saw the continued success of Ryback's book. The paperback edition of *The High Adventure of Eric Ryback* went through a second and then a third printing. This was the climate in which Winnett got a report from Jeff Schaffer in the field. Schaffer had run into a classmate, Phillip Kane, and he said he gave Ryback a ride. Thus was the seed of doubt planted.

OPPOSITE: Eric Ryback at Monument 252, finishing his hike at the Mexican border. Ryback finished 20 miles west of the present PCT's southern terminus. California's then-largest-ever forest fire forced him to end at the alternate location (left); 40 years later, Ryback returned to the spot of his finish wearing the pack he carried in 1970 (right).

Winnett sent out word to his trail scouts: find discrepancies in Ryback's book; find anyone that says Ryback didn't hike the whole trail. Winnett made the same requests in letters to many others. He wrote to Barry Murray, who thru-rode the trail over two summers during 1969 and 1970, "Dear Barry: In my book about the Pacific Crest Trail, I want to marshal some evidence that Ryback did not walk the whole trail."

Winnett was 51. Ryback was 20. Winnett made no attempt to contact Ryback, who by then was at Idaho State University working toward his degree in secondary education and writing about his CDT hike. Winnett also made no attempt to contact Ryback's publisher, who was actually Winnett's friend.

In December 1972, Winnett wrote what would become pages three and four of his new PCT guidebook. He edited and rewrote it four separate times. In bold-faced, quadruple-size type, Winnett titled the section "The Ryback Caper."

Winnett spent three paragraphs on supposition and math that ended with this question: "Could an 18-year-old American boy carrying 46% of his body weight average 30 miles per day on mountain trails day by day?" Then Winnett trotted out two specific circumstances. In the second, he challenged Ryback's account about hiking those last 65 miles with John Caragozian. How could Ryback have finished that distance in two days when "slowed down not only by a pack but by a Forest Service official?"

The Second Best Seller

The first PCT best seller was *The High Adventure of Eric Ryback*. The third and the most recent was Cheryl Strayed's *Wild*. But in between there was another. In 1975, National Geographic published *The Pacific Crest Trail*. It sold more than 320,000 copies and, like Strayed's and Ryback's works, it too changed lives. Perhaps none more so than those of the book's author and photographer.

During the summers of 1973 and 1974, author William Gray and photographer Sam Abell spent seven months on the PCT. Their packs weighed 50 to 60 pounds, a third of which was photographic equipment. Coming in at 200 pages with 123 photographs, the book wove in trail scenes with interviews with hikers, rangers, miners, ranch owners, mountaineers, climbers, loggers, firefighters, horsemen, geologists, a trail crew, and a smoke jumper. The book covered a joyous trail wedding. It covered a contentious land-use meeting where the speakers jousted like knights fighting over the PCT's future route. The Forest Service officer John Caragozian was there, the man who had accompanied Ryback on the last two days of his trek. In a short-sleeve shirt and black string tie, Caragozian raised his hand to make a point in one of Abell's photos, while on the opposite page Abell caught a Norman Rockwell–style frieze of stern-faced landowners.

Gray hiked 1,600 miles for the book. He re-soled his boots three times. When reached recently, he said the book "had a profound impact both personally and professionally." It kick-started what would become a 33-year National Geographic career ending with Gray's 12-year run as head of the book division. For Abell, of the photos gracing the book, none was more important than the ones on pages 25 and 77. They show a freckle-faced, long-haired Denise Myers, one of the PCT's earliest female thru-hikers. Abell and Myers married in 1977. They are still together.

When the book was published, Gray received a letter from PCT pioneer Warren Rogers: "I want to congratulate you and Sam for doing a splendid job!"

Photographer Sam Abell (left) and author William Gray (right) toast reaching Monument 78 at the PCT's northern terminus. Gray and Abell spent two summers on the PCT for their 1975 National Geographic book *The Pacific Crest Trail*.

Winnett wrote to Caragozian, "I don't want to detract from your accomplishment, but I must say that seems like an awful long way in two days." Caragozian wrote back and was emphatic: "No you have not misread the book. The portion of the book you are questioning is authentic."

Winnett sent the guidebook to the printer on February 15, 1973. This was seven days after he received Caragozian's letter telling him his challenge was wrong. Winnett sent the "Caper" text to the printer without any changes.

In May 1973, Winnett submitted a five-page article to *Backpacker* magazine. It bore the same title as the Ryback section in the guidebook. *Backpacker* rejected the article.

Question to Winnett in 2009: "Were you angry at Ryback?" Winnett: "Probably."

Kane had no idea he'd been the spark for Winnett's attack. In a 2009 interview Kane said, "I took [Ryback] north. . . . I was just giving a guy a short ride." *North*—the opposite direction for one skipping trail.

The publication of Winnett's guidebook devastated Ryback. It was a sucker punch that drastically changed the arc of his life.

Ryback's publisher took the lead, hired attorneys, and they sued. Libel suits are incredibly hard to prove. "It was kind of bizarre because the trail wasn't all established," Ryback said. "We could have never proven that I hiked every foot of the trail."

After litigating for a while the suit was dropped. Ryback moved on. He left the trail world far behind. He graduated college in 1976 and taught English for a couple of years. He moved back to Michigan in 1980, was a substitute teacher, and then got a job at Ann Arbor Trust Bank. He got married, raised a family, and settled in St. Louis, working as an investment manager. He bought the company in 1993 and retired seven years later.

His three children knew next to nothing about his Triple Crown feat. While he remained a hero to many PCT hikers who came after him, the controversy was always present. "The taint has never left," he said.

He said his boyhood dream of being an adventurer was certainly derailed. "After the Winnett thing, I was done," Ryback said. "Had Winnett not done what he did, who knows what would have happened. I most likely would have stayed in the outdoor industry. I am not complaining. I have had a wonderful life and perhaps all for the better. Life went on. I did really well anyway."

Coincidentally, in 2007, his nephews were hiking the PCT. They were at the annual Kick Off at Lake Morena and word got out their uncle was Ryback. They called and asked if he'd come down and give a talk. He could not get away.

But over the course of the next year, Greg "Strider" Hummel, a 1977 thru-hiker and Kick Off cofounder, convinced Ryback to attend. He spoke for the first time before a modern hiker gathering. He was warmly received. The prodigal child had returned.

"It was great," Ryback recalled. "It was actually a give back because the trail did a lot for me."

In 2009, Ryback joined the board of the Pacific Crest Trail Association. He took it upon himself to design and finance the modern PCT completion medal—his goal was to make it "Olympic quality."

Today, questions about whether Ryback hiked the entire trail seem all but irrelevant. What is unanimous—even from Winnett and others who held any doubt—is that Ryback, his incredible accomplishment, and his book had a tremendous positive effect on the trail.

CHAPTER FIVE

PEOPLE

Trail Angels

Even in Eric Ryback's day, the weary walker viewed folks such as Darlene Young, who delivered kindness out of instinct, as angels. Help for the Pacific Crest Trail hiker and horseback rider comes in many forms, from an unplanned lift to the trailhead or back to town to cold drinks and hot food where the trail meets a forest road. These instances of aid are called *trail magic*, and those who provide them are called *trail angels*, an amazing part of the PCT community. They may be people who've hiked the trail who are looking to give back, or angels may stumble into the service of hikers and horseback riders by accident. They may do it once or they may so love what they find and feel that they continue year after year.

In 2015, Cheryl Strayed's memoir *Wild* and the subsequent Reese Witherspoon movie brought the PCT out of the shadows and fully into the public consciousness, with good and concerning consequences. The growing popularity of the trail meant more hikers. More hikers meant more trail angels. And the growing presence of all these people raised questions about the need to understand and address the cumulative impacts on the landscapes through which the PCT travels. It's clear that PCT lovers and advocates will be wrestling with this issue forever.

Regardless of the long-term implications, it's impossible to write about the trail and the amazing people behind it without recognizing the valuable service trail angels provide. Here we tell the tales of two angels who've been around for a time and epitomize the spirit of giving that is true trail magic.

BOB RIESS

Bob Riess reaches into the battered cardboard hiking box on his kitchen table, pulling out the detritus of many a newly weight-conscious hiker. There were canisters of compressed cooking gas, parachute cord, and many other assorted items whose sole utility would be to contribute to the carrier's backache. He lifts a gallon-sized plastic bag filled with tent stakes, abandoned over many years by former owners who wisely exchanged them in favor of a lighter version.

"This is where tent stakes go to die," said Riess, a San Diego, California, trail angel, who since 1999 has picked up hundreds of PCT hikers at the airport, put them up for the night, and then shuttled them out to the PCT's southern terminus. He is but one in a dedicated cadre of San Diego trail angels who ensures that PCT hikers' journeys begin as safely and stress-free as possible.

Riess recalled one couple that went through their backpacks on his picnic table and mailed 12 pounds home. When they arrived at Warner Springs for their first resupply, 109 miles north of the Mexican border, they quickly shaved another 12 pounds.

It's a typical routine, played over and over. "My living room becomes like a cowboy camp," Riess said. "The packs are broken open; we're filling up water bottles and testing stoves."

Often hikers—especially those coming from far away—will have new gear mailed to Riess's house from the retailer. So the day before they are going to hike, they have to test the gear to make sure it's good enough and they know how to use it. "It's like Christmas. They're setting up their tent for the first time on my front lawn," he said.

PREVIOUS SPREAD: The moon rises over Oregon's Diamond Peak.
OPPOSITE: In a rare wet year, California poppies abound, covering the rolling flat country south of Warner Springs.

Riess is an unlikely yet elite member of the PCT community. He's a trail angel, a mercy man, who does favors for strangers for nothing more than the satisfaction of helping out. He said he's not much of a hiker, though he is getting into it more. He hiked part of the John Muir Trail section of the PCT in 2014.

Riess spent his first career in the US Navy. From 1972 to 1994, he served on seven ships in the Pacific Fleet, spending 13 of those 23 years at sea. He rose to the rank of commander, and was the executive officer (second in command) of a guided missile frigate in the Persian Gulf in 1987, the year the USS *Vincennes* accidently shot down a commercial airliner.

His ships took him to Karachi, Bahrain, and many other foreign and domestic ports. But the sea duty took its toll. He and his wife divorced after one of those cruises. They had two young children at the time.

When he retired in 1994, he and his son Bobby, then 10 years old, hiked the Tahoe-Yosemite Trail south to Tuolumne Meadows. "Every hiker we met northbound was a PCT thru-hiker," Riess said. "I was not aware of the existence of the PCT until 1994. I had no concept of what it entailed."

He was intrigued. He found the storied PCT online chat room, the PCT-L, and read. He did that for three years. One thing struck him year after year. When the thru-hikers finished, they wrote that their worst experience seemed always to be getting to the southern terminus from the San Diego Airport. Every single year, "Day Zero" in San Diego was hell. Hikers arriving in the afternoon could not make the one bus to the El Cajon Transit Center in time to get the next bus to Campo, so they'd spend the night in the bus station, often getting rousted by the sheriff or transit police.

In 1999, Riess was teaching high school algebra and geometry when he posted his first invite to hikers on the PCT-L. He said that year was a "slow start." He hosted 17 at his house. He felt like it was a no-brainer. "I have a six-passenger van, two empty bedrooms, an RV, and no wife to say no," he said with a smile.

That same year, he saw a post from Tom Reynolds on the PCT-L about the Annual Day Zero Pacific Crest Trail Kick Off (ADZPCTKO). It was the first year of the event that would host 75 hikers at Lake Morena County Park. The low-key event offers aspiring PCT thru-hikers a gathering where they can seek help with gear, get advice and encouragement, and tie in with other hikers.

Riess naively volunteered to bring Sunday breakfast for the group. To cook it, he brought a gas barbecue and before he realized what had happened, he was the Saturday night chef as well, cooking burgers on the only barbecue in the park. "I was waylaid," he said, grinning wide. "I got nominated by virtue of being there."

For the first 12 years, he was known to many thru-hikers as the "Food Dude," creating a smorgasbord. As the Kick Off event seemingly doubled in size every year, Riess added vegetarian meals and more elaborate fare. He enlisted teams of people to help cook and serve. A few times the event coincided with his birthday, April 28. On those years, his daughter Jeannie would bring birthday cake to the camp to celebrate, with enough plates and forks for 500 people.

Riess helped hikers with gusto. One year, a couple stayed with him for five nights because the wife was sick. They were 3,000 miles from home and knew one person in town: him. Riess shuttled them to the doctor. Once, a hiker at the trailhead realized he had forgotten his hiking poles at Riess's house. Riess figured out he could deliver the poles two days later as the hiker crossed a road.

Over the years, the routine at the house became as rigid as a Navy ship, only with softer edges. It had to. Collect hikers at the airport. Hit the gear or food store if needed. Come home and eat, repack backpacks,

OPPOSITE: Punchbowl Falls on Eagle Creek, the widely popular PCT alternate route descending to the Columbia River Gorge, just before the trail crosses from Oregon to Washington.

watch movies, tell stories, and crash, because at 4:00 a.m., it's wake-up time. On the road by 4:30 a.m. in the dark for the hour-long ride to the trailhead at the border. That gave Riess 10 minutes for good lucks and good-byes. He had another hour and 10 minutes to get back to town, get to school, and unlock his classroom by 6:50 a.m. Class started at 7:00 a.m.

He has made that drive more than 400 times, shuttling more than 600 hikers, and was never late for school. "Squeaky close a couple of times," he said.

After 12 years as a teacher, Riess retired. He gave up the Kick Off cooking duties after a 2011 bypass surgery. He's still single. The RV is still parked alongside the house and the van with the "Trail Angel" license plate holder is parked out front. The American flag towers on a pole in the front yard and Riess anxiously awaits another class of thru-hikers every spring.

Someday he wants to thru-hike the entire trail. By then, maybe he'll think he has hiker cred.

For some repeat hikers who've become true friends, it would be hard to imagine not showing up at the San Diego Airport to Riess's smiling face or knocking on his door at whatever time of the day or night to be greeted by his barking dogs, his joyous smile, and his worn-out Kick Off baseball hat.

The alarm goes off at 4:00 a.m. But it's a happy time.

"You make a lot of good friends here," he said. "It's enormously such a good time."

MEADOW ED

As the PCT Class of 1977 made its way through the High Sierra, Ed Faubert spent the summer nearby at 8,720 feet above sea level, cooking food for tourists at the Tuolumne Meadows Lodge.

They all but passed by his front door, but he never saw the thru-hikers or even knew of them. "Talking about it now," he said, "it's one of the funny things in life."

Faubert spent 30 years as a professional chef. He cooked at lodges in Yosemite and in the Tetons long before PCT lovers came to know him as "Meadow Ed" and even longer before many more would see him portrayed in a Hollywood movie.

Faubert stole one of the funniest scenes in *Wild*, the 2014 movie based on Cheryl Strayed's memoir about her 1995 PCT hike. Faubert helped Strayed sift many unnecessary items from her backpack, including a saw, binoculars, and a camera flash.

"I still have that saw," he said with a chuckle.

The movie scene, which took place at Kennedy Meadows, was pretty accurate, Faubert said, even though it was filmed somewhere in Oregon, not the southern gateway to the Sierra. Most importantly, that summer marked the beginning of a trail angeling (yes, it's a verb) saga that continues.

That year, 1995, Faubert turned 50 in Kennedy Meadows. He was living in Pasadena, California, and didn't want to wake up at home on his birthday.

"I brought a bunch of food from the house for me and my nephew," he recalled. "Back then they only had microwavable stuff at the store there." That's when it happened. "Seven hikers came through. Whatever food I put out they ate it all."

Faubert dropped off his nephew a week later. Then he loaded his coolers and went back to Kennedy Meadows with the goal of feeding PCT hikers. "That's when I met Cheryl," he said.

The hikers would have been fine without him, he admitted. But he realized how much he liked making meals for them. Maybe he needed them more than they needed him. At any rate, there was something special about cooking for hungry hikers that was different than loading plates in restaurants.

"It's a rare experience when you can mingle with the people you are feeding," he said. "We're all a community out here. That first day on the trail you get a bond going and sometimes it goes all the way to Canada. You get amazingly close to people. I could sense that."

In 1996, Faubert moved around, cooking for hikers at many places in the Sierra Nevada, including Kennedy Meadows, Reds Meadow, and Tuolumne Meadows. He saw many of the same hikers as they moved north. Faubert doesn't remember who asked him the vital question: "Where are we going to see you again, Ed?" "I said, 'Where's the next meadow?'" he recalled.

Meadow Ed had just received a trail name.

OPPOSITE: Tuolumne Meadows, Yosemite National Park, California.

In 1997, he added more stops, cooking for hikers all along the trail. He followed them for hundreds of miles. "You really get lock-stepped in with these people," he said. "It's really fun."

Faubert cooked meals for hikers every summer at Kennedy Meadows through 2006. The death of a good friend and PCT enthusiast, "No Way" Ray Echols, changed all that. Known for an infectious smile and his support for the PCT, No Way Ray was hiking on the trail near Deep Creek in Southern California when he fell about 200 feet. His wife, Alice Tulloch, was about 20 yards behind him on the trail and saw him walk around a bend. She didn't see him fall but spotted his body in a ravine. Alice later edited and published her husband's book about his years of hiking the PCT: *A Thru-Hiker's Heart.*

After No Way Ray's candle service in Kennedy Meadows, the place "became somewhat of a holy ground," Faubert said. He needed to move on. He'd also been getting some pressure from the owners of the store near there because he was, in essence, taking away business and they had to pay rent. Faubert sympathized and in 2007 moved his operation south to Walker Pass.

He kept up the routine year after year, but in 2013, things caught up with him. He was at Walker Pass and it was 110 degrees that day when he simply passed out, falling over backward. Doctors ran tests and treated him for seizures but weren't sure what was wrong. He skipped cooking in 2014 because he wasn't cleared to return to altitude.

At Kick Off in 2015, which he helped organize, Faubert said he missed cooking for the hikers. But that summer he went back to Walker Pass for five days. "There's no reason to stop this," he said. "As long as I'm healthy and getting involved, I'll still go."

He said he finds the company of hikers truly genuine. There's no pretense. They carry their whole worlds on their backs. "It's like group therapy," he said.

"You can tell your fellow hikers stuff that you would not tell your family," he said. "I've got brothers I don't ever talk to. The PCT is my family. The hikers are my brothers and sisters."

And just like family, Faubert has made arrangements for the day when he's no longer around. He has left instructions with another PCT trail icon, Jackie "Yogi" McDonnell, author of the well-known *Yogi's Pacific Crest Trail Handbook.* She is to spread his ashes where it all began, at Kennedy Meadows.

Meadow Ed will be home.

The PCNST Advisory Council

Less than a month after Eric Ryback completed his PCT thru-hike and barely two years after President Lyndon Johnson inked his signature on the National Trails System Act, the Pacific Crest National Scenic Trail (PCNST) Advisory Council held its first meeting at a Holiday Inn in San Francisco's financial district. There were 32 members, many far-flung, but only three missed the inaugural gathering.

As previously noted, the keynote speaker was Ryback, who'd flown in from Michigan. Chairman Richard Droege presented Ryback with a framed PCT completion plaque, the only one the council would issue.

The PCT passes through three Forest Service regions and the heads of each one personally welcomed the council—Vern Hamre from Region 4 (Intermountain); Douglas Leisz from Region 5 (California); and C. A. Connaughton from Region 6 (Pacific Northwest). For two days, council members rolled up their

sleeves. They learned how much work lay ahead to complete the 225 "non-existing" miles of trail in Oregon and Washington, and California's far larger trail construction needs. The daunting nature of the California work must have flummoxed the minute taker because there was no record made of the mileage number.

One item of lasting importance was choosing the symbol for the whole trail. After "considerable discussion" of "various suggested symbols" they coalesced around one: "the Alpine fir symbol now used in Washington and Oregon with an outline of mountains in the background would be acceptable."

From an April 3, 1974, Forest Service news press release:

NEW CONSTRUCTION FOR PACIFIC CREST TRAIL

San Francisco: More than $1,000,000 appropriated by Congress for the Pacific Crest National Scenic Trail will be used by the U.S. Forest Service for construction and re-construction activities on National Forests in California during 1974. California Regional Forester Douglas R. Leisz said, "More than 500 miles of the proposed 1,600 miles of the trail in California have already been constructed. During 1974, about 100 miles of new trail will be completed."

The PCNST Advisory Council existed for just more than 18 years, from November 1970 to January 1989. It held 21 meetings overseeing the setting of the initial official route, setting guidelines, and reviewing trail policies. The council continually, with uneven success, exhorted Washington, DC, to allocate more funds.

At its 14th meeting in Bakersfield in 1982, it heard that 98 percent of the trail was completed in Washington, Oregon, and Northern and Central California, but only 72 percent had been built in Southern California. A year later, at the 15th meeting, those numbers had been raised to 99.9 percent and 75.4 percent respectively. And at that same meeting at Timberline Lodge, high on the slopes of Oregon's Mount Hood, the minutes recorded a vote on a heated topic that "invoked a lot of discussion" despite the many heady topics before them: "Action—It was unanimously agreed to recommend to the Secretary that llamas be allowed on the PCT."

At the council's 19th meeting in 1987, the title of one hot topic was "Monumentation of PCT Termini." That classic example of government-speak actually covered something near and dear. The 20th anniversary of the National Trails System Act was approaching and they were considering erecting a monument at each end of the PCT to mark the occasion. Louise Marshall, who would go on in three years to become the first executive director of the Pacific Crest Trail Conference, precursor to today's PCTA, was then the council's communications committee chair. Marshall reported that she "reminded the Appalachian Trail Conference of the PCT and suggested that the Appalachian Trail Conference provide leadership for all other long-distance trail councils. That suggestion didn't go over well."

The congressional authorization for the council expired on January 24, 1989, and the council faded into history. But as one of its last acts, in September 1988, the council traveled as a whole 60 miles east from their San Diego meeting to Campo. There, at the PCT's southern terminus on the Mexican border, they dedicated a monument of five fir pillars. That monument still stands, as does so much of the council's work, which today can be seen in what took shape as the Pacific Crest Trail.

Early Thru-Hikers and the First Wave

After Eric Ryback, the next thru-hikers headed out in 1972. The Wilderness Press PCT guidebooks credit Richard Watson as the first to finish the designated trail route—September 1, 1972. Close on his heels were Dave Odell, Wayne Martin, Toby Heaton, Bill Goddard, and Butch Ferrand—September 5. After that came a solo hiker, Henry Wilds, and then a couple, Jeff Smukler and Mary Carstens—the first woman thru-hiker. All started at the Mexican border and went north.

From the Eugene, Oregon, *Register-Guard*: "Long Hike Cost Pair 75 Pounds: Toby Heaton, 25, Santa Monica, lost 45 pounds and Dave Odell, 21, Burbank, shed 30 pounds. The two bearded, bespectacled Californians hiked the length of the Pacific Crest Trail, longest in the world."

The year 1977 saw the first big wave of thru-hikers. That year some 47 are credited with finishing the trail. Carl "Kelty Kid" Siechert remains emphatic today: "Without a doubt, Eric's book was the main inspiration for every one of us 1977 PCT hikers."

Monte Dodge, another from '77, recalled how he started on April 1 with the snow level at near-historic lows, but then "the Sierra had their winter in May." The 19-year-old was the first to sign the Mount Whitney

ABOVE: Leaning on Monument 78 at the Canadian border, Monte Dodge wears a smile as big as his accomplishment— a 1977 thru-hike of the PCT. OPPOSITE: Hiker Don Molleur crosses swollen Bear Creek in the Central Sierra Nevada during 1977, a high snow year.

Ray Jardine: Backpacking Gear Revolutionary

Since the 1930s, backpacking gear has advanced in great leaps, a progression of ever lighter and more efficient equipment. The 1930s wood-and-rope Trapper Nelson pack boards gave way to World War II surplus gear, to external-frame, hip-belted Keltys, and to today's internal-frame, infinitely adjustable packs.

Each step was a revolution, but no advance claimed a single parent until the last one, some 20 years ago. Ray Jardine started the "ultralight backpacking" revolution when he published his *Pacific Crest Trail Hiker's Handbook* in 1992.

This was Jardine's second revolution. In the 1970s, the avowed mountain climber and space engineer whiz revolutionized technical climbing, inventing the climber's "Friend," the first spring-loaded camming device. One writer aptly dubbed it "the most famous piece of rock climbing gear of all time."

Jardine took up long-distance hiking in the 1980s and turned modern backpacking on its head.

With 15,000 miles of trail experience, he was like a preacher, espousing "The Ray Way." His dogma was simple—use a tarp, not a tent; a sleeping quilt, not a sleeping bag; running shoes, not boots. You couldn't buy "Ray Way" gear at REI or any established sporting-goods stores. Jardine gave out plans showing how to sew your own pack at home, one that tipped the scales at a pound, not the then-conventional five to seven pounds.

The first disciples became dozens and then a league of proselytizing pilgrims. Today many "ultralighters" don't even know Jardine's name, but carry his legacy on their backs. They pay homage to him every time they take to the trail in jogging shoes instead of boots.

Twenty years after storming the establishment citadel, ultralight gear has established beachheads in the big-box outfitter world and in *Backpacker* magazine. But it's still largely served by a host of cottage-industry sellers. Among these are Gossamer Gear, Tarptent, Six Moon Designs, Titanium Goat, and ZPacks. Tarptent's two-person, three-season Squall weighs two pounds. Gossamer Gear's popular Mariposa pack weighs 21 ounces, and a sleeping quilt from ZPacks is barely more than a pound.

Ultralight is not for everyone and many still swear by their leather boots. And if you do decide to make the switch, keep in mind this good counsel from Glen Van Peski. Called by some the "Guru of Lightness" and the founder of Gossamer Gear, Van Peski says if you are thinking of switching to ultralight, the "journey should be one of baby steps . . . trying a couple of new things each trip."

summit register that year on a still quite early May 15, and everyone who had tried it before him, Dodge said, "needed to be rescued." At the Mexican border, Dodge weighed 195 pounds, but upon reaching Canada, he weighed 157. When asked about the term "trail angel," Dodge said, "as far as I was concerned, the term trail angel was someone who didn't ask to see your photo ID."

Twenty-five years later, in 2002, the "Class of '77" held a reunion. Today, in faded photos from 35 mm film, those '77ers stand out, and not because they hiked in blue jeans. Dodge said, "I never saw anyone with hiking poles. We looked like a bunch of sheep all dressed in wool." But what's not unusual is to find out that some have "given back."

Dodge turned a penchant for old backpacking gear into what's now a museum-quality collection of backpacking stoves. He shows them far and wide. "Someday I want them to be part of a PCT museum," he said. Since 2001, Siechert has been a pillar of Kick Off, wearing many hats. Paul Hacker, most every year, gives one of the more popular Kick Off talks, *The Geology of the Pacific Crest Trail*. In front of standing-room-only crowds, Hacker, together with '77 thru-hiker and fellow geologist Greg "Strider" Hummel, made PCT geology interesting. In 2009, Hacker and Hummel's geology talk sprang to life before a worldwide audience as they were featured in a National Geographic hour-long PCT special. But if you talked to Dodge, Seichert, Hacker, and so many others, all would agree that "Strider" stood a head above the crowd.

Dodge recalled one of his earliest impressions of Hummel. In 1977, at Warner Springs Resort, 110 miles north of the Mexican border, "I saw him sitting in a lounge chair beside the pool drinking a can of Budweiser and noticed his legs. They extended a foot past the end. I thought, 'Man, he is tall!'" Hummel was six foot, nine inches.

Hummel stood out for what he did, more than for his height. He was a father of five and a petroleum geologist for 35 years. His PCT highlight reel of giving back includes cofounder of the Kick Off, serving as its president and "wagonmaster" until 2014; a long run as president of American Long Distance Hiking Association-West (ALDHA-West); and a myriad of PCT talks at outdoor stores, PCTA Trail Fest, and other gatherings.

But a scene that sticks forever in the memory of so many starting-out PCT hikers is "Strider's Welcome." That's what they called Hummel's lead-off talk on Friday nights at Kick Off. As the stars came out and the temperature plunged, before hundreds sitting in an open field, Hummel told them how special they were, and he reminded them that along with being special came a responsibility. "You are trail ambassadors. Every contact you have with others reflects on the trail," he said. Hummel always ended his talks with a trademark so well known many of the crowd joined along: "Sweeeet," he'd say with long, drawn-out vowels.

Hummel wasn't there in 2015. He died four months before of ALS, Lou Gehrig's disease. The month before he passed, long after the disease had robbed him of speech, he managed an e-mail to John Zant, a *Santa Barbara Independent* reporter. The e-mail reverberates with Hummel's childlike delight for the PCT and his 1977 hike:

> One sunny summer afternoon [in Oregon], I was leading and [my hiking partner] Paul began to giggle as I heard a loud buzzing sound. I asked him what's so funny, and he replied that I had a visitor. At that moment, the hummingbird that had been checking out my bright blue pack came around to face me an inch from my nose, matching my speed but flying backward! This flustered and surprised me so much that I misstepped and fell off the trail, hat going one way, sunglasses another, and pack twisting off into the dirt and branches. Paul was doubled up in laughter, pointing at the chaos that was me and choking out how a one-ounce hummingbird took down a 6'9" hiking machine!

At the 2015 Kick Off, Siechert asked the Friday night crowd to remember Hummel. Rather than a moment of silence, he asked them to join together and five hundred voices rose as one: "Sweeeeet."

Federal Agencies

It's true that the PCT would not exist without the hard work and dedication of many tireless volunteers, advocates, and donors who stepped up when it would have been easier, and perhaps more sane, to walk away.

The same can be said for the government employees charged with making the trail happen. In fact, without the sheer will and buying power of the federal government and the dedication of the agency employees who believed in the grand idea of national trails and what they could provide to the American people, the PCT would not be what it is today. Not by a long shot.

While Fred Cleator may have been the first in the government to grab hold of the idea of a long-distance trail along the Pacific Crest, he certainly wasn't the last. There were many who championed the cause and not only urged citizens such as Clinton C. Clarke and Warren Rogers, but also helped them navigate the sometimes slow-moving bureaucracies so they could get things done.

In the 1970s and 1980s, the United States Forest Service, Bureau of Land Management (BLM), and National Park Service made a big push to make the vision of the PCT, words on paper in the 1968 National Trails System Act, become an on-the-ground fact. While volunteer groups were working on small sections of the trail, the work was sporadic, incomplete, and largely uncoordinated. There were long stretches that didn't really exist. Road walks and temporary PCT signs were everywhere, and the federal agencies put manpower and money in the form of contracts to move the trail off these logging and backcountry roads to the crest, generally from one part of government land to another.

Many miles of trail also remained on private property, but in these decades, the land-management agencies—pragmatically realizing the complexity and expense of buying this real estate and creatively working with the budgets in hand—secured easements so that the trail could be considered complete, even if the term was loosely applied.

Regardless, with the agencies behind the idea of the PCT, a lot happened to improve the trail in a short time. To tell that story, we introduce you to two government employees. The fact that they're both military veterans says a lot about them and their belief in public service. And with their stories, we salute all our local, state, and federal government employees who continue to dedicate their careers in that same spirit.

SAM THARP

Looking at the PCT near the standout peak called Spanish Needle in Southern California's Owens Peak Wilderness, one wonders how the crazed folk who designed and built it could ever get past the doubts that it could be done. But many decades after that special section of trail came to be, Sam Tharp still remembers the agonizing pain and time it took just to lay out the flags for trail builders.

From 1978 to 1984, Tharp, now 74, was the outdoor recreation planner for the BLM's Caliente Resource Area based in Bakersfield, California. He served in the US Marine Corps for three years and spent 16 months in Vietnam in 1967 and 1968 before earning degrees in wildlife and marine biology.

At the BLM he was charged, among other things, with filling in the gaps on 135 miles of the PCT, from Tejon Ranch north to Sequoia National Park. To tell the truth, there was not much permanent trail in the area, he recalled. But flagging and building the PCT near Spanish Needle was by far the toughest spot.

OPPOSITE: The PCT crosses the southern end of California's Owens Peak Wilderness.

Tharp led a five-person team that included an engineer and an archaeologist. They were dropped by helicopter into desolate backcountry for 10 days at a time to scout the best PCT route. It was rough, dry, and filled with snakes and bears, he said.

"It was ugly. Once the archaeologist had to be flown out because she sat on a fire ant mound," he recalled. "The manzanita was 10 to 12 feet tall and was so thick you couldn't get through it. We would have to crawl under it on our bellies for a mile, flagging where the trail was going to be."

The PCNST Advisory Council toured the area during a November 4, 1982, field trip. *The Bakersfield Californian* reported on the visit and the difficulty of making the trail through seven miles near Spanish Needle. "In terms of physical barriers, the Spanish Needles section presents the greatest challenge in Kern County," the newspaper reported.

Prevalent signs of Native American tribes made the survey work more difficult because they didn't want to disrupt possible archaeological sites. Sheer cliffs also were obstacles, and the team had to scramble and climb across rock faces, flagging areas where contractors would come later and make the trail.

"They had to blast their way across the rock at $100 a foot," Tharp said. "There was no other way of going so we had to go across there. Trying to hang on and tie ribbons while we were flagging, I thought I was going to die."

Once the path was set, Tharp oversaw the construction and spent many days in the field supervising the contractors' work, which took about two years.

Tharp also worked on the installation of the PCT trailhead at Walker Pass. He and a colleague in the Forest Service came up with the idea and made it happen, much to his supervisors' chagrin. "I probably

stepped way over my boundary," he said. "I didn't even go to my director. I just said let's build the damn thing. I wanted to get it done."

When the dedication ceremony happened at the trailhead, Tharp was a little hurt that he was the only person with a direct hand in the project not invited onto the stage. His bosses, the ones peeved he moved ahead without approval, were up there though. He laughs about it now. "Sometimes you've got to move to get things done," he said.

Soon after his work on the PCT ended, Tharp and his wife, Patricia, moved to Northern California and owned and operated landscape nurseries in Morgan Hill and Gilroy. He helped a friend build the Gilroy Gardens Family Theme Park and worked for the United States Postal Service. He retired in 2008 and now lives north of Phoenix, Arizona.

Of the PCT, he feels like it was a career highlight.

"At the time I thought the PCT was pretty neat and a lot of other people I worked with thought so too," he said. "It was like being part of history."

He said he'd like to go back and hike "his" section someday while he still can. "I haven't been there in years. I think that would be kind of nice," he said.

BILL ROBERTS

If you've walked the PCT in Northern California anytime in the past several decades, chances are Bill Roberts had a hand in making your experience possible.

A Humboldt County native, Roberts moved to Seiad Valley, California, when he left the US Navy in 1971. He'd served three years during the Vietnam War on Midway Island in the Pacific and at age 24 was looking for a place that would put him close to mountains, trails, and solitude.

He'd been around trails since he was a boy. His father and uncle hiked through the Olympic Range in the late 1920s and he still recalls hiking with his dad in the Columbia River Gorge and seeing a man come off the trail with a wood-framed canvas pack and a shotgun.

"My dad bought lunch for him," Roberts said. "That impressed me and I've bought many a meal for hikers in my life."

He got a job as a seasonal employee with the Forest Service maintaining and building trails, including the PCT from the California-Oregon border south 50 miles to the Marble Mountains. At that time, a third of the PCT wasn't yet built through the region and hikers walked on roads outside the wilderness, he said.

Roberts was in Seiad Valley when Warren Rogers came to visit in 1971. Rogers was visiting trail towns along the PCT, giving talks and drumming up support for the newly minted national scenic trail. He showed pictures and spoke in inspirational terms about the history of the trail and what was needed to bring it into the future, Roberts recalled.

"It was an honor and pleasure to meet him," he said. "I remember the passion that he had. I was already working on the trails and I knew trails and the PCT. For me, the lightbulb was already on."

As a seasonal government trail worker, Roberts had lots of time off. For a few years, he worked for private contractors hired to build new trail in the off-season. But he quickly got into running strings of pack mules for the agency, and has been at it ever since, more than four decades. Today, he is one of only 12 Forest Service packers remaining in California. The program is much diminished from its heyday as the agency relies more heavily on volunteer packers from the PCTA, horsemen groups, and others.

For him, being seasonal meant that he'd take as much work as the Forest Service would give him, or could, for that matter. Some years, when money was tight, he'd work for free. More paid hours usually came his way.

"My life and job are kinda all tied together," he said, "and I love what I do. Somewhere along the line I decided this is what I wanted to do. If I had enough money to eat, well I could make it work. I knew I was going to get money eventually and there was stuff to do so I got to working on it."

As a packer, he remains invaluable, bringing in tools and supplies for crews that can spend up to five months in the backcountry building trail. Roberts said a 17-member crew needs about 100 mule loads of 150 pounds each load to get base camp set up and supplied. During a project, he'll bring in six or seven mules packed with supplies each week. Once he moved a whole camp in one shot, with several packers and 44 animals.

One of the biggest projects he was involved in was the realignment of the PCT along Grider Creek. The trail crossed the creek 14 times in 1971, with no bridges. By 1974, the realignment had reduced the number of crossings to four, all with bridges.

OPPOSITE: Members of the PCNST Advisory Council pose at the dedication of the PCT southern monument in September 1988.

Building those crossings was a herculean effort for the Forest Service crews and the private contractors. One bridge abutment took about 15,000 pounds of cement to make—that's 100 mule loads.

Even though the trail was much improved in the area, Mother Nature continues to take her toll. Of the four bridges, Roberts said, "Most either burn up or wash out eventually. I've been part of putting in eight bridges on that eight-mile section of trail."

After 31 years working season to season, the Forest Service hired Roberts as a permanent employee, though he still works only during trail-work season. The position gives him health coverage, which is good since he got tossed from his horse a couple of years ago, breaking his pelvis and ribs and rupturing his bladder.

Roberts spends some of his spare time writing cowboy poetry and he has published his poems and performed them publicly. He continues to look forward to the next season—packing mules, supplying crews, and maintaining trails—because it's not just a job.

"It's a real good excuse to be in the mountains," he said. "To me the mountains are almost sacred. I just like being out in the natural world and I'm comfortable being by myself. I also like meeting like-minded people. Even in California, it's a small world above 5,000 feet."

A Nonprofit Is Formed

The 1980s were lean times for the trail. The spurt of '70s hikers set loose by Eric Ryback and the first Wilderness Press PCT guidebooks had petered out. Money and interest in the PCT had grown slim. Volunteers caring for the Pacific Crest Trail not only had to contend with Mother Nature's zealous attempts to reclaim it—wind-toppled trees, ever-growing shrubs, and the erosion caused by wind, rain, and fire—they also faced the seemingly hopeless reality of a shoestring budget.

Warren Rogers had founded the Pacific Crest Club in 1972 and five years later followed with the Pacific Crest Trail Conference. The club was for individuals and the second for trail groups such as the Washington Trails Association. But by the 1980s, both foundered as Rogers's health, not his interest, waned.

As the history of caring for this trail had proven time and again, someone stepped up in this time of need and picked up the baton. Larry Cash was next in line.

Marion Lawrence Cash was born in 1915, in Bristol, Virginia, within 20 miles of what would become the Appalachian Trail. In 1942, he married Zlotta "Zotty" Risley in Oxnard, California, and served three years in the US Navy during World War II. The couple raised three sons and two daughters.

By 1977, the Cash family lived in Eugene, Oregon. Cash was 62, newly retired from Pacific Northwest Bell after a 31-year career. He wrote that his primary interest "moved from my job to my family and outdoor activities."

Cash's son, Dave Cash, said his father loved escaping to the outdoors, partly because he spent a career working indoors with the phone company. "For all of my life, the outdoors and being outdoors was really important to him," Dave said of his father. "The family vacations that I remember were camping and fishing."

Once Cash retired, he joined the Pacific Crest Club. Dave Cash was working as a reporter in Hood River, Oregon, when his father called and invited him to a PCT Conference seminar on how to hike the PCT. There they met Rogers for the first time. "I went along just to keep him company," Dave said.

OPPOSITE: Fall colors frame the trail in an oak glen south of Green Valley, Southern California.

When he returned home, Cash began planning a family hike across Oregon on the PCT. Dave recalls letters from Rogers and lists of items to bring. By 1979, the plan was set. Larry, Zotty, Dave, and his brother Jeff loaded their packs with heavy gear and bags of dried food.

They took a bus to Ashland, Oregon, and planned to ask the driver to stop when the road crossed close to the trail. From there they would head north. "The bus missed the trail, went by it by several miles," Dave recalled. "Dad stopped the bus and we got off. His plan was to hike north until we picked up the trail. That meant our great adventure started with bushwhacking through heavy wet brush in a cold rain with 65-pound packs on our backs."

By the time they reached Crater Lake, Zotty was not feeling well, Dave had a sty, and Jeff's knee was swollen. They made a side trip to the doctor and eventually Dave and his father rejoined the trail at Odell Lake. Things didn't go well. "We were post-holing in snow near North Sister," Dave said.

THE PACIFIC CREST TRAIL

They hiked out and arranged for Dave's sister, Christy, to pick them up. At the end of the summer, Dave, his brother, and his parents hiked from Timberline Lodge on Mount Hood to Cascade Locks. It was the most beautiful part of their summer adventure of starts and stops. Larry Cash was forever hooked by the PCT.

By the early 1980s, Dave had moved to Southern California and was working as a reporter at the *Press-Enterprise* in San Bernardino. His parents came to visit regularly and his father would find a new place to hike on the PCT. Cash often went alone, climbing into the Sierra or taking a ride into the Mojave Desert to check on trail conditions. Once he climbed Mount Whitney, the highest peak in the continental United States.

"I know it was a big milestone in Dad's life," Dave said. "It was the biggest one on the list. He was an older man when he did that climb. It was an emotional milestone for him."

On one trip to Southern California, Cash took time out to see Rogers, who lived close by. The two struck up a friendship. Dave recalled visiting Rogers's house and seeing his garage filled with PCT materials and records.

By 1984, Cash also was a member of the Eugene Obsidians board and, by then, a staunch PCT supporter. The Obsidians were charter members of Clinton C. Clarke's original PCT System Conference, the group of hiking, horseback-riding, and trail-building clubs and organizations that advocated for and maintained the trail. Cash attended the annual meeting of Rogers's reincarnated conference in San Francisco as the Obsidians' delegate and was elected conference vice president. In May 1986, when Charles Vogel, the conference's 90-year-old president, resigned, Cash became the conference's president.

With no real money or employees, Cash ran the conference out of his house and—like Rogers—often out of his own pocket. Family members said he worked 10 to 12 hours a day in an upstairs bedroom he'd converted into an office, writing letters, responding to inquiries, and monitoring trail conditions and register books. He got out on the trail when he could, but keeping the PCT Conference flame alive took almost all his time.

"Set up the PCTC national office in a spare room of our home, shared our home phone, and enlisted my wife and daughter to help with paper work," he wrote.

The conference and club merged in February 1987 during the conference's annual meeting. The club was insolvent and heading downhill and Rogers had little energy left to devote. It was Rogers's idea that the club should become part of the conference, Cash wrote in 1997. But despite their friendship, the two disagreed over the direction of the nonprofit. Rogers fought Cash's proposal that individual club members should be allowed to join the conference. Instead of including the club as a separate entity within the conference, Cash's proposal meant the end of Rogers's beloved Pacific Crest Club.

"We felt that having two similar names for the same organization would be confusing," Cash wrote. "In spite of Warren's pleas, the board agreed and we dropped the club name."

Soon, more than 100 club members joined the PCT Conference, the precursor to today's Pacific Crest Trail Association, the nonprofit whose mission is to protect, preserve, and promote the trail.

By then, Rogers's *PCT Quarterly* newsletter had not been sent in years. Cash revived it in July 1988 as one of the first responsibilities of the newly melded conference, paid for with membership dues. The first issue included a simple heading: *Pacific Crest Trail Conference NEWSLETTER* and Cash's address and phone number. It was a single page of type with the title "A word or two from the president's desk." He told members that the *PCT Quarterly* published for years by Rogers had not come out in several years because Rogers had

OPPOSITE: Crater Lake and Wizard Island, Crater Lake National Park, Oregon.

been in a car accident and suffered whiplash. Just a few weeks before the "new" newsletter was mailed, Cash said, Rogers had suffered a stroke.

Cash promised a newsletter once a month. Two months later, the second issue, dated September 6, 1988, carried the title *The Communicator* for the first time. (The name would change again in 1992 to *The Pacific Crest Trail Communicator*.)

The year 1988 was a big one for trails nationally. It was the 20th anniversary of the National Trails System Act, which named the Pacific Crest Trail and the Appalachian Trail as the first national scenic trails. The PCNST Advisory Council named Cash chairman of a committee to promote the anniversary. Governors in all three PCT states signed proclamations and various celebratory activities were held along different sections.

Most importantly, the monuments at each end of the PCT were designed and installed. The southern monument, according to Cash, replaced a shot-up metal sign that hung on a barbed wire fence. These permanent markers, touchable and real, gave Cash a great deal of personal satisfaction. Forever morphing, the trail and the perception of it were taking shape.

By 1989, Cash crowed in a letter to the membership that "our meager bank account" was up to about $1,500 and that he'd bought a better typewriter.

But despite this small victory, the PCT Conference, the citizen-led organization that maintained and protected the trail, was still tenuous at best. Like many a small, volunteer nonprofit, it had no real financial clout or the means by which to get it. Changing that would take bold new ideas.

Billy Goat, the PCT Guru

Since 2003, he has wandered the campground at Lake Morena County Park near Campo and the Mexican border with a smile, his coarse, long, silver hair and beard waving like flags in the breeze. He's such a recognizable fixture at Kick Off—the Annual Day Zero Pacific Crest Trail Kick Off—his legend betrays any possible anonymity. He's barely able to make it 10 feet, let alone to the restroom, without someone coming up to greet him, shake his hand, or take a photo.

"I met you hiking in 2012," one gushing fan exclaims, putting an arm around him while the cameras click. Billy Goat's face lights up. "Oh yeah, how are you?" Pleasantries are exchanged, hands shaken, questions about the year's plans asked, and advice given—all with the grace of a person who unwittingly finds himself at the center of attention. Except Billy Goat's 15 minutes of fame goes on.

"That's very typical of what happens 20 times a day," he said following the encounter. "I have no recollection of him. I'm sure I met him, but I meet lots of people on and off the trail. I talk with them. I pay attention to what they have to say. It's almost like it's my job, like I'm the ambassador."

Not surprising since he spends most of his days on a trail somewhere. It's his wisdom every new class of PCT hikers comes for. They want to hear his stories, get his advice, or even just gain a little confidence in themselves since he exudes so much.

"I tell people two things: give yourself three weeks to get your body in shape and get your mind in shape," he said with a happy chuckle. "Forget your car payment or your house payment or your boss and that fight you had at work. You just forget about all these things that seem so trying."

OPPOSITE: The Middle Fork of the Kings River winds through a Central Sierra Nevada meadow in California.
ABOVE: Billy Goat at the top of Glen Pass above Rae Lakes Basin, Sierra Nevada, California.

Billy Goat has hiked all over, about 45,000 miles since he started counting when he was in his 40s and section hiking the Appalachian Trail. He has hiked 13,000 of those miles in the last seven years. He said his goal is "50 by 80," or 50,000 miles by age 80. He's almost there on both counts. He has until 2019 to finish the last 5,000 miles.

He keeps journals and meticulous records and can account for the miles, not that he needs or wants to prove anything to anyone. "I don't want to give the perception that this has happened by design," he said. "I have become Billy Goat by happenstance. I don't do anything different than anybody else. I just walk. I might do more of it. Hiking is where I'm most comfortable."

And in that statement he reveals a lot about himself and his motivations. When pressed, the real guru comes out. "I have some discomfort with other situations in life, loud music and this rat race we all live in," he said. "I can socialize when I'm comfortable—if I'm where I want to be. With these people, I am. We have this thing in common that works."

He hikes alone a lot but is not averse to hiking with others.

"I can do it either way," he said. "There's a lot of give and take when you hike with a partner. If I waited for someone to hike with I would never go any place. I would think I'm a loner more than not."

Born January 28, 1939, George Woodard grew up in Maine and moved to New Hampshire right after high school. He has three younger sisters whom he calls on birthdays but rarely sees in person. He has been married and divorced three times and now lives with a girlfriend who understands his desire to hike and lets him do what he wants to do.

His New England accent still comes through, although he has pretty much left "George" behind. "No way, nobody even knows that name," he said. "My mother used to call me that. I hardly even recognize that name."

But he wasn't always Billy Goat. That's a person he became after he put his career behind him and made a choice to pursue his love of walking.

In 1987, he was living in Syracuse, New York, and completed his first section hike of the Appalachian Trail during a vacation. In 1989, he retired after a 30-year career as a railroad conductor. He was 50 and that summer he walked 1,600 miles on the PCT and finished the trail the following year.

"I knew that was what I wanted to do. It was just a matter of getting the numbers lined up." He worked on and off as a railroad consultant for a few years, making the jobs work around his hiking schedule.

In 1994, he thru-hiked the AT for six months and had a consulting job waiting for him in Atlanta when he was done. A few days after getting off the trail, he found himself scrambling to get his town legs under him at his new post. He had a pager and office phone, employees to manage, and a demanding boss. "It was too much," he said.

He found a way to live more simply. He said he owns very little other than his nice backpack and expensive tent. He doesn't own a car. "Stores just saturate you." He has enough money to live comfortably. "You make it work. We get into big holes, getting married, making babies, and getting a mortgage," he said.

While some might say he has sacrificed a lot for his lifestyle, he would disagree. "It's a trade-off, not a sacrifice," he said. "I think it's a fair trade-off for what I get out of it."

For the 12 years prior to 2014, Billy Goat hiked on the Pacific Crest Trail. Even he knows that his passion for the trail seems a little strange. But he equates it to gardening. A gardener works the soil into rows and

OPPOSITE: A lone hiker in Oregon's Sky Lakes Wilderness.

plants seeds and after the vegetables come ready, he eats some and gives some away. And the next year, he does it all over again. "For what?" he asks.

"I really like this trail. When I finish a hike, I start thinking about the next year a day after I get home. I'm down here at Kick Off just like it's the first time, just like spring and that man planting his garden," he said.

In January 2014, things changed. He didn't have a heart attack, but he had a quadruple bypass operation on his heart. "That really knocked me down," he said of the operation. "I've walked every day since then. I'm so focused on being able to backpack."

The PCT, he said in 2015, would have to wait at least another year. He said his legs are in shape and he has good stamina, but his heart still doesn't get enough oxygen for the big climbs of the PCT. His 50,000-mile goal looms, but Billy Goat is trying to keep it in perspective.

"I'm trying not to be so 100 percent goal oriented," he said. "I'm not thinking about 1,000 miles. I'm thinking about being out there in the summer—just being there and enjoying it."

Yet it's evident he's struggling.

"I've got to keep moving. It's so ingrained in me," he said. Then, in the next breath, "Probably those days are over. I just have to come to grips with that reality."

Ever the guru.

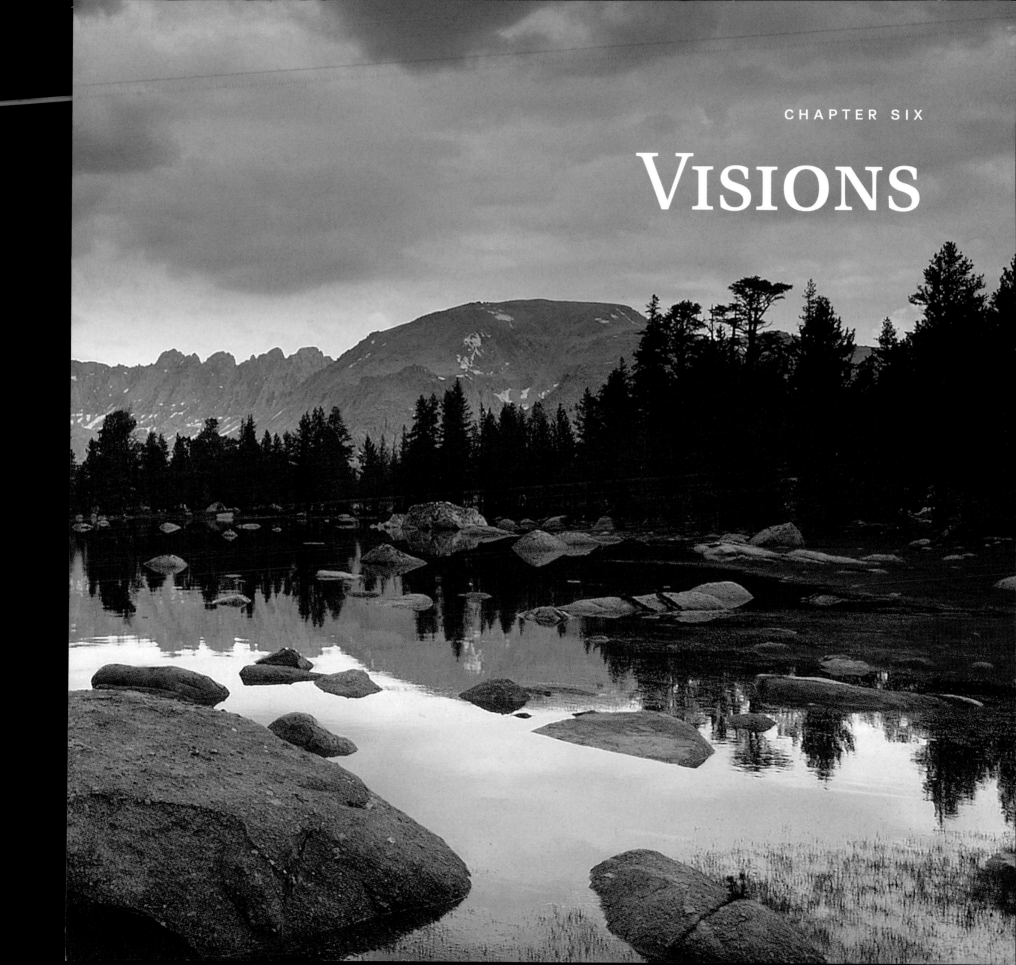

CHAPTER SIX

VISIONS

MT. BAKER National Forest

CLEAN UP
Campsite
...be a good neighbor!

Sock it up
Pack it home
Recycle it.

Louise Marshall and the Era of Grand Ideas

In mid-1990, Louise Marshall became the Pacific Crest Trail Conference's executive director. Marshall was seen at the time as a great hope for the PCT and the volunteers who worked diligently to keep the trail a going concern. A national leader in the hiking movement for decades, she brought a long list of credentials, the least of which included membership in the PCT Conference. She was a tireless advocate for trails in her home state of Washington and nationally, and was a tenacious volunteer organizer as well as a trail worker in her own right. In the 1980s, she had served on the PCNST Advisory Council, so she had firsthand knowledge about the goals for the trail.

Marshall came to the PCT Conference on loan from the American Hiking Society (AHS), a national organization she cofounded. She was president and chairman of the board of AHS at the time, making a "sideways" move, *The Pacific Crest Trail Communicator* declared, as part of the society's program to assist local and regional trail groups.

"Well, the PCT Conference has been burning three fires for a long time . . . and it certainly needs help," Larry Cash declared in an announcement to conference members in July 1990. "For my money, AHS couldn't have made a wiser choice."

Rarely mentioned was the fact that Marshall served in this position as a volunteer.

She was born Louise Burnett on May 7, 1915, in Boston, the daughter of an Iowa farm boy who made his way to Harvard Medical School, both as a student and professor. Louis Raymond Burnett was a flight surgeon during World War I and was a director of health and recreation in Paterson, New Jersey. He held similar jobs in Cleveland and Denver.

According to Ann Marshall of Port Orchard, Washington, one of Louise's two daughters, Louis and his wife, Isabel, homeschooled Louise until she was eight years old. Later, she attended the Wadleigh High School for Girls. "It was one of the turning points for her because everything was done by girls, which gave her confidence," Ann said.

Marshall enrolled in Columbia University and traveled several summers to Europe, where hiking in the Alps and the culture of outdoor recreation would shape her future goals for trails in the Pacific Northwest. She graduated from Columbia in 1938 with a master's degree. Influenced by her father's career in health and recreation, she taught physical education—swimming, dance, gymnastics—and ran recreation programs at community centers and schools on the East Coast.

She and her husband, William "Bill" Marshall, headed west in October 1951, settling in Seattle. Ann was three years old and her sister was still an infant. They drove a 1940 Ford and towed a homemade trailer containing their worldly possessions. Ann still has wooden packing crates her father made for that trip.

Soon after moving to Seattle, the Marshalls joined the Mountaineers, the local outdoors club and one of the nation's largest. Marshall started the club's international travel group, Ann said, drawing upon her European experiences. She served as trip chair, backpacking chair, and later was on the board of trustees. Marshall led the club's first overseas hiking trip to Germany.

"That was all my mom needed," said Ann, who also served as a Pacific Crest Trail Association board member and magazine editor in the 1990s. "She really felt at home with the Mountaineers club."

PREVIOUS SPREAD: Siberian Outpost just outside the boundary of Golden Trout Wilderness, Sierra Nevada, California.

OPPOSITE: Louise Marshall in 1965 at a trailhead in the North Cascades of Washington.

In 1966, Marshall founded and was editor of the magazine *Signpost*, noting that hikers wanted a forum to share information on trails. Soon she turned to advocacy, cofounding the Seattle-based Washington Trails Association (WTA) after it was revealed that off-road vehicle recreation was receiving more public money than nonmotorized recreation. She also fought to keep open-pit mining out of Glacier Peak Wilderness. Today, WTA is the state's largest and most active player in trail building, maintenance, and advocacy and its work includes the PCT.

By 1968, Marshall had put education behind her as a career and she was a professional writer. Among other things, she wrote a newspaper column for *The Enterprise*, a weekly that served South Snohomish County, and was a member of the Outdoor Writers Association of America. She authored *100 Hikes in Western Washington*, the first Northwest hiking guide and a forerunner to the still-popular "100 Hikes" series of hiking guidebooks. She also wrote *High Trails*, a guide to the PCT in Washington.

The list goes on. Around 1970, Larry Penberthy, the founder of outdoor industry mainstay Mountain Safety Research (MSR), suggested that she run for a seat on the board of directors for REI, the Seattle-based co-op. This was in the days when any member could run by collecting signatures on a petition, Ann said.

"My mother stood outside the doors of the old REI store on 11th and Pine with her petition, collected the signatures, and was elected," Ann said. "She was the first woman to serve on REI's board and stayed for a total of 19 years."

In a 1991 *Communicator* article titled "My Dream for the Pacific Crest Trail," right after she "took hold" of the executive director's job, Marshall wrote poetically of her memories and experiences on the PCT: seeing a grizzly near Red Pass; soaking in the warmth of Kennedy Hot Springs; wondering who might have found a camera she lost near Big Lava Bed. She told her stories as a way of urging her readers to share theirs.

But her dreams, like many who'd taken on the PCT cause before her, were as big as they were imperative if the organization was to succeed; and surely as difficult on a shoestring budget. For one, she wanted to make the PCT more widely known, and lamented that few even knew it existed, let alone understood the challenges and rewards it offered the world.

"I'm dreaming of brochures, newspapers, and magazine articles, a corps of volunteer advice givers, a network of volunteer Trail Watchdogs . . . and lots more hikers and riders traveling The Trail," she wrote. "I want to make the PCT better maintained. I'm dreaming that our volunteer and paid trail crews will go in and do the work and our membership clout will convince Congress that The Trail needs funding support. We will find ways to help the land managers. We can help them publicize their maintenance needs and recruit clubs or individuals who can improve the PCT. And I'm dreaming that we'll have lots more hikers and riders maintaining The Trail."

It was almost as if Marshall had a crystal ball. What she'd described was today's Pacific Crest Trail Association.

Marshall could be deadly serious and impatient, but her style, at least in the pages of the conference newsletter, was fun and campy. Soon after she started, she was producing the *Communicator* and doing much of the writing. She started one of her *Communicator* columns in 1991 this way: "Hi! My name is Louise Marshall and I'm your Executive Director tonight. (Grin, grin.) We have a lot of specials on the menu and I hope you will find one that pleases you."

OPPOSITE: Fall paints a hillside in Washington's North Cascades under the watchful eye of Glacier Peak.

She quickly got serious, listing a number of projects for improving the PCT Conference, including a membership campaign, drafting bylaws, developing a cost-sharing agreement with the United States Forest Service, trail work, and even paying a living wage to the executive director. "In general, we encourage more INVOLVEMENT from you, the members. Dues are great! Keep them coming! Yes! But there's more excitement than that available." She closed the plea with a rallying cry: "Let's make it a trail we're all proud of, every mile."

Despite the long odds, Marshall never seemed to lose her sense of humor. In another column in late 1991, under the title "You Can't Win Department," she wrote about choosing photos for a new membership brochure. Noticing that all the photos were of hikers, they rushed to include horseback riders since the conference was about both user groups. No one praised the horse pictures, she grumbled. Instead, one woman complained that the conference was "sexist" because the brochure mentioned only Boy Scouts, not Girl Scouts, and all of the photos were of men. "How she could determine that a little ¼-inch-high figure was male is amazing . . . especially as it happened to be female, and the third, smaller figure was me, and I'm female," she wrote.

Her stint as the conference's executive director, while filled with grand vision and much organization—100 new members joined after the new brochure went out—was short lived. On November 1, 1991, Marshall resigned the executive director position "for reasons of health," the *Communicator* said.

There is speculation that Marshall and Cash disagreed over the direction of the organization. Ann Marshall isn't sure but is not surprised by the notion. "That very well could be," she said. "They never saw eye to eye. He had his vision for PCTA and she wanted to change. When she took over she thought the organization needed to be managed. She grabbed it and took it along with her and gave it the structure it has today. Trails were changing, people were changing, and the PCTA needed to keep up with that."

Marshall couldn't stay out of the fray for long. By the following March, Cash had served as PCT Conference president for six years. PCT bylaws limited the president to two consecutive three-year terms. Marshall, still an active board member, was elected board president. They moved the PCT Conference office from Cash's home in Oregon to Marshall's in Lynnwood, Washington. Cash remained on the Board of Directors.

In October 1992, the conference board approved changing the name of the Pacific Crest Trail Conference to the Pacific Crest Trail Association. "The term 'conference' was confusing," the *Communicator* declared. "At least one foundation rejected our funding proposal on the grounds that 'we don't fund conferences.'"

Marshall liked the name change, Ann said. But all was not well. She complained to fellow board members in a November 12, 1992, letter that, among other things, she was uncomfortable having to dance around the fact that the association was not living up to many of the promises it was making to members.

"WE DON'T DO ANY OF THOSE THINGS. IT'S ALL TALK," she vented. "I don't want to continue to sign my WELL-KNOWN AND RESPECTED NAME to these untruths."

She went on to talk about lax financial accountability and oversight by her fellow board members. "Why can't you see as clearly as I do that we MUST get professional staff?" she wrote. She ended the letter this way: "I'll recover—I HAVE TO BECAUSE I'M THE PRESIDENT—but I certainly am not happy in my work. Please help me escape."

By the following spring, Marshall resigned her post as president. Her last *Communicator* entry is a simple statement of the PCTA budget. There was no final "President's Message."

OPPOSITE: On their 1969–1970 thru-ride, the Murray family heads up California's Vogelsang Pass just off the PCT.

The Golden Spike

June 5, 1993, was the first National Trails Day, created for the 25th anniversary celebration of the 1968 National Trails System Act. And the PCTA was set to celebrate. Interior Secretary Bruce Babbitt, appointed by President Bill Clinton, came to the trail for a ceremony in Southern California's Soledad Canyon, where he helped plant a Golden Spike celebrating the PCT's "completion." F. Dale Robertson, chief of the Forest Service, attended, along with many other dignitaries from federal, state, and local government and other PCT lovers. Babbitt's remarks included:

> I was walking through the audience and I met a young schoolteacher in a blue coat and she's wearing a button which symbolizes what this is all about. It says: "Everything is interconnected."

It was an incredible event for the trail and the PCTA. Stories of Babbitt's visit, and therefore the PCT, ran in many newspapers locally and across the nation, giving the trail a media blip. What they didn't say was that the trail was far from complete.

After the passage of the National Trails System Act, the Forest Service and other agencies still needed to acquire many private properties to truly connect the trail from end to end on public land. Throughout the 1970s, 1980s, and into the early 1990s, the agency worked diligently to secure right-of-way easements that gave hikers and horseback riders legal access to the trail.

An unsigned February 1993 memo to the Angeles National Forest supervisor is telling. It talks about the work being done by the PCTA to get Soledad Canyon in shape for the Golden Spike ceremony and Babbitt's visit:

> Just to get the two remaining pieces of trail completed prior to the event will take a major effort and priority on [sic] many people. The Soledad Canyon section still has not had the ROW [right of way] completed and on March 2, 1993, we found an adjacent landowner has encroached on the ROW and will require several work parties and volunteers to clear trash, relocate a chain-link fence, construct the trail tread, and install signs.

The trail was far from complete in 1993, and today, it still crosses hundreds of private properties. Federal conservation funds have been used for many key land-acquisition projects over the last decade, and those will continue to be key in years to come. However, the PCTA is ramping up efforts to facilitate purchases of remaining private parcels through partnerships with established land trusts and by raising private money on its own.

Why Marshall quit was never publicly stated. We can speculate from this letter that she was fed up. But Ann said her father, Bill, was seriously ill. Marshall set aside most of her work, resigning from the REI board and the Lynnwood Parks Department. "She took a year off to care for my dad. That's what she felt like she had to do," Ann said. "Dad died in the fall of 1993."

Marshall remained on the PCTA board for several years and received the PCTA's Lifetime Achievement Award in 1996. She died on August 24, 2005, at age 90.

Ann said her mother loved the trail, even in her later years despite failing health. They would often load her electric scooter in the car and drive to the PCT trailhead at Snoqualmie Pass, east of Seattle, where Marshall would engage PCT hikers.

"Sometimes they would recognize her and it would make her month," Ann said. "It was fun for me to stand behind her and listen to people talking to her."

PCTA Takes a Step Forward

In early 1993, with no ready volunteers to fill in for Louise Marshall, Larry Cash agreed to take the reins as president of the newly minted PCTA for one more year. The organization seemed poised to step it up, largely because of the tenacity of active board members and Marshall's grand ideas. And there was synergy to help it along. Under Cash, the PCTA named five regional coordinators to organize the various trail-maintenance crews and clubs in all three states.

Larry Cash on the PCT in his home state of Oregon, 1979.

With a Forest Service grant, the PCTA board hired Nancy DuPont as the organization's first full-time, paid executive director. DuPont was a longtime trails advocate and horsewoman who spent 12 years as the president of Heritage Trails Fund, a nonprofit raising money and public awareness about riding trails.

The Heritage Trails Fund was the 1980s brainchild of George Cardinet Jr., a California trails advocate "considered by many to be the father of the California trails system," the *Los Angeles Times* said upon his death in January 2007. The *Times*' article quoted Steve Elkinton, then the National Trails System program leader for the National Park Service. "Without George, the national trails system wouldn't have the shape or breadth it does today," Elkinton told the *Times*. "George was larger than life, one of those giants on whose shoulders we all stand."

DuPont and Cardinet were friends, and when she lost her job as an advertising representative for the *Oakland Tribune*, he helped arrange an interview for the PCTA job, she said. She attended a board meeting and was immediately hired.

DuPont's job was to spearhead a public awareness campaign to increase membership and support for the PCTA. "She was the best candidate . . . She's a trail rider herself and she knows what we're about and she understands us," Cash wrote in the *Communicator*.

In her first month on the job, DuPont went to Washington, DC, to meet with the Forest Service and proposed an expanded partnership with the agency beginning that summer. In a May 7, 1993, letter, Lyle Laverty, director of recreation and cultural resources for the agency, wrote that he had pitched the idea to all the regional recreation directors. "Everyone is in agreement that the benefits to such a plan can be great," he wrote. And he laid out a framework for developing the agreement through the regional Forest Service offices for California, Oregon, and Washington.

The PCTA signed its first memorandum of understanding with the Forest Service in 1993, paving the way for a partnership that continues to endure and mature. This was an era when the agency was shrinking because of politics, budget cuts, and reduced timber sales because of environmental concerns, among other things. With decreasing recreation budgets, federal land managers struggled to maintain trails and other amenities, such as campgrounds.

But relying on volunteers and citizen stewards was part of the direction of the National Trails System Act, which states:

The Congress recognizes the valuable contributions that volunteers and private, nonprofit trail groups have made to the development and maintenance of the Nation's trails. In recognition of these contributions, it is further the purpose of this Act to encourage and assist volunteer citizen involvement in the planning, development, maintenance, and management, where appropriate, of trails.

Federal agencies needed groups such as the PCTA to get the work done. The PCTA was likely an attractive option at the time, and with seed money, one that could turn its loose but standing organization into a well-honed entity.

Cash's final term as board president ended in April 1994. In an address to the members on the occasion of his last board meeting as president, Cash marveled at all the association had accomplished: the organizational progress, the regional coordinators, and maintenance success. "We know we have the potential for tremendous growth and we have a unique opportunity, working in partnership with the U.S. Forest Service, to help achieve the highest and best use of this long, narrow piece of real estate we call the Pacific Crest National Scenic Trail," Cash wrote in the spring 1994 edition of the *Communicator*.

Cash stayed on the board of his beloved PCTA. In 1995, he took on the role of PCTA historian and the group's files show much correspondence toward this end. In 1997, he received a well-deserved PCTA Lifetime Achievement Award.

In 2002, at age 86, Cash gave an interview to a son-in-law for a college paper. The transcript survives in the Cash family archives. "My hope for the future of the PCT is a long, happy residence in the hearts and minds of people who love and respect the great outdoors," he said. By then, Cash's health made it nearly impossible to get out on his beloved trail.

Dave Cash laments that his father spent much of his early retirement working in his home office on behalf of the trail rather than out hiking. But for those who love and care for the trail, it's hard to imagine where the PCTA might be today without his dedication and intervention. He was a true volunteer.

"It's pretty clear that he felt good about it," Dave said. "It was hard, it was demanding, and there were some sacrifices, but he felt it was a really worthwhile thing to work on behalf of the trail. The notion that everything has grown in such a great way and that so many people are involved in stewardship would please him."

Larry and Zotty Cash observed their 67th wedding anniversary in September 2009. Zotty passed on the following April. On July 25, 2010, Larry Cash died in Eugene, Oregon. He was 94 and held the trail close to his heart until the end. For his memorial program, his five children chose a famous John Muir quote: "The mountains are calling and I must go."

The Wonder That Was Alice Krueper

If you could make a mold of the perfect trail-maintenance volunteer, Alice Krueper would be the model. Like most things she did in life, she took care of the Pacific Crest Trail in Southern California with her entire spirit and seemingly boundless energy.

OPPOSITE: The PCT above Whitewater River in Southern California's San Gorgonio Wilderness (left); Alice and Harry Krueper never let their children stop them from hitting the trail (right).

At the PCTA, Krueper is a legend. The association's top honor, named for her, is given only to the most outstanding volunteers, those who go well beyond what anyone could reasonably expect. Her story is both inspirational and bittersweet, the latter only because she died in the middle of her tireless effort to make the trail in Southern California safer and a better experience for hikers and horseback riders.

Even without her volunteerism, Krueper is worthy of marveling. She bagged peaks around the world, rode a bicycle across the country, won the Ironman triathlon in her age group, and section hiked the PCT.

In addition to raising four sons, she was one of the key people who fought to create the San Gorgonio Wilderness, one of the country's first wilderness areas. Her efforts before and after the 1964 Wilderness Act's passage helped save San Gorgonio Mountain from becoming a ski area.

She was born October 1, 1927, in Campbell, California, near San Jose, the daughter of Knud and Sarah Jensen. Knud Jensen, who immigrated to the United States from Denmark as an orphan after World War I, was a carpenter and owned a prune orchard in the Santa Clara Valley. Krueper and her older brother Tom worked the farm as kids and spent weekends combing the trails of the Sierra with their parents, said Ron Krueper, Alice's oldest son.

"She would tell us that she was a tomboy growing up," Ron said. "Tomboy was her nickname because she helped so much on the farm."

She went to Campbell High School and attended the University of California, Berkeley, where she earned a degree in nursing. While there, she got involved in the campus hiking club. She also met her future husband, Harry Krueper, a UCLA graduate who was attending Berkeley for his master's in traffic engineering.

After college, Krueper and a girlfriend planned to bicycle for six months around Europe, warming up with an 800-mile trip in the Canadian Rockies in the summer of 1953. The following summer, the ladies traveled more than 2,000 miles around Europe by bike and train and, among other things, climbed peaks in the French and Swiss Alps using crampons and ice axes.

"For two women to do that in 1954, I would say, was exceptional," Ron said.

On June 11, 1955, Alice and Harry married and eventually settled in San Bernardino because it offered them easy access to the desert, beach, and mountains of Southern California. Harry's family had a cabin near Big Bear Lake, which played into their decision. Krueper was a stay-at-home mom and Harry was a Division of Highways (now Caltrans) engineer. They took their boys all over the southland on weekend excursions—hiking the mountains, camping at the beach, sleeping under the stars, or spending time at the family cabin.

"When I was six and my younger brother was four, we had already climbed to the top of San Gorgonio," Ron said. "My mom made all these unique ways of carrying the smaller kids. She made a papoose board. One parent would carry that and the other parent would carry the sleeping bags and food for a one or two nighter."

In the early 1960s, there was a proposal to build a road to the base of San Gorgonio and install ski lifts on the northern slope. At that time, the mountain was part of a primitive area, before there was official "wilderness." It became a touch point in a rising national debate over the proposed Wilderness Act. The Kruepers and others came together to stop the ski area. They formed the Defenders of the San Gorgonio Wilderness to draw awareness to the ski area interests. Krueper was the group's secretary, drafting monthly newsletters and helping build a coalition of conservation groups to lobby state and federal lawmakers.

Ron, today a retired California Department of Parks and Recreation ranger, recalls monthly backyard gatherings in which the adults would operate a mimeograph machine and crank out letters to lawmakers and supporters. The kids would get involved in folding the papers, stuffing envelopes, and licking stamps. It was true grassroots activism.

With the passage of the Wilderness Act, signed into law by President Lyndon Johnson on September 3, 1964, the San Gorgonio Wilderness was one of the first areas protected.

Despite the wilderness designation, Defenders of the San Gorgonio Wilderness decided to stay vigilant. Krueper spearheaded an effort to make a user-friendly map of the area, which they sold in Forest Service ranger stations for $1. The money helped keep the nonprofit afloat. Sure enough, in 1967, the ski area interests sought an exemption to the wilderness designation. Opponents mobilized again, backed in part by the money Krueper's maps were bringing in.

"As I reflect on her life, her motivation, leadership, and organizational skills really showed through," Ron said. "She used the same skill organizing work parties on the PCT, making sure there was enough food and water."

By the early 1970s, the wilderness battle was over. She had young children to care for, but Krueper got back into bike touring and hikes for herself, among other outdoor pursuits. She loved snowshoeing and backcountry ski touring. In 1980, she began volunteering for the Forest Service on PCT trail crews.

OPPOSITE: A hiker strides through sparse sage desert near Whitewater Creek at the southern foot of California's San Bernardino Mountains.

She trained to climb Denali in 1981, though never made the trip. But she and Ron did summit Mount Rainier in 1980. She also climbed Mount Hood in Oregon and Mount Baker and Mount Adams in Washington.

In 1981, Ron came in 10th in the Hawaii Ironman, sparking his mother's interest in long races. She ran the San Bernardino Marathon that year. And Ron, a high school swimmer, coached his mother, first in a pool, then in the open water. In 1982, at age 56, Krueper won the Hawaii Ironman in her age group. "She felt so accomplished," Ron said. "She put her mind to stuff and got it done."

In 1984, she climbed Communism Peak (today called Ismoil Somoni Peak)—at 24,590 feet, the tallest peak in the former USSR, now Tajikistan. She was one in a party of six Southern Californians. A climber above her broke free and started to fall, passing two others in the party before crashing into Krueper. Her rope held and both were saved.

Hiking the PCT was next. Ron recalls having a conversation with his mother in which she said she wanted to walk from Mexico to Canada. She section hiked the PCT in six legs over six years, from 1987 through 1992. "I knew I couldn't consider doing the trail until my boys were out of the house," she told *Communicator* Editor Lee Terkelsen in 1995. "Still, we did a lot of hiking. The boys practically grew up in the backcountry. But as they got older and busy going to college, I got less busy and began to think of the PCT again. I convinced my husband that I didn't think he would miss me for five or six weeks a year."

On the last day of her last section on the PCT, she crossed into Canada in a snowstorm. When asked if she was glad she was done, she said, "I was really depressed. I just wanted to keep on going north into British Columbia."

She found that many sections were either overgrown or nonexistent. A lot of the trail was unprotected. The PCTA was still a fledgling organization made up of volunteers. All this galvanized her volunteer work and the PCT became the cause to which she devoted her energy and passion.

As the volunteer trail coordinator for Southern California, she was in charge of organizing maintenance projects on the southernmost 700 miles of the PCT. This could be considered the toughest section of trail to care for. Thick brush grows fast there and desert heat can zap even the most dedicated volunteers.

Krueper pulled in volunteers from the local Sierra Club. Working with the Bureau of Land Management and the California Department of Parks and Recreation, she organized and led projects to build an eight-mile section of trail through the lower Whitewater Canyon near Interstate 10 at San Gorgonio Pass, taking the trail off a road with no shoulder.

She slowly built a faithful following of trail maintainers, the precursor to today's PCTA Trail Gorillas, one of many organized volunteer groups that tackle maintenance and restoration work. "She had a way of convincing people to help," said Pete Fish, the Trail Gorillas' leader, who credits Krueper with getting him involved in maintaining the PCT. She conducted appreciation ceremonies at the end of each work project, giving each worker a gift and a hug.

As the chair of the PCTA's now-defunct Trail Water Committee, she worked to enhance natural springs and other water sources along the trail, making it safe to cross dry sections. She built relationships with state and federal land managers. She organized the 1993 Golden Spike ceremony and was widely praised for her efforts, receiving letters of thanks from California Governor Pete Wilson, California Senator Barbara Boxer, and Interior Secretary Bruce Babbitt, who gave the keynote address.

OPPOSITE: Trail building takes place circa 1935 in the San Gabriel Mountains of California's Angeles National Forest, high above metropolitan Los Angeles.

"I only wish my schedule had allowed me time to get out for a hike along the trail," Babbitt wrote.

The following year, Krueper started feeling tired. Low energy was not who she was. She knew something was wrong. On her way to a PCT work project, she stopped off at the hospital for some tests. In 1995, exploratory surgery found pancreatic cancer. She was 68.

More surgeries to remove the cancer and chemotherapy followed. Krueper dug into researching the disease with the same zeal she'd done everything else in life. "It was tough," Ron recalled. "They said it was inoperable but she said she was going to find the best treatment that she could and live her life the best she could." Still, she continued to organize PCT work parties and attended when she could, despite the drug pump that she wore in a fanny pack.

When she began her cancer treatment, she told a newspaper reporter, "Everyone is born and everyone dies; you just do your darndest to do your best in between." When Terkelsen interviewed her for the *Communicator*, she shunned the attention, saying, "We've got to get publicity for the trail."

At the end of 1995, Krueper received the first Alice Krueper Award during a public ceremony. PCTA President Ben York presented it. In old photos of the occasion, it's clear that the cancer had taken its toll, though it's equally clear that Krueper was happy and at peace.

A few months later, in February 1996, Krueper had a stroke. She died March 16, 1996, at age 69, nine months after being diagnosed. Family members scattered her ashes near a lake tucked into the Kern-Kaweah River drainage, southeast of Mount Whitney. Krueper traveled there back in her Berkeley days and it was one of her favorites, Ron said.

Krueper did all she could and much more for the PCT. She was a supernova of a volunteer, devoting the last years of her life to the trail. Her example sets the bar for today's and tomorrow's volunteers and the fact that so many others have stepped up in her absence would clearly make her proud.

And her husband, Harry Krueper, continued to be a PCTA and wilderness supporter until his death on February 26, 2015.

A Course Correction

When Larry Cash stepped down as president of the PCTA in the spring of 1994, the group was riding high. A year earlier, it had hired its first paid executive director, Nancy DuPont, and the organization was becoming more involved in the United States Forest Service's plans for care and management of the trail.

DuPont, a lifetime equestrian who lives in Walnut Creek, California, said she worked hard for the PCTA. She said she helped organize dozens of much-needed maintenance projects, hired an office assistant, organized an extensive project to map the trail with GPS technology, put together a brochure, and used her newspaper background to improve the *Communicator* by printing it on newspaper stock.

Outwardly, the PCTA seemed to be doing well, but DuPont and the PCTA board members, Cash among them, did not see eye to eye. As she described it, she was told by her Forest Service contacts that the agency's grant money should get spent, and she saw her role as making sure the agency got what it wanted. But she said some board members pushed back about the way she spent the grant money and disagreed with agency priorities, such as the GPS mapping project.

OPPOSITE: Sunset bathes the PCT's classic scene—Thousand Island Lake and its twin massifs, Banner and Ritter Peaks.

"I was always loyal to the Forest Service and they didn't like that," she said of the board. "Yes, I was their executive director. I just knew where the money came from. I was accountable for that money to the Forest Service, not so much them."

Enter Alan Young. Young was a Boy Scout and in high school, living in Milwaukie, Oregon, when he read Eric Ryback's book about thru-hiking the PCT. He loved the book and thought that when he graduated high school he'd hike the trail, or at least part of it. He wrote to every national forest along the trail and they sent maps, which he pinned to his bedroom wall.

"My mother asked me what I was doing and I said I'm going to walk from Mexico to Canada, and she said, 'Oh no, you are not!'" he recalled. "I might as well have been talking about walking on the moon!"

In 1979, he thru-hiked the PCT.

Fifteen years later, he was in the San Diego Adventure 16 store looking at backpacking gear when he saw a stack of the *Communicator* and took one. "I always loved the trail but I didn't know what the PCTA was," he said.

He filled out a membership form included in the newsletter, which, among other things, asked for skills and talents. By then, Young made his living organizing fundraising campaigns and nonprofit organizations. "You write that down and you get a telephone call," he said.

It was DuPont who called Young and asked for help. He quickly volunteered. But the more questions he asked, the more he learned that the PCTA was in financial trouble. It had roughly 800 members but only about half were paying annual membership dues, he said. The others were kept on the rolls for a year or longer and sent membership materials and newsletters, an expense the organization could ill afford.

Young said he was dismayed by what he learned. The PCTA's small board would come together a couple of times a year. It had no real strategy, no plan. It was, he said, "one step up from a mimeograph machine."

The 1993 Forest Service's grant to the PCTA, used to hire DuPont, was also meant to grow the organization, said Bob Ballou, a former professional Boy Scout executive and nonprofit organizer, who would take the PCTA's executive director job in 1996. The money was gone in about a year and a half and didn't produce the results the agency was looking for, he said.

DuPont disagreed. She said the agency wanted her to spend the grant money on trail-maintenance projects. She said she also worked hard to build awareness, connect people to the trail, and increase membership. But in the end, she said, she and board members could not agree on how best to make progress.

"The bottom line is that the Forest Service didn't get what they hoped for, which was a larger organization that could do the work that was needed on the trail," Ballou said.

Ballou said Young saw that the PCTA was going to hit a financial wall and that its relationship with the Forest Service was in jeopardy. Young suggested a new direction in a document that he submitted to PCTA President Ben York and the board. It became the PCTA's first long-range plan. "It really defined the mission and described how we would go about advancing that mission," Young said.

Among other things, the document laid out a strategy for increasing lagging membership to 2,000 through a direct-mail campaign. It included direction for how the board should operate, how membership money and gifts should be used, and how to put a good accounting system in place. The plan also called for annual membership meetings and other gatherings and improved relationships with the Forest Service

OPPOSITE: The trail heads north out of Bighorn Plateau in California's Sequoia National Park.

and other agencies. And it addressed the benefits of membership and called for a permanent office with a staff of professionals.

"They asked me to join the board but I refused until they made these changes," Young said. "They worked hard and they met those conditions and I eventually joined the board."

At the February 4, 1995, board meeting in Oregon, the board adopted Young's plan. Also on the agenda was to "review and evaluate the executive director." DuPont was told the next day by phone that she had been let go.

In a March 6 letter to DuPont, which was published in the *Communicator*, York wrote, "It is regrettable that this situation has occurred. You have been very faithful to the organization and have put forth a tremendous amount of energy. I have known you to be honest with lots of enthusiasm."

DuPont said it all boiled down to the fact that she and most board members didn't have the same ideas for building the organization. "We all loved that trail. Man, I loved that trail. There's not one of us that didn't," she said. "But when it came to what we had to do to keep it alive, we had different approaches."

DuPont remained a PCT advocate, despite it all. She and the Heritage Trails Fund stayed on as regional coordinator for a section of the trail in Central California and she wrote for the *Communicator* in June 1996 about the GPS mapping project.

Today, she breeds Arabian horses and has a business organizing horse camps and riding lessons for children. She also is president of the Amigos de Anza, a nonprofit started by her friend, George Cardinet Jr., to support the Juan Bautista de Anza National Historic Trail, which runs from Mexico to San Francisco.

CHAPTER SEVEN

VOLUNTEERS

Trail Gorilla Emeritus: Pete Fish

Pete Fish raps on the side of the van at 6:00 a.m. sharp with a wake-up call.

"Coffee's ready!" he yells.

It's not just any coffee; it's Fish's infamous cowboy coffee, legendary rotgut and a necessity on any trail project. It was especially welcome on a chilly morning in May 2015 in Angeles National Forest as the sun just began to shoot its warmth over the horizon. Other cooks in the Trail Gorillas crew try to emulate the brew, but Fish jokes about his special golden touch when making hot, brown water.

"You float a raft of coffee grounds on the water," he said, as if he's describing a delicate procedure for a cable TV cooking show. He gestures with hands that have tended to thousands of campfire meals and hefted countless tools. Then smiling, he said, "Then you swing it over your head."

Behind his aging face—Fish was born May 6, 1931—his bright eyes flicker with happiness and determination. His hearing is going and even his eyesight is bad up close, but none of that stops him.

When he hits the trail for a day of backbreaking work, he jumps in with the spring of a man 20 years younger. The transformation is as unbelievable as it is palpable. Watching him pull the cord on a chain saw and dive into thick manzanita growing over the trail makes you wonder if you'll be able to keep pace with him all day. The fact that he has been building and maintaining the PCT for two decades might seem impossible to believe until you see Fish in action. Talk to him about trail work and you begin to understand the definition of obsession.

He's clearly a legend in the Pacific Crest Trail Association (PCTA) community. He took over maintenance responsibility for the southernmost 702 miles of the PCT from Campo to Kennedy Meadows in 1996, after Alice Krueper's cancer made it impossible for her. Fish had been a volunteer on her crews. He was also a PCTA board member for two terms, from 1993 to 1999. All this effort came in retirement.

He has built the Trail Gorillas into a powerhouse, with seven section chiefs who steward various parts with his oversight. He still procures, wrangles, and maintains tools—from hand tools to chain saws and powerful brush saws—and drives his 4x4 pickup hauling a trailer to remote campsites miles off the pavement.

It's familiar territory. When he was a young man, he and his dad joined the Sierra Club together. His father was a horseman who helped build hiking and riding trails, some of which became part of the PCT. During high school, Fish worked as a packer out of Onion Valley, taking clients into the High Sierra backcountry. "I've always thought some of my best friends on the trail are mules and horses," he said.

Fish's parents lived in Warner Springs, California, where he remembers visiting once and seeing PCT hikers stumbling into the local store to resupply. "I stood on the trail and had the realization that Mexico was that way and Canada was that way," he said. It's an old refrain, but one that is familiar and has deep meaning to many PCT fanatics. "It stayed in my mind and when I retired I thought it was something I thought I'd like to do."

Fish spent a career as an exploration geologist in the oil business, working fields and drilling rigs from Bakersfield, California, to Alaska and as far as Indonesia. Today, he and his wife, Joyce, live in Ventura, California. They raised three children. Their home, decorated elegantly with mementos from their time in Asia, is where Joyce's car shares garage space with a rack of chain saws, various power tools, picks, McLeods,

PREVIOUS SPREAD: Looking east from the trail across the Suiattle River drainage onto Vista Ridge, Glacier Peak Wilderness, Washington. OPPOSITE: Conifers young and old in California's Tahoe National Forest.

and pulaskis—all tools of the trail-building trade. Out front, a Trail Gorillas tool trailer takes up a parking space in the driveway.

Fish retired at age 59, and in 1991 began section hiking the PCT. In 1993, he joined the PCTA Board of Directors and was put in charge of membership. "I got in touch with all 300 members," he joked. "It didn't take that long."

That same year he attended the Golden Spike ceremony when Interior Secretary Bruce Babbitt dedicated the PCT in an emotional speech. But it was Krueper who inspired Fish that day. "She had put this whole thing together," he recalled of the ceremony. "She had rented chairs and tables and was going to camp and take it all back the next day. I thought I could help."

Fish stayed the night, too. Soon after, he joined one of Krueper's 10-day trail crew projects. "I just got swept up," he said.

He finished section hiking in 1994 and was one of Krueper's regular crew. In 1996, when she could no longer handle the responsibility, Fish took over. He cajoled and organized. He took a lesson from Krueper, who was impossible to turn down when she called—because she wouldn't take no for an answer.

Fish received the PCTA's Alice Krueper Award in 1997, presented by Alice's husband, Harry Krueper.

Today "Pickaxe" Pete Fish and the Trail Gorillas are a tight band of 50 diehards and another 200 occasional volunteers who lop and beat back brush, build rock structures, and crosscut and chain saw their way through 700 miles of terrain that is as hot, dry, and difficult as it is beautiful. They do about 50 projects every year, including several extended projects, which Fish still calls "full-court-Alice projects."

The group's name came during an evening campfire. Fish doesn't remember when or where, but he said there may have been cheap beer or boxed wine involved. Several folks were sitting around and Fish was off doing something. "When I came back, they were standing there beating their chests, shouting, 'We are Trail Gorillas!' The name stuck," he said.

They are a diverse group that has no business being together—pilots, a glassblower, a banjo maker, and even a nuclear submarine skipper. Fish is sure of the differences in the group, not so sure of what makes the individuals tick. "I guess for all of us, it's the people," he said. "It's like family. We have a lot of experience together. It's just fun to do. For me, the work is its own reward and you have a feeling like, 'That's my trail.'"

In the early days before the PCTA hired regional representatives and the Trail Gorillas had section chiefs, Fish would set up the projects and gather the tools. He met with the agency folks and lived and breathed trail. His wife would shop for food for the crews and put up with her husband's obsession. "Joyce has been very understanding and has helped a lot," he said.

In those days, the PCTA's relations with the United States Forest Service were fairly new and evolving, Fish said. He made a big effort to play the role of partner, making sure the agencies were aware of any projects the volunteers were going to set themselves upon. Individual forests decided which projects needed to get done and how much money they had to support the crews. Every November, Fish would visit each ranger district separately and set up budgets for the coming year.

"It was just a road race. It was a hunt for money," he said.

The volunteers regularly dipped into their own pockets to make sure they could keep the trail open in areas where the agency couldn't come up with food and gas money. Gradually, the partnership with Southern California forests improved. "We built up credibility and that allowed us to work on our own, but it took a while to get to that point," Fish said.

When he was fully engaged, Fish spent about 100 days a year out on the trail. He still gets out for about 30 days, maintains tools, and teaches others in the use of power saws and how to care for them.

In 2004, the PCTA gave Fish its Lifetime Achievement Award. More than a decade later, he's still going strong. There's little sign that he's going to quit doing that. When he's out hefting a chain saw, he is happy.

Asked to explain the drive, he smiled knowingly. If you've never worked the trail, you might not get it. If you have, and you believe that the PCT is bigger than the sum of its parts, that it's special, you understand the glint in his eye.

In 1995, he wrote in *The Pacific Crest Trail Communicator* that after the euphoria of hiking the PCT wears off, the learning associated with the hike continues. "You realize that the trail didn't just happen," he

OPPOSITE: Mount Adams peers over the shoulders of a PCTA trail crew in Snowgrass Flats, southern Washington.

Trail Towns: Milkshakes and Economic Boot Prints

A well-known commercial once asked, "How do you spell relief?" For PCT hikers, horse riders, and lovers of the outdoors, relief is spelled "T-r-a-i-l T-o-w-n-s."

Towns are a PCT common denominator. Near trailheads, cars gas up at rural corner stations. Hikers guzzle cold sodas. Horseback riders rinse chapped lips with the froth topping frosty beer mugs. Eyes bulge at Nelda's Diner in Lake Isabella, California (population 3,466), trying to pick just one milkshake from 108 named choices. And near where the PCT crosses Pines to Palms Highway, famished PCT travelers devour famed Jose burgers at the Paradise Café. Tens of thousands of hiker resupply boxes overflow the shelves of dozens of rural post offices. And the faint smell of pine duff rises from hard-to-clean shower stalls in near-trail hostels, motels, and trail angels' homes. At nighttime, grateful heads bed down to fluffy pillows.

Just north of the Mexican border it starts with Campo, Lake Morena, and Mount Laguna, California, and then ends up north with Skykomish, Stehekin, Mazama, and Winthrop, Washington. The towns run the alphabet's breadth, from Agua Dulce, a forty-minute drive north of Los Angeles, to ski area White Pass, three hours southeast of Seattle. In Northern California, Old Station claims a population of 50, barely enough bodies for an army platoon, while west of the Mojave Desert, the town of Tehachapi (population 14,500) could fill all the billets in an army division.

A sliver, not even a tenth of a percent of the PCT, is on an asphalt road, but in northernmost California, the trail marches on black tarmac through Seiad Valley, where the single business establishment, no larger than a suburban home, houses the post office, general store, and the café. It's obvious that PCT aficionados love trail towns. But do trail towns feel the same? The Washington towns of Stevenson, Carson, and North Bonneville are not far from where the PCT exits Oregon and crosses the Columbia River. Stevenson Mayor Frank Cox writes, "This past year, Stevenson, Carson, and North Bonneville were blessed with recreation users who came for the trails and . . . then went shopping and stayed for beer, food, and a place to sleep. Our businesses had a record number of customers leaving an economic boot print in the communities." Underscoring all this he added, "Trail systems . . . are very important to our businesses." In a separate letter, 29 local business owners echoed Cox's sentiment.

Cox spoke locally, but nationwide, that same trend is evident. In 2013, across the United States nearly 35 million went out for a hike. More than nine million backpacked at least one night. Spending for outdoor recreation in 2012 topped $640 billion, all of which supported six million jobs. In all, almost 150 million Americans participated in at least one outdoor activity. The economic boot print of the PCT and other trails looms large.

Just as Martin Luther nailed his manifesto to the church door, the following sent from Oregon's Cascade Locks could serve as a PCT trail town manifesto:

The steady stream of dusty adventurous thru-hikers and section hikers visiting our community each year provides an important contribution to our local economy. You are welcome here. We will store your resupply boxes in every nook and cranny of our rural post offices. We will provide you soap for your showers. . . . We live vicariously through your stories. Thank you for your business. Thank you for recreating responsibly and respectfully. Thank you to the organizations and volunteers who build and maintain our beloved trails. Be safe out there!

By the way, try the "Green Finger" shake at Nelda's—pistachio almond ice cream and Butterfinger chips.

wrote, crediting people and their mules and horses for keeping it open. "With luck, you meet some of these dedicated people whose example may spark within you the desire to make a positive contribution, to give back to the trail. This is where the real commitment begins. It is measured in years."

Twenty years later and still beating back brush, Fish explained it this way: "You are prepared to stay out there until the job is done. I think you never get over that. Either that or you take up golf."

In his garage, there are no golf clubs, just chain saws.

Camp Cook: Doris Peddy

A large pot of red chili bubbles on the stove. Next to it there's another smaller one for the vegetarians. Salad fixings are plentiful; the cornbread is homemade, just like the after-dinner brownies. And it all comes with a smile. It's a meal that would satisfy anyone, let alone a hungry trail crew, all served up by Doris Peddy, a longtime Trail Gorillas volunteer trail worker turned cook.

Peddy might be one of the smallest Trail Gorillas, but she likely has one of the biggest hearts. The San Bernardino, California, resident has been volunteering for the PCTA since 1989 after reading an ad looking for trail workers in the Sierra Club newsletter. She was 64 years old.

"My husband had passed away in 1988 and I needed something to do," she said. "I joined the Sierra Club."

On that first day, she could have easily quit. "I went out and nearly killed myself because I tried to keep up with the youngsters," she said. "My neighbors thought I was stark raving mad for doing it. I was always hot, tired, and dirty or cold, tired, and dirty."

Coincidentally, Peddy and Alice Krueper lived close to one another. They met on a trail crew and became good friends. Peddy remembers when Krueper would swing by and pick her up for a trail project in her yellow Volkswagen. Peddy received the Alice Krueper Award in 2007.

Approaching her 90th birthday on November 13, 2015, Peddy said she had no intention of giving up her volunteer gig with the PCTA. She cooks for five or six crews a year and for Trail Skills College, the PCTA's training program for volunteers.

Born and raised in Fresno, she is a graduate of mechanical engineering at the University of California, Berkeley. She and her husband, Jack E. Peddy, lived all over California for various jobs—they both once worked for the state highway department in Fresno—before settling in San Bernardino. They raised two sons and a daughter and Peddy said she now gets to enjoy her four grandchildren and two great-grandchildren.

She has never thru-hiked the PCT, though she wishes she had started hiking 40 years earlier. "Maybe I would have done it," she said.

She loved doing trail work, but when she could no longer handle the physical aspects of it, decided to stick with the crew as a cook. Her motherly touch is evident. "The crews are so appreciative of anything you do," she said. "They come back from the work site; they're so tired. It's fun to be with them and know that I'm helping in my small way."

One of her favorite tasks is cooking for school groups who join trail projects. "It also brings back memories of when I was a kid," she said.

Looking back, she's amazed at some of the places she has been able to visit along the trail. She recalled driving to a campsite on a rough dirt road. The next day, she was a passenger on the same road with Pete Fish behind the wheel. "If I had driven it the first time with Pete I don't think I would have driven it myself," she said.

For now, she said, Trail Gorillas can look forward to her meals for years to come. She'll continue to load her small car to the roof with supplies for hungry trail workers. "I'll keep going as long as I can," she said, "as long as I can drive there. It has never not been fun, even though you're always hot or cold. I enjoy it."

Ben York Rides into PCTA History

In early 1995, with Nancy DuPont's departure, the burden of running the PCTA again fell to a volunteer. To retake that old path felt like a setback. Despite the heartache of having to fire a fellow trail lover and horse person, Ben York was a pragmatist who kept the best interest of the trail in mind.

York was a retired veterinarian who had brought much attention to the trail with a successful 1992 ride of the entire PCT on horseback. He and his daughter, Valerie York-Watts, moved the PCTA's office files from DuPont's home in Walnut Creek, California, to theirs in Alpine, a rural community east of San Diego near the trail's southern terminus. York-Watts remembers making the drive on a rainy weekend in her father's pickup.

York-Watts had just moved back to the United States after eight years in Heidelberg, Germany. She was living with her parents and looking for work when her father offered her an administrative assistant position with the PCTA. She began culling through membership files, making a list of current members, and contacting those whose memberships had lapsed. She provided information to trail users, supported the maintenance groups, and answered the hotline.

"We just wanted to nurture the membership, making sure people got their *Communicator* and patches or whatever it was we were sending out at the time," she said. "If they had a question, it was answered right away. I even ferried people from the airport to the trailhead."

It was a time of transition and turnaround for the PCTA. York had been on the PCTA board for about a year when he took the president's post. But the job was not unfamiliar to him. He'd also been president of the Backcountry Horsemen of California and believed deeply that the nation's trails system should be valued and well maintained.

Born September 3, 1924, in Pleasanton, California, Ben York Jr. graduated from Amador Valley High School and served in the US Army during World War II. He and Adeline Wright were married August 30, 1952. He graduated as a veterinarian from University of California, Davis, three years later and opened York's Animal Clinic in Brawley, California, where he cared for animals for more than 30 years. He retired in 1987.

In 1992, the year before joining the PCTA board, York and Adeline planned a thru-ride of the PCT to take a detailed look at the trail's condition and to bring attention to it. They left the United States-Mexico border on April 21, her 61st birthday, riding horses and pulling a string of three mules—Texaco, Molly, and Queenie. York was 67.

"We want to prove to ourselves that we can do it before we get too far over the hill," he told the *Communicator*. Adeline was forced to quit the ride when she broke her arm, but York, his horse, and the mules kept on. He learned to love the solitude.

OPPOSITE: Ben York leads a string during his 1992 thru-ride. He often would pick up another rider for a day or two as he made his way north.

THE PACIFIC CREST TRAIL

"He would say that so many times he'd find himself somewhere where he could have yelled his fool head off," York-Watts recalled, "but he just wouldn't because the place and the stillness itself was so awesome he felt like it would be wrong to speak above a whisper."

He did another thru-ride in 1996. A year after his first thru-ride, York was interviewed by the *Los Angeles Times*. "There's a tendency to think you're closer to the Lord when you're out there," he said. "You have the quietness and the solitude and the awesomeness of it."

Many involved at this time in the PCTA's history said one of York's greatest talents was inspiring people and bringing together the sometimes philosophically divergent hikers and horse people. He fostered an understanding that horses and mules were necessary to maintain the trail in remote areas, an idea that prevails.

One of those hikers was Pete Fish. Fish was section hiking in 1992 when he came upon York with a horse and two pack mules near Golden Oaks Spring. The two men camped together that night and Fish recalls being low on food. "I thought to myself, I am in luck," Fish said. "Everyone knows what good providers backcountry horsemen are."

As he helped York unload his mules, there was plenty of food for the animals. But all York had in his saddlebags for humans was a half-eaten burrito a TV cameraman had given him during a trailhead interview earlier in the day.

"We wound up eating dinner mostly out of my pack," Fish said. "Ben would dispute this account later, but as we became much better acquainted over the years I learned that Ben took much better care of his animals than himself. On trail projects, we learned to always pack a lunch for Ben, and were glad to do it."

Fish woke up the next morning and York was gone. But he said he spent the rest of his hike that summer following the horses and mules. Their large feet stamped down tall grasses, and Fish made up rhymes about the mules' names as a way to pass the time.

They got to know one another later on trail projects. York and his mules often packed in the crews and he regularly worked in the dirt. Later on, as they worked together on the PCTA board, Fish recalled that York was constantly talking. "You couldn't turn him off," Fish said.

That served the PCTA well most of the time. Once, on a scouting mission, they were driving on a remote dirt road when their vehicle was hit head-on by a pickup. Fish said the truck, driven by a young man, was brand-new. Fish was talking to the driver and York was consoling the man's passenger, a young woman in tears. "I realize he's trying to recruit her to join the PCTA," Fish said, laughing. "Typical Ben." It turned out that the new truck was not insured and the woman was not the driver's wife, Fish explained. "That guy was in a peck of trouble," he said.

Fish recalled another time when he and York went to an AmeriCorps meeting in San Diego to give a pitch to hundreds of potential volunteers. The PCTA was close to last on the bill and time was dragging, Fish said. York finally stood up in front of the crowd in his trademark cowboy boots, hat, and thick red suspenders. It was clear he was a cowboy and had the grizzled face, gray messy beard, and booming voice to prove it. He told the crowd to get on their feet because they had to sing.

"He had a song about horses and hikers on the trail," Fish said. "Everybody is singing and they are doing the wave. It made the day for us. Ben was besieged with volunteers. He carried it off."

Though he was a horseman, York served both horseback riders and hikers with equal zest. He once told Fish, "I must be doing something right. Both groups are complaining."

Alan Young, who served as the PCTA's vice president of finance under York, said York made tough decisions about the direction of the association that were right for the group even if they might not have been perfect for him. In April 1995, Young was living in Portland, Oregon, and had picked up York at the airport for a Board of Directors meeting. On the way he told York that PCTA board members should each be required to give $1,000 a year to the organization and pay their own expenses, a major shift for the group.

"Ben York was quite the talker and he could go on and on about every mud hole on the trail," Young said. "I was in a car with him. He was going on and on, and I said, 'Ben, this is the moment, will you make a gift of $1,000 and set a standard for others?'"

York got uncharacteristically quiet for several miles. Young said he could see him thinking about the proposal. Then he agreed. "Once he did it, he turned to the other board members and asked that they do it, too," Young said. "Many of them did. That's when the finances started to turn around. They realized that no one would make a gift unless the members of the governing body did so first."

PCTA board members still hew to the same spirit, but they have taken York and Young's lead to another level. Not only do they give expansively of their expertise, contacts, and time; in 2014, board giving alone nearly topped $100,000.

OPPOSITE: Ben York on horseback at age 12 in Pleasanton, California, circa 1936 (left), and as the grizzled veteran in the Sierra Nevada, 1992 (right).

The PCTA's financial turnaround can be charted back to Young and York's conversation in the car followed by York's challenge to the board as a whole. York's dedication and charisma paid off, York-Watts said.

"He could hold the attention of the entire room and he loved the spotlight," she said. "He loved the trail. He was a very charismatic man, and I didn't realize that too much growing up. It was a sweet time to be working for him. I had a chance to know him in a way I had not gotten to before that in my life."

York stepped down from the PCTA board in 1998 after two three-year terms, most of it as president. For a time, he continued as area coordinator for the southernmost section of the trail, working on trail-maintenance projects. He and Adeline traveled extensively in retirement. While making a round-the-world trip in 2005 at the age of 80, he suffered a massive stroke in Siberia. It left York, a former toastmaster, debilitated, without the ability to speak clearly. "At some point they told him he wouldn't be able to walk again and he proved them wrong," York-Watts said.

He would still try to tell stories about the PCT. "Because I'd heard those stories so many times, I was able to tell people what he was trying to say," York-Watts said. "I could understand a few words and I knew the story. Riding the PCT was the feather in his cap. He was a veterinarian and he had a lot of accomplishments, but this was his proudest accomplishment."

A year later, the Yorks were living a quiet life at the ranch in Alpine. They had been married for 53 years. Adeline decided she was going to sell the horses and buy a condo in nearby Coronado. But before she could do that, she was riding behind a horse on a light two-wheeled buggy when she was thrown from the buggy and hit her head. She died from the injury. York-Watts became her father's caretaker for the rest of his life. Ben York died on October 19, 2011. He was 87.

Legacy Member: Paul Cardinet

If the PCTA were a college fraternity, Paul Cardinet would be its legacy pledge. Cardinet's uncle—his father Robert's older brother—was George Cardinet Jr. As previously mentioned, George Cardinet founded the Heritage Trails Fund in 1980 and was considered a pioneer of trails in California.

Paul Cardinet, a retired public health nurse who lives in Pleasant Hill, California, east of San Francisco, leads the PCTA's Can Do Crew, which maintains a 30-mile section of the trail from South Crater Meadow in Ansel Adams Wilderness north to Donohue Pass in Yosemite National Park.

George Cardinet was a horseman. Paul never rode. But he was a hiker and he shared his uncle's love for trails. It was in the mid-1990s on a Sierra Club trail project near Yosemite's Tenaya Lake, organized by his uncle, that Cardinet got the bug for trail work.

"George wanted to get hikers and horsemen together because he knew there was animosity between those two groups," he said. "He knew that if he could get them together, there would be better understanding. The horsemen pulled up in their rigs with their trailers and whipped out their hot hors d'oeuvres and their cocktails. We hikers pulled out our bota bags. That really broke the ice."

At one of those early projects, he met Priscilla Johnson, whose husband Paul was on the PCTA board. She proposed teaming up to form a maintenance group. She organized crews and food while Cardinet contacted the Forest Service to find places along the PCT that needed attention. For the first few years, they

OPPOSITE: From the summit of Tinker Knob in California's Granite Chief Wilderness, sunset lights the clouds over Lake Tahoe.

worked in the northern Sierra and at Castle Crags. The crews were small and inexperienced, but Cardinet said he learned more and more with each project.

In 1999, they were asked to tackle a horrendous 10-mile section of trail north of McArthur-Burney Falls Memorial State Park that was overgrown with brush. High winds had blown down hundreds of trees, covering the tread. The section was impassible and hikers were detouring along a road. PCTA member Tony de Bellis created a stir with a *Communicator* article about how this section had been neglected and was "the worst" place on the trail. Interest in rectifying the problem grew.

They planned for a crew of 40 to 50 people, including the entire PCTA Board of Directors. PCTA volunteers from Southern California wanted to come help. That spring, they organized a short trip to Castle Crags where they worked to get people certified to use chain saws.

The six-day Burney Falls trip was set for September. Everyone was excited to put their newfound chain-saw skills to work. But the night before the project started, rangers informed Cardinet that they had gone in and bucked out all the fallen trees. They left the overgrown brush. Cardinet suspected the rangers were concerned about all those volunteers handling chain saws.

"We had a lot of saws but only 20 pairs of loppers," Cardinet recalled. "The board was there. Everybody was there. We tried to go into town and buy some weed whackers and other brushing equipment, but couldn't. We decided we would do what we could do."

In six days, the crew cleared nine of the 10 miles. "That really endeared me to the PCTA," Cardinet said. "What really impressed me is that the board paid its own way and got out there. I liked that integrity."

In 2000 he was asked to steward trail in Inyo National Forest, the heart of the High Sierra. "We really lucked out," he said. "We're just in the jewel, with high drama when it comes to scenery."

He loves the work and runs up to three crews a year, depending on need. He said he enjoys looking back on the day's accomplishments, the camaraderie, and the shared sense of purpose.

"It's really important to the health of the country and the world," he said. "We create these trails where people can get out and walk. That's special."

The Horse Folk

When the PCT was first envisioned, horseback riding was a big part of the equation. By the time the PCT was named one of the first two national scenic trails in 1968, it was already long considered a resource for equestrians as well as hikers. Early proponents of the trail wanted to preserve what was a big part of the culture of the American West. They wanted people, such as Ben York and George Cardinet, to be able to taste the early pioneer experience.

Congressionally designated wilderness, as we know it today, was an infant, created just a few years before the National Trails System by the 1964 Wilderness Act. As wilderness areas were added over the decades and the commitment to preserving the country's most pristine and wild landscapes became deep rooted, using stock animals to maintain backcountry trails became the norm out of sheer necessity, especially in the mountainous West. Wilderness rules prohibit the use of motorized equipment and mechanized transport, so horses remain the only means to get heavy hand tools and supplies deep into the backcountry.

OPPOSITE: The Murray family pack train high in California's Ansel Adams Wilderness, 1969.

The Forest Service's history of trail building and maintenance is deeply entwined with packer and service animals. There are still a few remnants of what was once a great and mighty force of government packers out there. But today, as volunteer citizens perform much of the backcountry maintenance, many packers are citizen stewards.

The PCTA has long and fruitful partnerships with equestrian and livestock groups in all three states. These men and women are dedicated volunteers who use their own animals to bring crews into backcountry camps. In many cases, they are the volunteers doing the first "log-outs" of the season—clearing trees that fell across the trail during winter. They often ride into a distant camp, set up for a week or more, and stay to do the trail maintenance as well.

They are certainly too numerous to count, let alone individually thank. But here we give a nod to a few of the trail's longtime horse folk and the rugged lifestyle in the saddle that helped open the West and still holds an attraction, thankfully, for many.

JERRY STONE

When defining a volunteer, the words "personal sacrifice" often come to mind. Jerry Stone personifies those words.

The tragic death of two of his horses on the trail has not stopped him from continuing in a leadership role with the PCTA Trail Gorillas in Southern California. His is a story of dedication to a cause, despite the cost.

Stone is the 2004 recipient of the Alice Krueper Award. He got into volunteering and horses by accident. His two daughters were the horse folk in the family, but as they grew older and their interest waned, he started riding the animals himself. The family lived in the Leona Valley, not far from California's Mojave Desert and three miles from the PCT as the crow flies.

In 1991, a couple of work friends invited him on a pack trip into the Sierra. Riding those high mountain trails changed his life. "When I got back from that trip I said this is what I want to do," Stone recalled. "This is going to give me the opportunity to see country that I wouldn't normally see."

Stone soon joined the Backcountry Horsemen of California (BCHC) and started learning packing skills. He figured getting into trail maintenance would be a way to learn more about the best access points to the mountains. In early 1996, he was on a BCHC ride where he met Mike Kearns, a PCTA member. Kearns told Stone to call Pete Fish. That October, Stone showed up unannounced to a Saturday morning PCTA work project that Fish was leading.

"The rest is history," he said. "I continued to do day rides. But pretty soon, there was no pleasure riding. It just evolved. By 2001, anything I did with my horses was in conjunction with trail maintenance."

It was July 2000 when Stone and a friend headed north from Walker Pass to clear a tree that was down across the trail. It was in a precariously steep section on Mount Jenkins in Owens Peak Wilderness. The PCT had been closed to stock for several months because there was no safe way for animals to get around the obstruction. Near the log, a small rock wall supported the trail. Stone tied his two horses to a scrub oak, admittedly not the best or most secure place, but the only one he had available. He described them as "savvy and calm" animals. His riding animal was blind in one eye.

"In turning around she loses a leg over one side of the rock wall and falls to her belly," Stone said. "While scrambling to get up, she pulls her line free and she falls backward over the side. She rolls over several times."

The horse was now 150 feet down the side of the cliff, tangled in deadfall. Stone got to her quickly. One of her hind legs was broken badly. "It's only being held on by a couple of ligaments," he said. "I have to put her down."

It was tough, but it was the logical and humane choice. Meanwhile, the other horse panicked. Stablemates generally stick together and this horse wanted to come down. Still below with the wounded animal, Stone said it was one of the craziest, most awful things he'd ever seen.

"She pulls herself free of the oak and throws herself down the hill," he said. "We look over our shoulders and she is doing somersaults all the way down. It was like something you see in a movie."

The horse fell 1,000 feet to her death. Stone, without a pistol, had to slit the first animal's throat to put her down.

"It's not something you really like to do," he said. "They bleed out. It's not painful. She rolled over and got behind a tree and she lay there and finally fell down the hill."

The two men went back to work. They cleared the log. Then Stone either walked out or rode his friend's second animal. It's one of the few details he can't remember about that day.

"I beat myself up for a while after that one," he said. "Anytime there is an accident you always look back and wonder what you could have done differently. You do the stuff we do—we tackle big jobs—and you be as safe as you can. But you're dealing with animals."

OPPOSITE: Volunteer Jerry Stone (left); the trail climbs between junipers in California's Owens Peak Wilderness (right).

He went for six months without a horse before purchasing his current animal. If he's packing in tools, Stone walks the horse on a lead.

Stone moved to Palmdale, California, in 2006. He is a Trail Gorillas volunteer section chief for 84 miles of the PCT from Highway 58 to Highway 178—Tehachapi to Walker Pass. The area is filled with sections of thick chaparral that he joked creates "job security" for the Trail Gorillas.

"I keep saying every year I don't know how long I'll do it but I'll keep going as long as I can make a difference," he said. "I like seeing the work at the end of the day. It feels good that you've made a difference."

KATE BEARDSLEY

In 2010, PCTA volunteer horse packer Kate Beardsley took on a gargantuan project installing new directional signs along the PCT in the Deschutes and Willamette National Forests of central Oregon.

From July 13 to October 20, Beardsley and a couple of friends installed 52 signs along a 160-mile stretch from Windigo Pass to the South Breitenbush River. Her pack strings carried eight-foot-long juniper posts and oak signs. She dug the holes by hand in which to install them.

Beardsley was no stranger to hard work, horses, or the PCT. Born in 1966, she has been a horse trainer for more than half her life and today packs tools and supplies into the wilderness for PCTA trail crews and Forest Service fire crews. She also runs a nonprofit animal rescue program, Mustangs to the Rescue, which has saved, trained, and found homes for hundreds of once-wild horses.

In 1994, she moved to the wilderness gateway town of Sisters, Oregon, from Prescott, Arizona, a town with a similar climate to the dry ponderosa forests prevalent on the eastern side of the Cascade Range.

It wasn't long until she met a PCTA volunteer named Curtis Hardie, who had transplanted to the nearby small city of Bend two years earlier. Hardie convinced Beardsley to use her horses to bring trail tools and kitchen supplies to a backcountry PCTA trail crew he was organizing. He was 72 at the time and was a very active recreationalist. He still had wisps of blonde in his hair.

"He skied, mountain biked, or hiked every day," Beardsley recalled. "He was very active and he felt community was important. I was so inspired and I decided I also would pack for the PCTA until I was 72. I'm only halfway done."

Hardie, a PCTA board member from 1995 to 1997, founded the PCTA Mid-Oregon Volunteers, organizing people and groups to take responsibility for sections of the trail. While he loved the work and being outdoors, friends have said he got involved in caring for the PCT because it was necessary. He received the Alice Krueper Award in 1998. Hardie died on August 13, 2011, at age 85.

Beardsley has been a PCTA volunteer for more than 20 years. Today, as a member of the PCTA Mid-Oregon Volunteers, Beardsley stewards a 10.2-mile section of the PCT south of McKenzie Pass near 10,085-foot-high North Sister. The first time she rode it there were 10 trees down across the trail in a quarter mile. She cleared it with a crosscut saw.

"I still walk that section and still look at all the cut faces that are there and I don't know how I did it," she said.

What she does know is that it's important for communities to have "very open access" to long-distance trails. "I think they're undervalued in our society," Beardsley said. "The ability to go for a long excursion in

OPPOSITE: A lavender sky paints North Sister a burnt red, as seen from Middle Sister in Three Sisters Wilderness, Oregon.

the backcountry really contributes to my life. The PCT enhances the health of our communities. Our society needs to have greenways for individual wildlife species as well. We need to allow other species to thrive so that we don't have even bigger problems."

She said she loves the work and the freedom of being on the trail, whether on foot or horseback. She said the history of the trail is palpable.

"There are times when I am traveling and I know I've just come through a pass that 150 years ago, very few people had come through," she said. "But you can tell that a population of Native Americans had come through there. I go along wondering what it was like for people to see it for the first time. When I'm out there, I feel like a part of a continuum."

JOHN LYONS

The trail crew has already started walking when John Lyons slowly makes his way up a steep grade from a car camp on the Sisson-Callahan Trail, which intersects the PCT in Shasta-Trinity National Forest near Mount Eddy in Northern California.

He stops to kick a rock or two off the trail and to catch his breath. At 76 and with decades of experience volunteering with the Backcountry Horsemen of California (BCHC) and PCTA, he's entitled to the respite. Also, on this drop-dead gorgeous July 2015 morning, he laments the left knee replacement he had in February.

"Too many birthdays," said Lyons, the leader of the PCTA Lyons's Pride crew.

The miles weigh on him. Being in the backcountry is what he loves most, whether he gets there on horseback or driving a bumpy and dusty road with his pickup. His body no longer performs the way he'd like, and he wonders how long he can keep it up.

Lyons is a beloved crew leader who knows the end of his volunteering days is near. Talking about it brings him to tears, so he doesn't say much. His regular volunteers—many have been coming on his hitches for more than a decade—wonder who's going to hold it all together and how.

Lyons spent a career as an underground plumber on construction sites in the Monterey Bay area, but he lived the horseman's lifestyle even then. In the early 1980s, he led trail crews for the BCHC in Los Padres National Forest along California's Central Coast. He and his wife, Gail, used to horse pack for fun.

In 1997, when he was 57, he took an early retirement. He and Gail purchased 10 acres in Etna, California, in the heart of Northern California's rugged mountain country. With the BCHC's Top of the State Unit and eventually the PCTA, Lyons and his volunteer crews have scoured the Trinity Alps, Marble Mountain, Castle Crags, and Russian Wildernesses.

He's legendary for taking care of his volunteers. His eight-day trips are well known for great meals and lots of friendship, and many of the volunteers have come back year after year. When they are car camping, he sets up hot showers and a pit toilet. "I've been doing this so long I've gotten to know these people and they're like my family now," said Gary Lee, who has volunteered with Lyons's Pride for 12 years. "We've grown old together. There's something special going on."

It was around 1999 that Lyons got a call from the PCTA's first trail operations director. Reuben Rajala, who was recruiting new volunteers to work the trail, was persistent when he called Lyons. Lyons said he eventually got talked into leading PCTA crews. He has been at it—unrelentingly—ever since. He was the 2005 recipient of the Alice Krueper Award.

It's tough to see him struggle with the idea that it has to end. He talks about needing help loading heavy packs on his mules, a task he relished and used to do alone. His pack animals are getting older and he's down to three from six. He said several times that Gail wants him to let it go. A couple of years back he had to ask for help in planning and putting on the three hitches he does every year. Buying supplies, working out logistics, and loading the tools are all too much for him to do alone these days.

"Physically, the body is worn-out," he said.

When asked about what it all means to him—the volunteering, the camaraderie—he said little. When told about how his crew members feel about him and how much the time they spend together means to them, his armor cracks and he tears up.

"Basically I do it for them," he said. "It makes me feel good. It's a great experience for all these people to get together. I've built up great friendships. How do you exit something?"

He describes himself as more of a camp host than a trail worker these days. But he still loves walking to the worksite to see what the crew has accomplished. "Now I just sit back and make sure it's done my way," he joked.

Then he comes back to the time in his life and what he can do and what he and Gail can afford to do. "One of us is going to be taking care of the other one sooner or later," he said.

He turns to look up the hill. "I've had many good times," he said. "It's just become part of my blood."

OPPOSITE: Cliff Lake in Marble Mountain Wilderness, Northern California.

CHAPTER EIGHT

STEWARDS

The Editor: Lee Terkelsen

Lee Terkelsen was another of those who read Eric Ryback's book in high school and got a bug for the PCT. Sometime in the 1970s, he wrote a letter to Warren Rogers and joined the Pacific Crest Club.

"I got these quarterlies in the mail and every one of them had these pictures of people doing thru-hikes," Terkelsen said. "It was inspiring."

It was his dream that far back to hike the PCT, which he finally did in 1991.

By then, Terkelsen was a veteran high school journalism teacher in Visalia, California. Now retired, he began teaching in 1975, quit to become a newspaper reporter for three years at the *Visalia Times-Delta*, then went back to teaching in 1982 when a new high school opened. He stayed for 26 years.

After completing his thru-hike, he volunteered for a trail-maintenance project with Alice Krueper. Pete Fish was on that trip and the two hit it off. "Shortly after that, Pete contacted me and asked if I would be a member of the board," Terkelsen said with a laugh.

He was elected to the Pacific Crest Trail Association (PCTA) Board of Directors in 1995. There were 923 eligible voters and 387 ballots were cast. Among six elected, Terkelsen was the sole unanimous choice. When Terkelsen attended his first board meeting in April 1995 at Timberline Lodge on Oregon's Mount Hood, he was surprised to find a "make or break" atmosphere.

"What Pete didn't tell me was that the organization was on the verge of collapsing, that there were some significant issues facing the group," Terkelsen said.

It was at that meeting that Alan Young presented an ultimatum. Terkelsen described the scene: "Young went around the table, asking each board member if they were committed to donating $1,000 to keep the PCTA afloat."

"Most of them said yes," Terkelsen said. "I was pretty nervous because I couldn't afford $1,000. When he got to me, because of my background in journalism, I said I could help with the *Communicator.*"

At that time, the PCTA was an all-volunteer operation. Every board member was contributing something significant to make the association successful.

Louise Marshall's daughter, Ann, was the magazine editor at the time. When Terkelsen took over in 1995, it was a home operation. He would gather materials for articles, do the typesetting and pasteup, then run finished pages to the local print shop, the same place his high school students printed their school newspaper.

From his first issue, July–August 1995, his imprint is evident. There's a full-page picture on the black-and-white cover. His third issue, February 1996, had the first color cover. By 1998, all the covers were color, and by 1999, the magazine went from newsprint to slick shiny stock.

"I knew that [by] printing the pictures in color they would come out sharper and better looking and would be more inspirational," Terkelsen said. "That was the goal all along. How do we grow our membership? The way we did it was communications and through the magazine."

As the association's membership grew, so did the job of putting out the publication. "We had to mail those things out too, remember. Pete Fish would come over. We'd have 5,000 magazines in my living room and we had to label them, separate them into zip codes, and bundle them up and haul them to the post office in Fresno for bulk mailing. My car started to drag on the ground it was so heavy," said Terkelsen.

For the last issue of 2001, he didn't have time to get the stories together, so he put together the PCTA's first calendar issue with photos he had taken on the trail. This lasting tradition, he said, began out of desperation.

Terkelsen was the PCTA's last volunteer editor. He served two terms on the PCTA board until 2000 and continues to volunteer, coordinating the judging of the PCTA's annual photo contest, which he started as a way of getting great photographs for the magazine and calendar.

"It was a very positive experience despite the long nights and complaining and all the work," he said. "The fact that I had even a small part in helping the organization succeed and getting people involved is the tops on my list."

PREVIOUS SPREAD: Evolution Lake, Sierra Nevada, California.
OPPOSITE: Lower Twin Lake in Lassen Volcanic National Park, Northern California.

Forging His Own Path: Steve Queen

For Steve Queen, it began high on the southwestern flank of Oregon's Mount Hood. Queen was eight years old when he became mesmerized by the PCT. He was hiking with a friend and his uncle when they came to the well-worn tread in the loamy sands of the sleeping volcano near Zigzag Canyon. The man pointed north, telling the boys that the trail they had just joined could take them all the way to Canada. Then he turned south and made the same, seemingly impossible claim about hoofing it to Mexico. Queen was forever transfixed.

"There are moments in your life that you realize are special," he said. "That was one of those moments for me. I felt like I was on holy ground. It overtook me."

Growing up in Portland, Oregon, every time Queen stepped foot on the PCT he felt a twinge of something special. Like many boys his age, Queen hiked on the PCT with his Boy Scout troop. In ninth grade, he read the school library's copy of *The High Adventure of Eric Ryback*, the 1971 account of the first PCT thru-hike. He reread the story every year until he graduated Jackson High School in 1980. "He was my hero. He still is my hero," Queen said.

A thru-hike was no question. "It was just a thing I was going to do. I wanted there to be a thing in my life that I could point to and say, 'I did that.'" By the time he graduated, he was already planning the hike. It was an era in which the trail still was more mystery and potential than sure thing, especially for a young and impressionable man. His 1981 thru-hike shaped his life.

In due time, he would take on his hometown section of the trail as his personal project, forming and shaping the PCTA's Mount Hood Chapter as a way of giving back to the trail that gave him so much.

He followed his 1981 PCT hike with a thru-hike of the Appalachian Trail in 1983 and the Continental Divide Trail in 1991, the "Triple Crown" of America's long-distance hikes. But the PCT was the most special. It changed him in ways that, to this day, he has a hard time describing succinctly.

"Answering that question is trivializing the experience," Queen said. "I cannot say what it has meant to me outside of this indescribable feeling inside my body. When I stood on the Mexican border, I was a completely different person than when I finished. All of the experiences, all of the people I met, all of the trail angels, all the bulls**t—the entirety of the experience completely changed me."

Pushed to explain, he told stories, many of which he kept in his journal of the trip.

Camping near the border in Campo on the eve of his hike, Queen stared at the sky in dusk. In his mind's eye, he saw a black-and-white silhouette of mountains. "That's all I could think of, not knowing what I would really see," he said.

Coming off Muir Pass in Kings Canyon National Park, he struggled with late-season snow. Postholing every step for miles, he struggled with the immense physical challenge. All the while his mind was also working on his life, the expectations placed on him and those he had for himself. His journal entry for that day is one word, over and over and over: "F**k." The burden of life he'd been carrying around, the uncertainty of the future, and the pressure put on a young man by his parents finally bubbled to an uncontrollable boil.

"My entire life had been 'What I should do?'" he said. "I was so irritated. I hated everything and I needed to put it into words. It's telling that I walked [nearly] 1,000 miles before I could write a curse word in my journal." And the frustration with his upbringing? "I wouldn't say I shook it. I was able to wrestle it," he said.

OPPOSITE: Muir Hut at the crest of 11,995-foot Muir Pass. Constructed in 1930 by the Sierra Club and the Forest Service, the stone hut is dedicated to John Muir.

The trail register entry he made in Manning Park, the day he finished his thru-hike, says it all. It begins, "I have arrived."

Queen completed grad school at the University of Connecticut, defending his dissertation in 1992. He and his wife moved back home to Portland later that year. They bought a house in early 1993. He was in the throes of a busy life in his early 30s—new job, young marriage, new home. Still, he felt strongly that he wanted to give back to the PCT because the trail had given him so much. The other trails were great, he said, but in the end, were just long walks. The PCT magic that captivated and pushed him as a boy had not worn off. "You never forget your first love," he said.

In early 1993, Queen answered the PCTA's call for new "regional coordinators" and by June, the first printed tabloid issue of the *Communicator* listed as him as the Region 4 Oregon coordinator.

Queen took the volunteer position in an era of both possibility and challenge. The 1993 snowpack and resulting runoff left many areas of the trail severely damaged. Queen and the other newly named regional coordinators—Alice Krueper in Southern California; Peter McGee in Central California; Paula and Hazel Shewell in Northern California; and Brian Booth in Washington—had their work cut out for them.

THE PACIFIC CREST TRAIL

Queen said he set out to mobilize people across Oregon, hoping that they would adopt 75- to 100-mile sections of trail, coordinating work projects. The job was harder than he thought and by the winter of his first year, he realized it wasn't working. "It was a bust," he said. "I didn't have enough time to do that job properly and people didn't understand what the job needed."

Queen had volunteered because he wanted to give back to the trail in a meaningful way, but instead of building new trail or maintaining the PCT, he was dealing with the frustration of trying to organize people across a large area and receiving direction from others he didn't always agree with. It was not in his wheelhouse. Something needed to change. "I started focusing on what I could do that would put me near the dirt. I said I'd take care of Mount Hood," he said.

His first Mount Hood work party in 1993 attracted about 20 volunteers. It was a good start. In 1994, he went on a trail project organized by fellow Portlander and 1996 thru-hiker Roger Carpenter on the Washington side of the Columbia River Gorge National Scenic Area. He met local trail volunteers and made lasting contacts within the United States Forest Service.

The Mount Hood Chapter has evolved into one of the PCTA's most sophisticated and successful groups, caring for more than 200 miles of trail in the Mount Hood National Forest in Oregon and the Gifford Pinchot National Forest in Washington. In 2014, its members tallied more than 11,000 volunteer trail-maintenance hours. Queen, recipient of the Alice Krueper Award in 2002 and the PCTA Lifetime Achievement Award in 2011, stepped down from the leadership role in 2012, though he still is involved.

Today, the chapter boasts more than 500 active members. Its list of annual projects has expanded to include many of the trails in the Columbia River Gorge, even those that don't connect to the PCT. In winter, much of the PCT in Oregon is covered in snow, so working in the low elevations near the river gives volunteers projects to do and helps maintain strong partnerships with land managers.

Queen is clearly one of a handful of dedicated volunteers who can be called crucial to the PCTA's success in the early years.

The Tween Years

PCTA Vice President Alan Young's strategic plan ushered in a new era for the organization. One of the plan's main goals was to hire a new executive director and Young headed up the search party.

It was May of 1995 when Bob Ballou saw a PCTA ad looking for volunteers for trail projects. When Ballou called the number, he reached Valerie York-Watts, who passed him on to Young. "It was what I call a God-interfering moment," Ballou said.

Ballou had spent 23 years as a professional in the Boy Scouts of America and then worked for a company that made investments in inner-city neighborhoods to make them a better place to live. When he called Young, Ballou was looking for something different for the final stop of his career.

By June, Ballou had a job offer with a catch. The federal budget for the fiscal year 1996 was delayed in a fight between President Bill Clinton and Congress, which delayed the Forest Service grant to the PCTA. Ballou started work on the promise he'd someday get paid. He set up an office at his home in North Sacramento, California, and went to work. He thought the funding might come in by January 1996. It didn't arrive until May.

OPPOSITE: Bear grass, azalea, and paintbrush near Lolo Pass, Oregon, with Mount Hood in the background.

While he found that the volunteer board members and others shared a vision, they did not have all the skills to make it happen. Nonetheless, he set out to reshape the PCTA. Ballou said one of the first things he did as executive director was seek a grant from REI to do a direct-mail campaign to increase membership, another of Young's many ideas. The board set a large fundraising goal of $112,000 for the year, which included the $50,000 Forest Service grant and $7,000 from board members. The membership goal was ambitious as well, from 800 in mid-1996 to 5,000 in five years. It's a goal Ballou called "seemingly impossible."

Fundraising was taking all his attention and Ballou needed someone to take charge of the trail and nurture the membership. In 1996, Ballou hired Joe Sobinovsky, a 1995 PCT thru-hiker who had also hiked the AT in 1988, the year he graduated high school.

After hiking the AT, Sobinovsky went home to Ohio, got a job, and got married. Sobinovsky and his wife spent years renovating an Ohio barn, turning it into their dream home.

"I kind of forgot about hiking," he said. But the infection was working on him. Eventually, he bought a Wilderness Press PCT guidebook.

"I had it shipped to my mom's house because I didn't want my wife to see it," he said. "She caught me reading it. I tried to explain to her how people get the bug for this. She said go ahead and do it but when you come back we're going to have kids."

A year after his PCT thru-hike, he answered Ballou's "help wanted" ad and got hired at the PCTA. He and his wife moved to Sacramento, had three daughters, and helped raise a trail organization. He stayed for seven years.

"The organization was on life support," Sobinovsky said. "We were barely staying alive and I doubled the payroll. It was all done by volunteers and shoebox accounting. If we needed something we had to have a volunteer write a check. I remember Bob saying, 'Don't buy stamps this week.' It was that bad."

Still, by the end of 1997, they had increased membership to 2,500, installed accounting and member-tracking software, and moved the office from Ballou's house to an actual commercial space—a 12-foot square, windowless office in a Sacramento strip mall. It was anything but glamorous, Sobinovsky recalled.

"If you backed up your chair, you had to tell the other person to scoot in," he said. "We worked without benefits. In the bottom drawer of his desk, Bob had a blanket and pillows. He actually slept there sometimes. I'd get e-mails at midnight, one in the morning. He slugged away at it, incrementally bringing up the membership and the stature of the trail. Nobody else in their right mind would have done that in the prime of their career."

In 1998, Ballou was able to exercise the rebooted PCTA's clout. The PCTA board learned of a plan to develop a subdivision where the PCT crossed Bureau of Land Management (BLM) property near Agua Dulce, California. The PCTA spoke out and the BLM eventually relented.

That same summer, the PCTA signed a new memorandum of understanding with the government. The PCTA was now the major partner in the management and operation of the PCT. The PCTA board also asked the Forest Service to engage a full-time PCT administrator from within its own ranks, which was done for the first time in 2000. By May 2001, private donations were making a huge difference, and advocacy efforts were paying off. Regular funding from the Forest Service made it easier to keep the organization going. The PCTA worked closely with federal land managers to prioritize property purchases and select optimal locations for trail reroutes.

PCT Manager

The National Trails System Act of 1968 called for oversight by the land-management agencies in charge of national trails, but until 2000, the Forest Service had always assigned the work as "collateral duty," meaning it was a job someone did in addition to other work.

Mike Dawson, the PCTA's trail operations director, said several people in the agency were responsible in the years before 2000, and that they made significant contributions to moving the PCT forward.

"By choosing to fund the position full time, the agency recognized the importance of strengthening the program," said Beth Boyst, the Forest Service PCT program manager since 2007. She is the second person to hold the full-time job. Tim Stone was the first.

Boyst has spent her career with the agency. She holds a master's degree in forestry from Colorado State University and was a student hire in 1987, assigned to Gila National Forest in New Mexico. In 1991, she transferred to White River National Forest in Colorado, working in a variety of wilderness and trail-management roles.

As a student, she hiked the Appalachian Trail in three sections in 1982, 1983, and 1985. And she did long PCT sections in 1991 and 2000. Her professional background and love of distance hiking set her up perfectly when the PCT job opened. It was an ideal fit for her interests, avocation, and ties to special places.

"It is definitely a dream job," she said. "To me it was one of three jobs that spoke to me in terms of being an outstanding opportunity in doing a different type of public service."

Dawson credits Boyst with embracing the idea of using a mostly volunteer force to maintain the trail, something others in the agency had doubts about. "She didn't need any convincing," he said. "Her background and personal experience told her it was the way to go. She has been a big proponent for building our volunteer program."

But Ballou was feeling burned out. He'd spent five years working nonstop on behalf of the trail. He told the board he wanted to retire and set out to find his replacement. He retired that October. When he started, the PCTA had 800 active members. At the end of 2001, the association had grown to more than 4,000 members.

The following year, Ballou formed the Carsonora Crew, taking volunteer maintenance responsibility for about 70 miles of the PCT between Yosemite National Park and Blue Lakes Basin, south of Carson Pass. Ballou took a fledgling organization and turned it into a thriving adolescent with tons of potential. Today, he lives in Carson Valley, Nevada, east of Lake Tahoe.

Sobinovsky left the PCTA in 2003. Sacramento was becoming too expensive for him and his young family. He took a job as statewide trails coordinator for Washington State Parks. Four years later, using skills and contacts acquired at the PCTA, he joined the National Park Service's National Trails Land Resources Program Center, which purchases private land for the Appalachian Trail, the Pacific Crest Trail, and other projects in the National Trails System. He lives in Martinsburg, West Virginia. "These trails really did set my career path," Sobinovsky said. "They made the decision for me, the trails. I just thank God I found them."

The Mapmaker: Lon "Halfmile" Cooper

Lon Cooper had been running the information technology department at *The Bakersfield Californian* newspaper for five years when he knew he needed a break.

It was 2003, and the Texas native and photojournalist was riding a wave of technology, when a newspaper photographer's world was morphing from a career spent in darkrooms filled with enlargers and the smell of chemicals to one that happened on a keyboard as much as behind a camera. Digital cameras still weren't very practical. Film negatives were turned into digital images using desktop scanners.

Cooper said he loved hiking as a kid in the Boy Scouts, so he decided he would take his vacation by walking the John Muir Trail (JMT). He took JMT hikes in 2003 and 2005.

"I suppose what got me back into hiking was that it was sort of a refuge from a high-pressure job," he said.

In 2006, he moved to San Diego County to run the computer technology department at Southwestern Community College in Chula Vista. The following year, with his first summer off because the school was closed, he decided to start a PCT section hike. He walked from Campo to Truckee, California, some 1,160 miles.

Before his PCT hike, the techno-junkie was trying to figure out a way to get the PCT route loaded into his GPS. "In 2007, that was hard to do because GPS units were not nearly as capable as they are today," he said.

The year before, Jack "Found" Haskel, now the PCTA's trail information specialist, was thru-hiking the PCT while on contract for *Backpacker* magazine to gather GPS data for the trail. Cooper took Haskel's data, converted it into half-mile points, and loaded it into his GPS. Then he made his own maps for the PCT and "off I went on my two-month summer section hike." Cooper's trail name—"Halfmile"—was self-fulfilling.

He also recorded his own data from that trip. Back at college after the hike, he loaded all the information into his computer. The following spring, he made the Halfmile map series, which includes most of the PCT from Campo to Truckee, available to the public online. And that's where his maps lived, in obscurity.

In the summer of 2008, Cooper took another PCT hike, this one from Truckee to Oregon Highway 138, just north of Crater Lake. "I remember running into a hiker in Ashland who really liked the Halfmile maps and how disappointed he was that they were not available for the section he was on," Cooper said. "I was surprised anybody used them."

Cooper found another hiker online, Craig "Sunwalker" Stanton from New Zealand, who had collected geo-reference points such as road crossings and campgrounds. He incorporated those points into his maps as well.

He pointed out that the iPhone and app store, so ubiquitous today, were still in their infancy in 2007 and 2008. Still, each year Cooper hiked a new section of the PCT, refining the data, making it more accurate. In 2009, he hiked from Crater Lake to Snoqualmie Pass in Washington. That same year, he released his first maps to the public.

In the ensuing years he took several trips, covering new sections of trail, recording new data, and refining his maps, which by 2013 were becoming standard issue for PCT hikers.

In 2012, David Lippke developed a Halfmile map application for iPhones, and in 2013, he added an Android app. The electronic databook became real and readily available. More than 11,000 phones carry the app.

In March 2014, Cooper retired. That year he thru-hiked the trail, for most of it carrying a custom GPS unit built by friends. The antenna stuck out of his pack, like a Google car cruising a neighborhood.

"As it's recording location information it's also recording information about the satellites and how good the signal is," Cooper explained.

Cooper carried the GPS unit from Big Bear Lake in Southern California to Manning Park. John "Dirt Stew" Haffner carried an identical unit southbound, from Cascade Locks to Campo.

Back at their computers after the hikes, Cooper and Lippke used location data and signal strength data to determine the best information. In some cases, when Cooper had to take an alternate route through the Sierra because of snow, for example, they used Haffner's track.

The Halfmile track released for the 2015 hiking season contained 3,100 waypoints, including campsites, road crossings, and water sources, up from 2,000 points the version before. The maps are wildly popular with PCT long-distance hikers. Cooper thought briefly about selling them, but the idea of starting a business did not sit well. "I did not want to have to worry about the business aspect," he said. "I decided ultimately that I would make it freely available and encourage people to donate to the PCTA."

One of the app's features allows hikers to tell how far away they are from the PCT. From this a contest developed among comment users, with the winner being the person who was then the farthest away.

OPPOSITE: An artisan spring feeds Little Crater Lake some 200 yards east of the PCT in northern Oregon.

In Southern California's 700 miles of trail, a second online resource was near the equal of the Halfmile maps. The "PCT water report" listed every water source and its present condition. Hikers sent in updates and it was all maintained by Bill "AsABat" Jeffrey. Jeffrey was an organizer of the Annual Day Zero Pacific Crest Trail Kick Off, and by 2011, he had hiked a substantial portion of the PCT. On August 10, 2011, on the PCT at Charlton Lake, Oregon, Jeffrey died in his tent of natural causes. He was 54. After a period of shock and sorrow, Cooper quietly stepped in and re-created Jeffrey's online water report, making sure that must-have tool for hikers remained available.

Reflecting on all he has done for the PCT and the reason he started hiking again (remember the job stress?), Cooper said it's more than that. "Of course I don't have that high-pressure job anymore and I still want to be out there," he said. "The best parts are the wild parts. You see little things along the way that you would probably not normally see. You meet people along the way and have experiences you wouldn't otherwise have. I'm sure I'll be back on the PCT again. In a way, it's kind of a crazy thing to do to walk for five and a half months. But it's a great thing to do, too."

Building Today's PCTA

Liz Bergeron came to the PCTA by coincidence. She was happy in her job as the development director for the Stanford Home for Children (now called Stanford Youth Solutions) and wasn't looking to change. But in mid-2001, she attended a luncheon held by the California Capital Chapter of the Association of Fundraising Professionals, where she ran into Bob Ballou. He told her he was retiring and urged her to apply for his job.

Bergeron was a backpacker and she had heard of the PCT but didn't know much about it or the PCTA. "I thought, 'Why should I do that?'" she said. "I loved what I was doing."

Still, she went home and pulled up the PCTA's website and read the job description. The association was looking for a fundraiser to lead the group. She was intrigued, so she applied, one of 19 candidates. Six board members interviewed her on a Sunday, the day after Bergeron returned from a seven-day backpacking trip. The trip, planned for months, was a coincidence, but it put her in an appropriate frame of mind.

She started her new job on October 1, 2001, with the nation reeling from the recent terrorist attacks on the World Trade Center and the Pentagon. She was one of three employees, including Joe Sobinovsky and an office assistant. By then, the PCTA had 3,900 members and a $350,000 annual budget. The numbers looked good, but the association was struggling.

"What I heard overwhelmingly was that they needed someone to keep the organization afloat," Bergeron said. She knew little about managing a trail but she knew how to raise money. But before she got started, she wanted to see just what kind of shape the PCTA was in. Bergeron immediately began a 90-day assessment of the organization, looking at books, databases, and even the trail, hiking a 30-mile section in her first month. Despite a respectable annual budget, growing membership, and Forest Service assistance (about 10 percent of the annual budget), there were problems. The association had no short-term plan and its thick, long-term strategy, despite some good ideas, was unworkable.

For one thing, the Sacramento office's relationship with distant maintenance groups, such as the Trail Gorillas and the Mount Hood Chapter, was weak. There was little oversight. Volunteer hours were not

OPPOSITE: Below the PCT, the headwaters of the Little Wenatchee River wind through Meander Meadows in the North Cascades, Washington.

tracked. The PCTA in Sacramento had no idea how many people were working the trail, where they were working, or for how long. "We didn't know half of what was going on out on the trail," Bergeron said.

Early on, when Bergeron picked up the telephone, she heard a beeping and crackling noise. That's how she found out that her desk phone—hooked to one of just three lines in the office—shared a line with the fax and credit card machines. Bergeron called Eugene "Bud" Reid, a PCTA board member. Reid was fully vested in the PCTA, donating $60,000 to $70,000 a year at that time. He bought the PCTA's new phone system.

In her assessment phase, Bergeron made a point to talk to as many people about the PCTA as she could. One of the calls her first week was to Dave Sherman in the Forest Service's lands office in Washington, DC. He told her to focus at first on stabilizing the organization and to let the agency worry about the maintenance efforts going on in the field. "As the new executive director, it was helpful for me to get a handle on where I should focus," Bergeron said. "We were at such a critical juncture in our organizational development."

Following her 90-day assessment, Bergeron went to the board and asked them to help raise $25,000 for a new database, accounting software, and a financial audit. It was the beginning of educating the all-volunteer board on the proper oversight, governance, and leadership needed, as well as building the foundation for what is today's PCTA.

The first two years were very stressful, in part because Bergeron didn't know much about managing trails even though people expected her to since she was leading a group with responsibility for a national scenic trail. The lowest point came, she said, in November 2003. The PCTA had just $5,000 in the bank. "I didn't know how we were going to pay the bills," she said. Also during that time, Bergeron's mother was dying. Dealing with that while worrying about keeping the lights on at the PCTA was a lot to manage. But year-end funding came through, which helped take some of the pressure off.

"It was mentioned that maybe we should get a loan and I said no way," Bergeron said. "That's how organizations get into trouble." The association has never had to borrow money to stay afloat.

Throughout all the early trials, Bergeron said she never had second thoughts about taking the PCTA job. "I always felt like I was in the right place," she said. "I believed in what we were doing. There is something about the PCT that when we needed something to happen, it did."

There are many examples of that and it still goes on today. "I truly believe it's because the PCT is bigger than all of us," Bergeron said. She led the organization as it built up its foundation and organizational infrastructure, including computer and phone systems, donor databases, accounting systems, and financial audits. At the same time, she guided the growth and maturity of the organization's Board of Directors, staff, and government partnerships.

"As this foundation began to take shape we were then able to focus on growing our membership and our trail-maintenance volunteer program," she said. "It's difficult to grow these types of programs without a solid foundation to support these large groups of people who are so vital to our success."

By late 2003, Sobinovsky had left the PCTA and Bergeron needed to make a hire.

About that time, Mike Dawson was working for the Pacific Northwest Trail Association when he joined the PCTA as a member. Bergeron, who personally signed thank-you letters to everyone who made a donation, recognized his name. The two had met at national trail conferences. She scribbled a note atop Dawson's letter.

OPPOSITE: The view south between Chicken Spring Lake and the south boundary of California's Sequoia National Park. The meadow in the distance is Boreal Plateau.

"Mike, might you be interested in a position with the PCTA?" Dawson recalled.

In February 2004, Dawson started as the PCTA's director of trail operations, bringing more than 20 years of experience working with volunteers and government agencies. Most of his career he spent as a regional representative for the Appalachian Trail Conservancy in southwest Virginia.

He spent time with the small staff and figured out what the PCTA was doing from Sacramento, then drove the trail from northern Washington to Southern California, meeting with agency partners and volunteer leaders to get a sense of what was happening on the ground.

The road trip introduced him to the PCT culture, and he said he quickly realized that oversight of this long trail from an office in Sacramento would be near impossible. He proposed setting up regional offices manned by professionals with backgrounds in trail maintenance and construction as well as working with government partners and volunteers.

"When I came, there were various groups doing work on the trail," Dawson said. "Many were single crew leaders organizing projects in a particular area. They were working independently of the PCTA. They were nominally under our umbrella, but we were providing minimal support for them."

There were no trail-wide programs or training efforts and no standards for worker safety outside of what had been developed between local volunteers and agencies. Dawson's job was to change all that. From 2005 to 2009, the PCTA hired five regional representatives and a trail operations manager.

The first was Ian Nelson, who started overseeing the PCTA's Big Bend region in Northern California and southern Oregon in January 2005. Dawson and Nelson had known each other on the Appalachian Trail. As a student at Virginia Tech in the mid-1990s, Nelson was a member of an outdoor club that maintained 30 miles of the trail and Dawson was the regional representative.

By 2005, Nelson had been working for the ATC for two years when his wife spotted the PCTA job announcement. They wanted to move back to the West, having lived in California after college teaching environmental education and doing seasonal work on trail crews. He jumped at the chance to work for the PCTA.

Nelson said he started by meeting with existing volunteers such as John Lyons and began the difficult grassroots work of finding new volunteer leaders in local communities. Another foundational leg was building trusting relationships with the land managers, Forest Service, National Park Service, Bureau of Land Management, and California State Parks.

"That's something we all take pride in," Nelson said. "We've built a lot of mutual respect amongst our agency partners. They know we're here to work and advocate for the trail, but also to support them in their work for the PCT."

Also in 2005, Bergeron realized that the expanding sophistication of the organization needed firm financial expertise and oversight, so she hired Finance Director Teresa Fieth. "She was such an important part of our growth," Bergeron said of Fieth.

By 2007, the PCTA had added regional offices in Southern California and the Columbia River Gorge, and hired Jennifer Tripp, trail operations manager, to build, manage, and support the volunteer program. She worked with the new regional representatives, adding efficient and more effective ways of tracking how much work was being done, where and by whom, and ensuring that the work was being done safely.

OPPOSITE: Lupine and Indian paintbrush in Cispus Basin, Goat Rocks Wilderness, Washington.

In her first year, Tripp said they held a trail-wide conference for volunteer leaders and agency staff to share experiences and knowledge. They asked volunteers what they needed to be more successful. "Hands down it was training," she said.

Regional Representative Dana Hendricks, also hired in 2007, had been working on training with the Forest Service in the Columbia River Gorge and there were a few other isolated efforts. But in 2008, the PCTA applied and won a $20,000 grant from REI, which it used to create the now-renowned Trail Skills College program. The PCTA hired John Schubert, Forest Service trails expert and instructor, as a consultant. With Tripp and Hendricks, he helped write the original curriculum. In 2009, the first weekend session was held in Cascade Locks, Oregon.

Today, Trail Skills College programs are held all along the trail, on weekends or in concentrated sessions, and the course materials are available online as well. The program has been expanded to include a saw safety certification program, approved by the Forest Service, which has volunteer trainers certifying other volunteers in proper use of crosscut and chain saws. "We are building the capability of individual volunteers to get the most out of their work and to do so safely," Dawson said. Since the program started, the PCTA's volunteer hours grew from 34,500 in 2004 to 96,500 in 2015.

With the building of a region-based program supported by the home office in Sacramento, the PCTA has gone from a small shop with a loosely knit group of volunteers just trying to keep the trail open to a sophisticated advocacy group fighting for the protection of the PCT experience. Its training and safety programs are nationally recognized.

"They point to us as a program for volunteer development, trail management, and collaborative planning that should be emulated throughout the National Trails System," Dawson said. "We have gone from being a bit player on the PCT to being a nationally recognized example of how public-private partnerships should work."

Despite that, there is still much to be done. In 2015, the PCTA hired Megan Wargo as its first land protection director. A 2008 land inventory identified 1,500 private properties along the trail that needed protection. They either held the trail easement or were important because of the scenery they provided. The PCTA is still working with that information today.

While the ultimate goal is to raise money to purchase these private parcels, work on that front has been going on for decades. Over the last 15 years, approximately $25 million from the federal Land and Water Conservation Fund has been used to acquire and permanently protect more than 17,000 acres along the trail. The fund sets aside a small percentage of the royalties from offshore energy production for state and federal conservation programs. Increasingly, through the PCTA, private-sector funding is also taking on a role.

Private landowners along the trail could still build homes, install power lines, or clear-cut their trees—a sad truth for a national scenic trail. Taking Nancy DuPont's 1990s GPS mapping into the 21st century, the PCTA added GIS mapping expertise to its arsenal in 2015 and it's now building an effective land-protection program through partnerships with established land trusts, government agencies, and others.

The PCTA also has become a force in the effort to build and nurture the National Trails System. Bergeron and Dawson are board members for the Partnership for the National Trails System, which today includes 30 scenic and historic trails around the country.

OPPOSITE: The gushing Tuolumne River in Yosemite National Park, California.

Today, the PCTA has 19 full-time employees and several contractors working on everything from organizing volunteers to land protection, communications, advocacy, fundraising, and administration.

Beth Boyst, PCT program manager for the Forest Service, summed up the importance of the PCTA and its 11,500 members: "The long-term benefit of having citizen stewards is not just the number of miles maintained or the amount of trash picked up, but it's the connection of people to the landscape," she said. "It's wonderful."

The Next Generation of Warriors

During a PCTA volunteer maintenance project in Northern California in the summer of 2015, one thing stood out—most folks working the trail were new to the organization. This crew was relatively young; many were still in college.

One woman, an undergrad at a nearby university, laughed about the fact that she thought she'd be the only woman on the crew, hanging out with a bunch of old guys. Not so here, but in some cases, that's not far from the truth.

It's no surprise that many of the PCTA's volunteers are older because retired people have more time to devote to public service. These veterans understand the importance of the long haul. Their expertise and dedication is unparalleled.

Yet, for the PCT to stay alive for future generations, young people must be inspired to get out on the trail, experience the magic, and make it part of their lives. More importantly, though, we must continue to draw talent and energy from all ages, as it will take both unbridled energy and wisdom to maintain and protect the trail experience long term.

A new crop of stewards has established itself along the trail in recent years. The PCTA is always looking for the next person to make a commitment to shepherd a section of trail and build a core group of volunteers. These relative newcomers join the ranks of longtime dedicated crews. Here are some of their stories.

NORCAL TRAIL CREW LEADER: JANETTE STORER

It takes love to take care of the trail. Janette Storer has it and then some. The energetic creator, detail-minded organizer, and leader of the NorCal Trail Crew was all smiles during a 2015 trip to mend the PCT near California's Castle Crags State Park. Her love for the trail, backcountry, and volunteers is always apparent.

"There's no such thing as an unhappy volunteer," she said.

It's a little strange to credit divorce for the creation of this important PCTA volunteer crew. But it was around 2005, following a painful breakup, that Storer sought solace in the wilderness near her home in Redding, California.

"I don't think there's any better healing thing than getting outdoors in the wilderness," she said.

She took her then-10-year-old daughter, Mariah, on an early season backpacking trip on the Pacific Crest Trail. There was a lot of snow in the high country, and lower the trail was running with water, like a creek. "I started wondering who took care of those trails and that's when I found the PCTA online," Storer said.

She joined the association, made regular donations, and, with her daughter staying with her father every other weekend, Storer started looking for things to occupy her time.

In 2009, during a National Trails Day gathering at McArthur-Burney Falls Memorial State Park, she signed up for a trail-maintenance project and met PCTA Regional Representative Ian Nelson, the PCTA employee in charge of coordinating trail management and maintenance in Northern California and southern Oregon. Soon after that, she joined a weekend project of the now-defunct Northwest Service Academy.

"It was a great, great crew and I had so much fun," she said. "I actually called in sick on Monday and stayed an extra day."

For the next two years, she did one-off projects and attended classes at the PCTA's Trail Skills College. She learned about moving dirt, stacking rocks, and leadership, among other things. By 2011, with the help of the PCTA, she started leading her own crew. She now leads up to six projects a year plus a trip for the local Boy Scout troop. She has built a base of core volunteers and welcomes newcomers on almost every project.

For her, Storer said the path from avid backpacker to trail caretaker was obvious. She was born in the summer of 1969, a year before the first Earth Day, when the environmental movement was just taking off. Today, she worries that there are not enough trail lovers giving back.

"I don't see a lot of activism in the younger generation," she said. "If we don't get the word out, trails and wilderness areas are not going to be around for my grandkids. There used to be a level of funding from the federal government to protect these areas that's not there now. It's important for people to step up and protect them."

OPPOSITE: Trail work in the 1930s on what would become the PCT through the San Gabriel Mountains near Los Angeles, California (left and right).

That all sounds serious. But Storer is lighthearted in her approach to spreading the word about the trail and its maintenance needs. While she and her crew are out working, she talks to hikers. "A lot of them have great stories to tell," she said. "I don't think there's a better volunteer base than those people who love the trail."

But she said she's amazed at the number of people in Redding who don't know the trail exists. "It's right there in our backyard and people aren't really aware of this national treasure. I want to encourage people to get out more," she said.

Storer is a marketing executive for 11 radio stations in Redding and Chico. She loves playing outdoors—hiking, biking, skiing—and is an avid target shooter who has won competitions. "I was pretty good," she said. "I grew up in a hunting family. I don't like to deer hunt but I like to shoot."

She has enlisted her family to get involved in trail work. Her sister, Erin, of Sacramento, is a regular; her dad and stepmom, Gary and Gail Gilbert, volunteer to cook for the crew; and her stepdad, Smokey Silva, sharpens tools and maintains the tool cache.

"I keep it all in the family," she said.

THE NORTH 350 BLADES: BARRY TESCHLOG AND JIM MILLER

They live in the same city—Seattle, Washington—and came to the PCT naturally, as hikers looking to get away from busy lives. Teschlog is an aeronautical engineer with Boeing and Miller is a retired general contractor.

But while they shared an interest in the trail, both avidly hiking and volunteering to maintain it with the Washington Trails Association (WTA), they'd never met. By coincidence, at a 2009 event held by REI, they met Suzanne Wilson, then the new PCTA regional representative for northern Washington.

Both men separately asked Wilson about the PCTA. By then, Teschlog had thru-hiked the trail (in 2006) and Miller had been section hiking and volunteering with the WTA for years.

Miller and his wife Dona walked from Stevens Pass to Snoqualmie Pass in 1982. "We didn't even think of it as the PCT back then," he said. "We went on a week-long hike, that's all." More than a decade later, he joined his brother on a WTA crew. The weekends became more regular. "Before I knew it I was an assistant crew leader. It sort of evolved on me," he said.

Miller said he volunteered on the PCT and other trails but didn't really get the thru-hike concept at first. "There were people who would disappear because they went off to hike the PCT," he said. "Over time I realized it was a continuous thing."

In 1987, he and Dona walked south from the PCT's northern end at Manning Park to Rainy Pass, and between 2001 and 2014, they section-hiked some 1,600 miles from Mexico to Northern California.

Teschlog was a section hiker who walked through Washington from 2001 to 2005 before taking a summer off in 2006 to thru-hike. When he turned 40 in 2009, he hiked 40 miles to celebrate—Snoqualmie to Stampede Pass and back. "The trail was in bad shape, so I bought some loppers and started cutting brush," he said. Eventually he found the WTA and PCTA. After meeting Wilson at REI, the formation of a new group to steward the PCT in northern Washington "kind of just happened," he said.

"Suzanne led the first work party," Teschlog said. "But she made it clear to Jim and me that it was up to us. We were the early prime movers. We talked it up to people we knew from WTA."

OPPOSITE: Hikers move north along the Los Angeles Aqueduct in California.
FOLLOWING SPREAD: A hiker heads down to Cajon Pass, Southern California.

It evolved quickly, both men said. They picked a name: "North 350" for the 350 northernmost miles of the trail, and "Blades" because all the tools have blades on them. "It's where we hike," Teschlog said. But they don't yet touch all the miles with annual maintenance crews.

"It was an ambitious name when we started," he joked. "That's the long-term goal: to have stewards on all 350 miles. Ten years from now we'll be working all 350 miles. We'll keep chipping away at it."

Both men say they enjoy it and are determined to make their group a success.

"I'm inspired," Miller said. "I like to be outside. We get a bunch of people together who want to do good work and we work hard. It's very satisfying to see what you've accomplished at the end of the day. I think the PCT is a national asset."

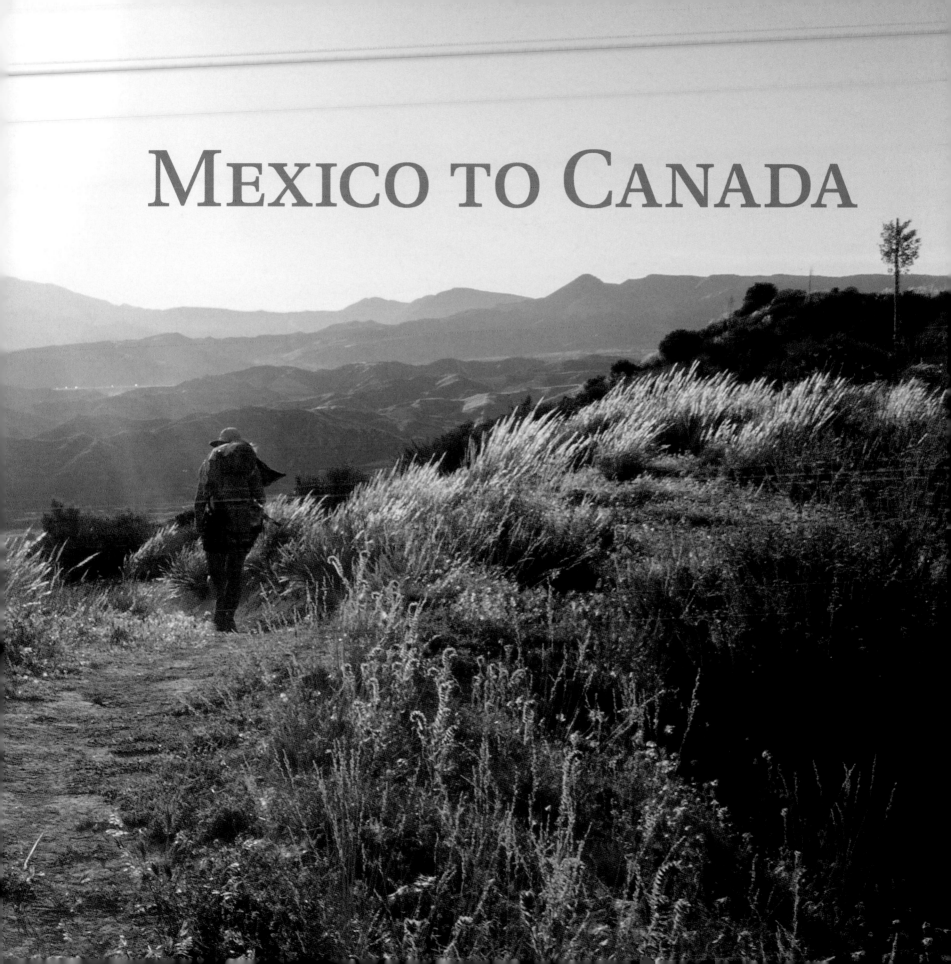

MEXICO TO CANADA

SOUTHERN CALIFORNIA

YOSEMITE NATIONAL PARK

Truckee

South Lake Tahoe

Sacramento

Bridgeport

Mammoth Lakes

San Francisco

Bishop

Independence

Lone Pine

SEQUOIA-KINGS CANYON NATIONAL PARK

Kennedy Meadows

395

Onyx

Lake Isabella

Tehachapi

Mojave

Agua Dulce

Wrightwood

Big Bear City

Los Angeles

Idyllwild

Palm Springs

Warner Springs

Mount Laguna

San Diego

Campo

N

The Pacific Crest Trail

Interstate Highway

US Highway

0   50   100   200   300   400

PREVIOUS SPREAD: The trail winds through thick chaparral in McCain Valley.
ABOVE AND OPPOSITE: The varied flora near Lake Morena, 20 miles north of the Mexican border.

Hauser Wilderness

One hour east of San Diego, California, and about eight miles from the Mexican border, the 7,547-acre Hauser Wilderness is the first of 48 wilderness areas northbound PCT thru-hikers cross. The trail cuts for less than a mile along the southeasternmost corner as it climbs up onto Morena Butte in the Laguna Mountains. Here you test your mettle on the first of many classic PCT climbs. With switchbacks the length of football fields rising above you, the exposed slope is a stairway to a 1,500-foot elevation rise. This is the southernmost wilderness area in California, part of Cleveland National Forest. Congress designated it as a wilderness area in 1984. Its steep, mountainous terrain, granite boulders, and chaparral comprise a quintessential Southern California landscape. Mule deer, golden eagles, and mountain lions make this place home, as do rattlesnakes and San Diego horned lizards. Think dry. There's very little water except for seasonal runoff.

OPPOSITE: Approaching a misty descent toward Hauser Wilderness. ABOVE: A velvet ant scurries along in Hauser Creek. FOLLOWING SPREAD: Snow blankets the high country in Cleveland National Forest (left); a cholla cactus grows in Rodriguez Canyon (right).

PREVIOUS SPREAD: There are more than 250 bighorn sheep in Anza-Borrego Desert State Park (top left); cholla and barrel cactus, framed by spiny ocotillo, thrive in the San Felipe Valley, Anza-Borrego Desert State Park (bottom left); the trail approaches Scissors Crossing (right). ABOVE: The famed Eagle Rock near Warner Springs. OPPOSITE: The PCT passes through a lush stand of oaks outside Warner Springs, about 100 miles north of the Mexican border.

Beauty Mountain Wilderness

A latecomer to the PCT wilderness family, Congress designated the 15,628-acre Beauty Mountain Wilderness in 2009. Until then, it was easy for PCT travelers to worry about threats to this vital landscape. You passed visible harbingers of encroaching development, including well-worn jeep roads and private lots with "For Sale" signs. Its namesake, 5,548-foot Beauty Mountain, with strange rock formations and stream-filled canyons, is a wildlife sanctuary and home to more than four dozen endangered, threatened, or declining species of plants and animals. Endangered species include the California gnatcatcher and the Quino checkerspot butterfly. It's also habitat for mountain lions, golden eagles, Cooper's hawks, prairie falcons, San Diego horned lizards, and northern red-diamond rattlesnakes, to name a few. The eastern boundary follows the alignment of the old California Riding and Hiking Trail and today's PCT.

OPPOSITE: Spring blooms across the desert in Beauty Mountain Wilderness.
ABOVE: Combs Peak, near Beauty Mountain Wilderness.

San Jacinto Wilderness

The San Jacinto Wilderness was
permanently protected with the original
Wilderness Act, signed by President
Lyndon Johnson on September 3, 1964.
In its 32,186 acres, split by Mount San
Jacinto State Park, terrain runs from
desert to alpine in dramatic fashion. On
the flanks of 10,834-foot San Jacinto
Peak, conifer forests shelter year-
round streams and lush meadows, a
destination for weekend backpackers and
horseback riders. In winter, boots and
saddles are replaced by cross-country
skis and snowshoes. At lower elevations,
chaparral abounds. The wilderness
includes Tahquitz and Suicide Rocks,
both world-famous rock-climbing areas
and popular day trips from the nearby
town of Idyllwild, California. Just more
than 28 miles of the PCT run through
the wilderness, and the trail drops an
astounding 8,000 feet in 20 miles as it
skirts to the west and then due north
of San Jacinto Peak into Snow Creek
and San Gorgonio Pass. The descent
is a rite of passage. It's not steep, but
it's agonizingly slow. You stare for hours
down to your first water in 20 miles,
which never seems to grow closer.

OPPOSITE: Footprints lead the way across Fuller
Ridge on San Jacinto Peak.

San Gorgonio Wilderness

Protected in the original 1964 Wilderness
Act and not far from metropolitan Los
Angeles, this is one of the most-visited
wilderness areas in the nation. Center stage
is 11,502-foot San Gorgonio Mountain,
the highest peak in California south of the
Sierra. Twenty miles of the PCT wind up its
eastern flanks. The 96,572-acre wilderness
is located in the southeast portion of the
San Bernardino Mountains mostly above
7,000 feet. It includes the Santa Ana and
Whitewater Rivers, fed year-round by
snowmelt. Still, while many streams tumble
out of its steep canyons, the extremely
long dry season means late-summer hikers
can have trouble finding drinking water and
this landscape is marked by fire. Dramatic
turns of conditions in this desolate and
beautiful place are commonplace. Bears,
deer, mountain lions, coyotes, and bighorn
sheep live here. Just more than 19 miles
of the PCT wind up Mission Creek in this
wilderness, once an oak-shaded sylvan glen.
But in July 2006, the Sawtooth Fire ravaged
the drainage. The following year, hikers
slept on ash, a mute testament to how fire
continually reshapes the landscape.

OPPOSITE: Rolling hills mark time in
San Gorgonio Wilderness.

Sheep Mountain Wilderness

Included in the California Wilderness Act of 1984, this 43,883-acre tract is a 90-minute drive from downtown Los Angeles. It's a popular recreation destination, but the ruggedness of this territory keeps it pristine. The alpine forests, streams, canyons, and pocket lakes provide a spectacular backdrop for hiking, camping, and fishing aficionados. Elevations range from 2,400 feet to more than 10,000 feet. Northbound PCT hikers make a huge zag west as they skirt the wilderness on the eastern and northeastern boundaries for fewer than two miles, with wonderful views of the San Gabriel Mountains, essential habitat for mountain lions, Nelson bighorn sheep, and the rare and endangered California condor. You may get lucky and see one of these majestic birds in flight as you walk the northern wilderness boundary high on 8,000-foot Blue Ridge. More likely, your thoughts will fill with visions of the approaching village of Wrightwood, California, 2,000 feet below, where town food, showers, and clean clothes beckon.

ABOVE: Hikers pause for shade in Sheep Mountain Wilderness. OPPOSITE: The PCT passes through high country in Sheep Mountain Wilderness. FOLLOWING SPREAD: Lupine and phlox on the ascent of Mount Baden-Powell (left); a gnarled limber pine shows its age near the Mount Baden-Powell summit (right).

Pleasant View Ridge Wilderness

Designated in 2009, the 27,040-acre Pleasant View Ridge Wilderness is a pristine transitional landscape. It is the north slope of the San Gabriel Mountains, falling from spectacular peaks to the floor of the Mojave Desert. The PCT crosses the wilderness for 10 miles, beginning a 120-mile stay in the high-desert foothills until it crosses Highway 138 and finally enters the Mojave. Whether on foot or horseback, descending out of this wilderness you must face the reality, and perhaps even dread, that it will be another 150 miles before you'll rise into another pine-forest sky island. In the desert, wildly changing conditions go from blistering hot to bitter cold, sometimes changing from one to the other on the opposite sides of a single sunset. The wilderness is aptly named, providing world-class vistas of the iconic San Gabriel range, a landmark, and, more importantly, a close getaway for millions of Los Angelinos. Along with Sheep Mountain Wilderness, it is included in the 346,177-acre San Gabriel Mountains National Monument, designated by President Barack Obama on October 10, 2014. Incredibly, these protected areas and the San Gabriels as a whole provide 35 percent of the Los Angeles region's drinking water.

OPPOSITE: Eastward from the PCT, the Mojave Desert stretches to the horizon. FOLLOWING SPREAD: The duff-covered trail on Mount Gleason (top left); yucca blooms heading north above Mallox Canyon (bottom left); Vasquez Rocks, famous for film appearances, just south of Agua Dulce (right).

Kiavah Wilderness

This 88,290-acre tract includes wildly divergent portions of the Mojave Desert, the Scodie Mountains, and the southern Sierra Nevada. You enter the wilderness, created as part of the California Desert Protection Act of 1994, on the PCT at Bird Spring Pass, and do not leave it until nearly 21 miles farther north at Walker Pass. Just before the five-mile descent into Walker Pass, you may glimpse the dust-veiled San Gabriel Mountains far to the south, and then scant strides farther along catch your first view of the Sierra Mountains circling Mount Whitney like King Arthur at his roundtable. This landscape showcases eroded rock formations, iconic clusters of shaggy Joshua trees, and a museum's worth of Native American heritage sites. There is a wide variety of plant life, such as piñon pine, juniper, live oak, and the ubiquitous chaparral, all of which shelters and feeds many animals, from mule deer, quails, and hawks to yellow-eared pocket mice, a variety of lizards, and small birds.

PREVIOUS SPREAD: California poppies in Antelope Valley, an old trail location now seven miles from where the PCT crosses Highway 138. OPPOSITE: Heading north, the trail approaches Walker Pass and the start of the Sierra Nevada. ABOVE: Chaparral for miles marks the PCT in Kiavah Wilderness.

Owens Peak Wilderness

Protected by the California Desert Protection Act of 1994, these 73,868 acres range over the rugged eastern face of the Sierra Nevada. Just under 30 miles of the PCT traverse the west side of the wilderness and the trail is a tease; one moment you're immersed in Sierra pine forests and the next you're surrounded by the scratch and prickle of sage scrub. After a dogged climb out from Walker Pass, you'll eventually be rewarded with views of Scodie Mountain to the south and Lake Isabella. Owens Peak, 8,445 feet, is the highest point. At the rare natural springs, Joshua Tree and Spanish Needle, you'll enter lush riparian areas. Creosote, yucca, cactus, and flowering annuals give way to the megaflora species such as cottonwood, juniper, oak, and pine. And the fauna is just as diverse as the plants. Golden eagles and falcons watch from above as mule deer, black bears, and mountain lions roam.

OPPOSITE: A large yucca blooms in Owens Peak Wilderness in the southern Sierra.

Chimney Peak Wilderness

Named for 7,994-foot Chimney Peak, this wilderness is surrounded on all sides by other wilderness areas—Domeland, Owens Peak, and Sacatar Trail—and is the smallest of the four by far at 13,140 acres. Pine forests dominate. The northern boundary has more bulges than a gerrymandered legislative district and the PCT crosses through two for a total of 2.6 miles. Chimney Peak Wilderness continues the rocky, mountainous landscape of surrounding areas. This is the northernmost wilderness area protected by the California Desert Protection Act of 1994. Springs and streams provide riparian habitat for many species, including black bears, bobcats, and mountain lions. The area is rich with native archaeological sites.

OPPOSITE: The PCT crosses rocky slopes in the southern Sierra Nevada wilderness areas near Chimney Peak.
ABOVE: A desert horned lizard hides in plain sight.

Domeland Wilderness

Rugged and dry, the Domeland Wilderness is aptly named since it sports an abundance of smooth, white-granite domes buttressing rocky ridges, hillsides, and granite spires. Once mostly hidden from the PCT by dense forest cover, today you'll find these sights in plain view. This is a result of the Manter Fire in the summer of 2000, when a majority of this wilderness burned, leaving 74,000 acres of leafless charred limbs and trunks. Elevations range from 3,000 to 9,730 feet and the wilderness remains a backcountry rock climber's paradise. The wilderness is in the elite company of those areas protected by the original Wilderness Act of 1964. Its original 62,695 acres were more than doubled in 1984 to protect sensitive transitional ecosystems to the east, south, and north. It is now 133,971 acres. The PCT crosses the wilderness for 13 miles, most of which follows the South Fork of the Kern Wild and Scenic River. The river has cut deep gorges with bold rock outcroppings interspersed with meadows and cottonwood trees. If you have time to linger, this is excellent trout habitat.

OPPOSITE: Fire-scarred remnants near Rockhouse Basin, nearly 700 miles north of the Mexican border.
FOLLOWING SPREAD: The gateway to the Sierra Nevada, Kennedy Meadows offers a respite and resupply point for weary PCT hikers.

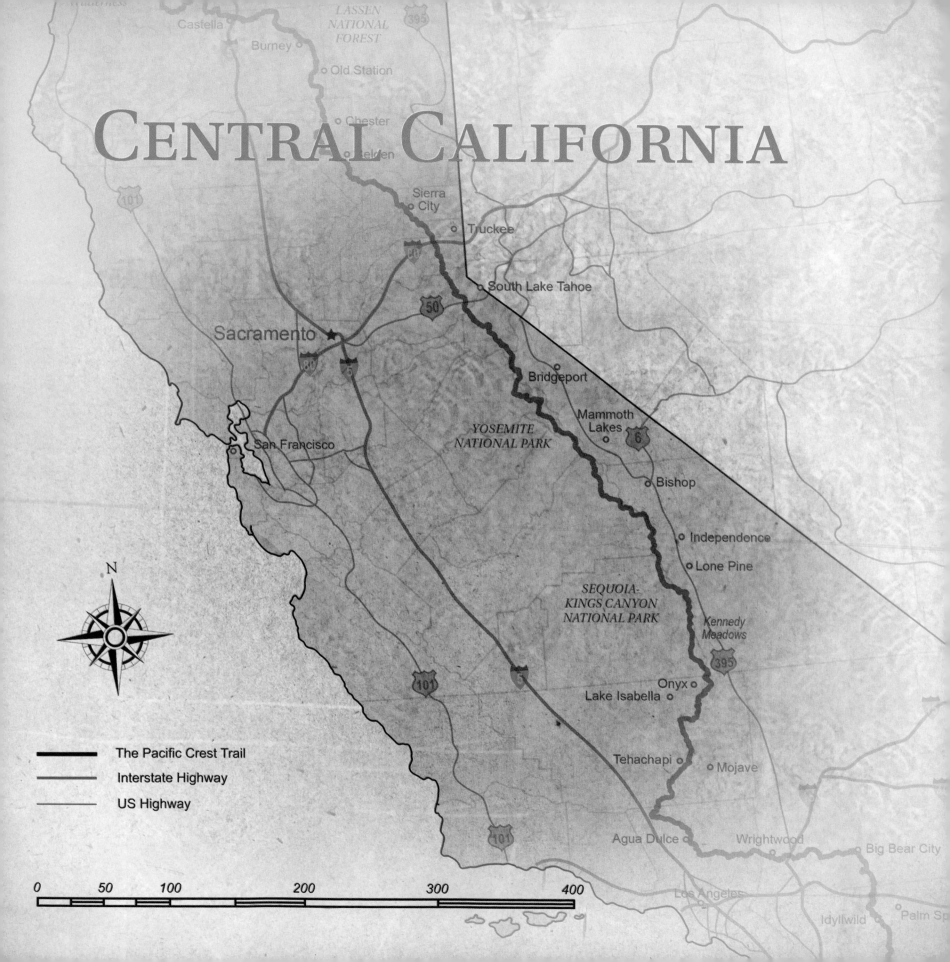

CENTRAL CALIFORNIA

Castella

Burney

Old Station

Chester

Helden

Sierra City

Truckee

South Lake Tahoe

Sacramento

Bridgeport

Mammoth Lakes

San Francisco

YOSEMITE NATIONAL PARK

Bishop

Independence

Lone Pine

SEQUOIA-KINGS CANYON NATIONAL PARK

Kennedy Meadows

Onyx

Lake Isabella

Tehachapi

Mojave

Agua Dulce

Wrightwood

Big Bear City

Los Angeles

Idyllwild

Palm Spr.

LASSEN NATIONAL FOREST

N

—— The Pacific Crest Trail

—— Interstate Highway

—— US Highway

0   50   100   200   300   400

South Sierra Wilderness

The gateway to the Sierra Nevada, the South Sierra Wilderness was designated in 1984. Its 62,700 acres hug the crest, spanning both the eastern and western slopes of the mountains. Your entry from the south at Kennedy Meadows is notable not only because the trail follows the South Fork of the Kern Wild and Scenic River, but also because most hikers and riders are carrying a new load of supplies. Also, bear country starts here and canisters to protect your food are required in many places ahead. The PCT runs just more than 20 miles across the wilderness in an efficient north-south transit. Both northbound and southbound travelers mark a major milestone here. It's either their first or last time crossing 10,000 feet in elevation. Abundant with diverse plant and animal life, the wilderness includes fragile meadows, forested ridges, rolling hills, and craggy peaks. Elevations range from 6,100 feet near Kennedy Meadows to 12,123 feet on Olancha Peak.

PREVIOUS SPREAD: Foxtail pines cling to life and granite at Trail Pass. ABOVE: Alpine Monache Meadows vies with Tuolumne Meadows for the title of largest in the Sierra Nevada. OPPOSITE: The Kern River cuts across a wide meadow in the southern Sierra.

Golden Trout Wilderness

This wilderness surely lives up to its name. Its 303,767 acres were protected by the Endangered American Wilderness Act of 1978 and include rolling forests and broad meadows ringed by rugged granite peaks. The colorful golden trout is the state fish of California and native populations still thrive here. This wilderness contains all of the Little Kern River's drainage as well as sections of the North and South Forks of the Kern Wild and Scenic River and 117 miles of smaller streams. It's an outdoor lover's perfect getaway. Anglers flock to the area and the raging North Fork is known for challenging multiday white-water rafting trips, which begin in the wilderness area. There are several hundred miles of exceptional backpacking and horse-packing trails, including almost 29 miles of the PCT.

OPPOSITE: A weathered juniper and snow-dusted Olancha Peak. ABOVE: A glassy Chicken Spring Lake in the Sierra high country. FOLLOWING SPREAD: Granite blocks and sunset at the top of Mount Whitney (top left); an icy tarn on the west slope of Mount Whitney (bottom left); hikers enter Crabtree Meadow, where conifers cling to life in the hardscrabble area near tree line (right).

Sequoia-Kings Canyon Wilderness

At 768,222 acres, this wilderness tips the scales as the largest on the PCT. Congress designated the area as part of the California Wilderness Act of 1984. This wilderness is largely synonymous with the now-merged Sequoia and Kings Canyon National Parks and is nearly surrounded by other wilderness areas. Spectacular to visit, here on 102 miles of the PCT you won't cross a single road as you stride through the heart of the High Sierra. A dizzying number of high peaks hugged by alpine lakes, wild resting meadows, and towering forests make this a place like no other. Kings Canyon splits the wilderness and rivals the beauty of Yosemite. The crest of the Sierra Nevada and the highest mountain in the Lower 48 states, 14,495-foot Mount Whitney, stand to the east. Many find the Mount Whitney summit irresistible and it is a well-traveled side trip for PCT hikers. Because of all this, the PCT and its sister trails are extremely popular. Make sure you check out the permit situation thoroughly and early.

OPPOSITE: Upper Rae Lake shows off the reason it is a destination for backpackers. ABOVE: Pinchot Pass, 12 trail miles north of Rae Lakes Basin. FOLLOWING SPREAD: Fin Dome towers over Rae Lakes Basin in Sequoia-Kings Canyon Wilderness. PAGES 216–217: Deer graze on the grasses of an upper basin, Sequoia-Kings Canyon Wilderness (left); Grouse Meadow (right).

John Muir Wilderness

Designated by the 1964 Wilderness Act, it's fitting that John Muir Wilderness was one of America's first official wilderness areas. In the late 1800s, California's mountains captivated Muir. He is considered one of the fathers of the idea of American wilderness and he fought especially hard for the protection of the Sierra, founding the Sierra Club in 1892. This 650,734-acre area is one he spent his lifetime exploring. Watch the sun rise or set on these peaks and you'll understand why Muir called the Sierra the "Range of Light." He urged others to venture into the wild, understanding that if more people could experience the splendor of the High Sierra, they too would be inspired to protect it. Here you can experience the largest contiguous area above 10,000 feet in the continental United States. Wildlife includes marmots, pikas, Clark's nutcrackers, golden trout, and black bears, and backcountry users are required to carry food in bear-proof containers. The wilderness is rugged and well traveled. This is the land of peaks higher than 12,000 feet, including 14,495-foot Mount Whitney. Canyons as deep as 5,000 feet and thousands of lakes and streams surround these granite towers. And the PCT basks in its splendor for 48 amazing miles.

PREVIOUS SPREAD: The PCT passes Wanda Lake (left); the Ritter Range towers above the Middle Fork of the San Joaquin River (top right); lodgepole pines ring Sally Keyes Lakes (bottom right). OPPOSITE: Marie Lake thaws at Selden Pass.

Ansel Adams Wilderness

The Ansel Adams Wilderness is the one with the most-photographed setting on the entire PCT. No PCT calendar is complete without a photo of Thousand Island Lake with the hulking massifs of Mount Ritter (13,143 feet) and Banner Peak (12,945 feet). Though the wilderness is now named for the famed photographer of Yosemite and the Sierra, when it was originally protected by the 1964 Wilderness Act, this 231,590-acre area was first called the Minarets Wilderness. The Middle Fork of the San Joaquin River flows from Thousand Island Lake, one of the largest backcountry lakes in the range. In 1984, the wilderness was renamed and enlarged to honor Adams, who in addition to his photography fame was an active Sierra Club member and helped organize the first Pacific Crest Trail System Conference in 1935. Adams's stunning black-and-white images brought a sense of this place to people far and wide, helping build support for wilderness protections that are in place today. Throughout the wilderness, there is evidence that for thousands of years native tribes gathered acorns, piñon pine nuts, and obsidian here, trading their bounty along routes that crisscrossed this beloved landscape. The wilderness includes just more than 24 miles of the PCT.

PREVIOUS SPREAD: The columnar basalt of Devils Postpile National Monument near Mammoth Mountain (top left); Rainbow Falls, Devils Postpile National Monument (bottom left); Tully Hole, Sierra National Forest (right).
OPPOSITE: Sunrise over Banner Peak and Thousand Island Lake.

Yosemite Wilderness

In 1864, 100 years before the Wilderness Act, President Abraham Lincoln set aside Yosemite Valley and the Mariposa Grove. While the Civil War raged, this was one of the first times that the federal government preserved an area for the people. In 1984, Congress designated 95 percent of Yosemite National Park as the Yosemite Wilderness, which is visited annually by millions from around the world. The wilderness, which includes 704,624 acres and 67.5 miles of the PCT, sweeps from Donohue Pass in the south to eminently swimmable Dorothy Lake in the north. Awe-inspiring granite cliffs and domes draw rock climbers and onlookers. West of the PCT, the accessible alpine landscape of Yosemite Valley is cut serenely by the Merced River. That landscape and the high, dome-laden expanse of Tuolumne Meadows offer countless jumping-off points for day hikers, horseback riders, and backpackers. Glacier-fed lakes feed streams and wispy waterfalls tumble and spill over rock formations. It's simply a place to see and be.

ABOVE: Hikers at Donohue Pass, the southern gateway to Yosemite Wilderness on the PCT. OPPOSITE: The Tuolumne River gently cuts the lush Lyell Canyon. FOLLOWING SPREAD: Lupine and the Tuolumne River below Lembert Dome in Tuolumne Meadows (left); deer grazing in Tuolumne Meadows (top right); marmot love (bottom right).

Hoover Wilderness

In this wilderness, near Kennedy Creek on the PCT, you feel a dramatic change. Granite is exchanged for lava. Peaks of gray-white jagged granite give way to slab-sided lava mountains. Rainbow-hued lichen brightens dark volcanic rock. This 128,124-acre area hugs the northeastern border of Yosemite Wilderness along the Sierra Crest. Despite steep, unforgiving cliffs that dominate tough terrain—elevations range from 7,000 to 12,000 feet—the area is popular among backcountry travelers and sees heavy use. It was established as a primitive area in 1931 and was among the many areas protected by the 1964 Wilderness Act. Its thin soils support no more than scattered groves of hemlock, pine, aspen, and cottonwood. The lack of timber means fires have been banned in the popular Twenty Lakes Basin above 9,000 feet. Wildflowers fill the meadows and black bears thrive. The PCT stays here for 11.3 miles.

OPPOSITE: The PCT approaches the southern edge of Hoover Wilderness.
ABOVE: Dorothy Lake sits just outside Hoover Wilderness.

Emigrant Wilderness

At the north end of this wilderness you might get your last views of the Yosemite highlands from the PCT before dropping to leave this tract at Sonora Pass at Highway 108, a possible resupply point. Like the High Sierra, alpine lakes, mountain streams, and deep canyons remain as dominant features in this 112,721-acre wilderness. Glacier-scarred rock is also evident. More than 200 miles of trails crisscross the area, including the PCT for more than four miles along the spine of the range, on the eastern boundary. The United States Forest Service first protected the area in 1931 and it won official wilderness status in 1975. Emigrant Pass is an important part of the West's history, as it was a major east-west route for settlers crossing the Sierra.

OPPOSITE: A view from the trail in Emigrant Wilderness.
RIGHT: Lake Harriet (top); a split granite bolder at Sonora Pass (bottom).

Carson-Iceberg Wilderness

It's not a real iceberg. The name comes from a granite formation along its southern boundary that resembles an iceberg. But it's the real Kit Carson. The Carson River in the wilderness was named after the famed 1800s scout and explorer. Entering the wilderness, northbound trekkers often experience a poignant moment: it's the last time on the PCT they will be above 10,000 feet. Either direction you travel you'll feel something's missing. For the 21 miles that the PCT runs the length of this wilderness there are almost no lakes, only Asa and Golden, two small hip-flask-size pockets. This wilderness is a spectacular chunk of rock, kept company by a dozen peaks rising above 10,000 feet and numerous others of lesser stature. The wilderness was designated in 1984 and includes 161,181 acres. The headwaters of the East Fork of the Carson River, the Clark Fork of the Stanislaus, and the Mokelumne River are located here. Jeffrey, sugar, lodgepole, and western white pines are prevalent, as are red and white firs. The 20.8 miles of the PCT are a small fraction of this tract's roughly 200 miles of foot and horse trails. For all these miles of trail playground, use is quite sparse compared with some of its neighbors. Think solitude.

OPPOSITE: Columns of volcanic basalt near Golden Canyon.

Mokelumne Wilderness

Here plant diversity reigns. Pronounced *moo-ka-la-mi*, this wilderness area brings together three distinctive botanic provinces in the Sierra. At summer's peak, the bush lupine and corn lilies are chest high and so dense that as you push through them you might even get grumpy. Created in 1964, Mokelumne Wilderness is 103,628 acres and rises from 4,000 feet near Salt Springs Reservoir to more than 10,380 feet at Round Top Peak in the north. Here again, think volcanic, not granitic. Mokelumne Peak is a fine example of the metamorphic rock pushed away by the rising Sierra's granite. Though wildflowers abound in late spring and early summer, the vast meadows dry up fast by summer, hence there's a campfire ban above 8,000 feet. The PCT crosses Mokelumne Wilderness for 16.2 miles.

OPPOSITE: The trail passes a grassy meadow and pond near Carson Pass.
ABOVE: The volcanic moonscape of the Eagle Creek area in Mokelumne Wilderness.

Desolation Wilderness

This beautiful, sparse, and high-alpine area is anything but desolate where humans are concerned. With nearby Lake Tahoe as a jumping-off point to the east, and access points on all sides, the area gets heavy use. There are more than 130 lakes dotted with campsites and for the entire PCT this wilderness is a contender for the top spot in mountain lake density. In all but the worst weather, shallow Lake Aloha will tempt you to pause for a swim. Designated as a primitive area in 1931, Congress upped its status to a wilderness in 1969. It's well worth a visit, so don't let the popularity scare you away. You'll draw a sharp breath more than once trying to take in a plethora of Kodak moments visible through the thin tree-line forests: jagged peaks, glacially formed valleys, and oh-so-many lakes. Elevations range from about 6,500 to almost 10,000 feet. The PCT crosses the wilderness for about 22 miles. Near perfection.

OPPOSITE: The three Velma Lakes—Upper, Middle, and Lower—sit at the heart of the serene and scenic Desolation Wilderness west of Lake Tahoe.
FOLLOWING SPREAD: Susie Lake offers yet another respite in Desolation Wilderness.

Granite Chief Wilderness

Edged alongside ski lifts and sweeping views of Lake Tahoe, this small wilderness, 25,111 acres, was designated in 1984 to preserve its beauty. Its glacier-carved valleys are filled with granite formations, fir forests, and inviting mountain meadows. Residents and tourists from Lake Tahoe access the area from a well-established system of trails, with 10.3 miles of the PCT weaving in and out of its eastern boundary. The PCT crosses the popular Five Lakes Basin, but you don't have to hike much farther along to find yourself in country that feels like the road less traveled. Elevations range from 5,000 feet in the valleys to 9,000-foot peaks. The northwest section of the wilderness is part of the French Meadows Game Refuge.

OPPOSITE: Rocky outcrops tower over the forests of the small Granite Chief Wilderness.
ABOVE: A large cairn along the trail.

NORTHERN CALIFORNIA

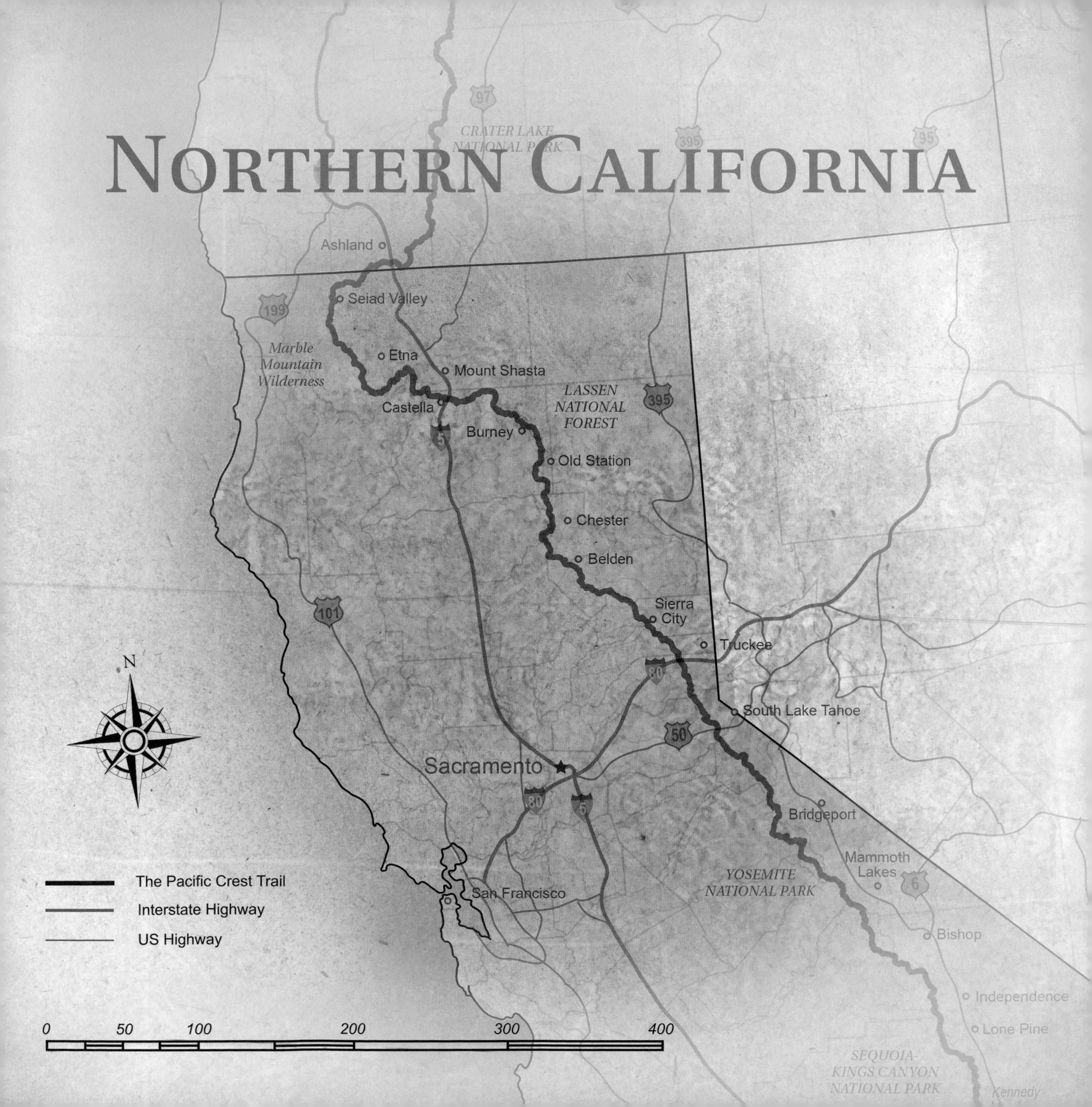

CRATER LAKE
NATIONAL PARK

Ashland o

Seiad Valley o

Marble
Mountain
Wilderness

Etna o

Mount Shasta o

LASSEN
NATIONAL
FOREST

Castella o

Burney o

Old Station o

Chester o

Belden o

Sierra
City o

Truckee o

South Lake Tahoe o

Sacramento ★

Bridgeport o

Mammoth
Lakes o

YOSEMITE
NATIONAL PARK

San Francisco o

Bishop o

Independence o

Lone Pine o

SEQUOIA-
KINGS CANYON
NATIONAL PARK

Kennedy

N

━━━ The Pacific Crest Trail

━━━ Interstate Highway

─── US Highway

| 0 | 50 | 100 | 200 | 300 | 400 |

PREVIOUS SPREAD: A windswept pine on Bunker Hill Ridge just north of Mount Etna. OPPOSITE: A natural rock arch near Lookout Rock in the Cascade Mountains. ABOVE: The PCT bridge over the Middle Fork of the Feather River.

Bucks Lake Wilderness

You'll dance as you sidestep your way through the PCT's longest stretch of poison oak on a six-mile, 4,000-foot descent Into tiny Belden, California. That's just one way you'll know that despite being part of the Sierra Nevada, you've left Central California behInd. This is officially Northern California. Another way you'll know is that you'll get your first views of Mount Lassen. Just more than 18 miles of the PCT course through this tract. Preserved in 1984, Bucks Lake Wilderness includes 23,710 acres. Elevations range from 2,000 feet in Feather River Canyon to 7,017 feet at Spanish Peak. Diverse vegetation—from brushy fields to oak and fir stands—offers northbound thru-hikers the variety of a break from the utter awesomeness of the High Sierra, yet this transitional landscape remains beautiful in its own right.

OPPOSITE: A lone pine on a ridge in Bucks Lake Wilderness.
ABOVE: Lichen-covered fir trees stand tall along the PCT.

Lassen Volcanic Wilderness

Noses wrinkle at Boiling Springs Lake just inside this wilderness boundary, while outside, a mile away, taste buds salivate at the thought of stopping for a gourmet meal at Drakesbad Guest Ranch. Designated in 1972, this wilderness includes 78,982 acres and is part of the 106,000-acre Lassen Volcanic National Park. A sliver of geologic time ago, Lassen erupted, flinging debris and volcanic ash and leaving a wide swath of destruction. That May 1915 eruption wasn't equaled on the West Coast until 65 years later when Mount St. Helens exploded. Today, Lassen Volcanic National Park is home to steaming fumaroles, hot springs, and sulfurous vents. This lava landscape hides many surprises, including meadows filled with wildflowers, thick forests of pine and fir, and clear mountain streams and lakes. At least 779 plant species have been identified here. Outside the wilderness area, the park includes 10,457-foot Lassen Peak, one of many inactive volcanoes. The PCT crosses in and out of the wilderness area for 12.5 miles.

ABOVE: The southernmost peak in the Cascades, Mount Lassen hovers in the eponymous national park. OPPOSITE: Volcanic steam rises along the PCT in Lassen Volcanic Wilderness. FOLLOWING SPREAD: Burney Falls, a popular attraction in McArthur-Burney Falls Memorial State Park (left); Hat Creek Rim is one of the driest stretches of the PCT (top right); Subway Cave, just half a mile off the trail, is a common side trip for PCT travelers (bottom right).

Castle Crags Wilderness

For the best part of a day you'll feel that you're scouting the perimeter of a vast granite fortress, but there's much more to Castle Crags Wilderness than this eponymous, amazing granite formation that reaches 7,200 feet and is visible from Interstate 5. These 10,609 acres, designated in 1984, are home to pine, fir, spruce, and cedar forests. Pitcher plants, with their cobra-shaped bells, trap insects for supper and more than 300 species of wildflowers have been identified here. One of these, the Castle Crags harebell, only blooms in this wilderness. Rattlesnakes, black bears, deer, and squirrels are as abundant as ticks. The wilderness, part of Shasta-Trinity National Forest, shares its southern border with Castle Crags State Park. The PCT crosses the wilderness for 15.5 miles.

ABOVE: A horseback rider climbs the PCT west of the majestic granite spires of Castle Crags.
OPPOSITE: Mount Shasta looms large from many points in Castle Crags Wilderness.
FOLLOWING SPREAD: The view of Mount Shasta from the Trinity Alps (left); moth (top right); columbine (bottom right).

OPPOSITE: Snow clings to the hillside in the Red Buttes. ABOVE: The serene alpine setting at Toad Lake, one of many lakes in Shasta-Trinity National Forest.

Trinity Alps Wilderness

Another of the California Wilderness Act of 1984 gems, this 537,360-acre wilderness (one of the largest in California) boasts high lakes, striking vistas, and 9,000-foot-high white-granite peaks that, to some, rival the High Sierra landscape in their beauty. Even amid all this beauty for hikers and riders alike, these 17 miles of the PCT can be maddening. Whichever way you're going, northbound or southbound, most of the time you are trending the opposite direction. This wilderness is a mere 50 miles west of Redding, California. It was formerly named the Salmon-Trinity Alps Primitive Area for the two Wild and Scenic Rivers, the Salmon and the Trinity, that are fed by 55 lakes. Virgin timber stands and large meadows known for wildflowers and butterflies flourish deep into summer. Black bears and other species thrive. As much as 12 feet of snow falls on the high country every year. At 17.2 miles, the PCT is a mere fraction of the 550 miles of trails that get hikers and horseback riders to amazing places with one thing in common—solitude.

ABOVE: A buck takes a break on the trail in Trinity Alps Wilderness.
OPPOSITE: The thriving Trinity Alps Wilderness high country.

Russian Wilderness

Gentle. Describing the 7.4 miles of the PCT that cross in and out of this wilderness, the venerable Wilderness Press PCT guidebook series uses the word "gentle" four times. One gentle ascent, two gentle descents, and a "gentle climb for about 15 minutes." More than one hiker has taken issue: it was a "strenuous half hour." The 12,521-acre Russian Wilderness spans the major ridge dividing the Scott and Salmon River drainages. Designated in 1984, it contains 22 lakes, most set in glacial bowls surrounded by granite peaks. This area is of national botanical significance because of the great diversity of trees and other plant species. There are 17 species of conifers here, probably more than anywhere else in the world. Elevations range from 4,000 feet to the 8,200-foot Russian Peak. It is not unusual for the PCT here to remain snow covered and difficult until well into the summer. Stock forage is limited, making pack trips a matter of tricky logistics.

OPPOSITE: Big Blue Lake, clogged with logs, is an oasis in Russian Wilderness.
ABOVE: "The Statue" is a landmark geological feature in Russian Wilderness.

Marble Mountain Wilderness

California's northernmost wilderness on the PCT is the 241,744-acre Marble Mountain Wilderness, a geologist's paradise. Alpine lakes—89 of them—meadows, and conifer forests surround its craggy formations and bare-rock outcrops, capped by Boulder Peak at 8,300 feet. Strangely named Man Eaten Lake, deep and a lustrous green blue, looks as if it migrated here straight out of the Sierra. It's close enough to the trail for a swim, but it's a 400-foot drop and scramble downhill. Some still yield to the temptation. The "Marbles," as the area is often referred to, was designated as a wilderness area in 1964. It's named for Marble Mountain, a bare red and gray formation of light limestone and darker metamorphic rock. Bald eagles and peregrine falcons are common overhead, and deer and black bears are also abundant. Wooley Creek and the North Fork of the Salmon River, both Wild and Scenic Rivers, run through, as do almost 35 miles of the PCT. This is a popular backpacking, fishing, and horse-packing destination, yet great opportunities for solitude also exist.

ABOVE: Well-made PCT tread climbs through the heart of the Marble Mountains.
OPPOSITE: Clouds float into Paradise Lake Basin, where snow still covers much of the trail.

OREGON

Seattle

Olympia ★

MOUNT RAINIER NATIONAL PARK

12

Goat Rocks Wilderness

97

○ Trout Lake

Cascade Locks

Mount Hood Wilderness

Portland

197   97

Salem ★

26   26

Three Sisters Wilderness

○ Sisters

20

20

97

CRATER LAKE NATIONAL PARK

395

95

Ashland ○

199

○ Seiad Valley

Marble Mountain Wilderness

○ Etna

Mount Shasta ○

LASSEN NATIONAL FOREST

Castella ○

Burney ○

395

Old Station

The Pacific Crest Trail

Interstate Highway

US Highway

N

0   50   100   200   300   400

Soda Mountain Wilderness

Welcome to Oregon! And get out your camera for famed Pilot Rock. Prominent, deep gray, and just off the PCT, this 5,908-foot volcanic plug unerringly guided the pioneers in their prairie schooners toward Siskiyou Pass. Designated in 2009, the 24,707-acre Soda Mountain Wilderness in southwestern Oregon is an important connective landscape in terms of biological diversity. You feel the tangible clash on its 4.8 miles of the PCT as eastern desert scrub meets tall fir forests and three mountain ranges collide. The Klamaths, the Siskiyous, and the mighty Cascades converge here. With the resultant varying landscapes, it's no wonder that it's a birder's heaven—more than 200 species have been identified here. And beyond that are the rare plants and a menagerie of wildlife, including a trifecta of megafauna: elk, cougars, and black bears.

PREVIOUS SPREAD: Ferns line the trail heading north into the Siskiyou Mountains. OPPOSITE: Fire is a natural occurrence and helps forests to rejuvenate and stay healthy. ABOVE: Aptly named Pilot Rock is a landmark for PCT travelers.

Sky Lakes Wilderness

Is it possible that there are more lakes than sky? It feels like it as you travel through the heart of this wilderness area and its three major lake basins that butt against the crest of Cascade volcanoes. Crater Lake National Park sits on the northern end of this 113,835-acre wilderness that was designated in 1984. Mount McLoughlin, at 9,495 feet, is the high ground. In the 1980s and '90s, the Environmental Protection Agency found some of these mountain lakes to have the most chemically pure water in the world. Shasta red fir, western white pine, mountain hemlock, and lodgepole pine surround the lakes, and older whitebark pine cling near the rugged summits of Mount McLoughlin and Devil's Peak. On a clear day you might spot Mount Shasta from the saddle just past Devil's Peak, an incredible 420 trail miles north of where you first spotted the snowcapped massif in California. Elk summer in the north, pine martens, fishers, black bears, cougars, coyotes, pikas, and golden-mantled ground squirrels thrive. The PCT passes all this splendor for just more than 40 miles and you'll likely have a hard time getting through it if you fall victim to temptation, stopping to swim at the many pristine lakes accessible from side trails and the old Oregon Skyline Trail near the PCT.

LEFT: Sweeping view from the summit of Mount McLoughlin (top); Snow Lake, one of dozens of alpine lakes in Sky Lakes Wilderness (bottom). OPPOSITE: Imported red cinder marks the trail through the lava fields below Mount McLoughlin on the shoulder of Brown Mountain.

Mount Thielsen Wilderness

One look and you'll agree that Mount Thielsen was aptly nicknamed the "Lightning Rod of the Cascades." The standout landmark in this 55,151-acre wilderness, the 9,182-foot needlelike volcanic plug towers over Crater Lake, which lies a few miles to the south. The PCT crosses the western shoulder of this wilderness for 25.2 miles. Congress designated this area 80 miles east of Roseburg, Oregon, as wilderness in 1984. Mountain hemlock, fir, and whitebark pine forests are thick and healthy here in a high-alpine setting flush with meadows and, in the spring, mosquitoes. Thielsen Spring, gushing from the ground clear and cold, provides the most refreshing and sweet drinking water on the PCT in Oregon, period. And this is one summit that's a relatively quick diversion for PCT thru-hikers and day hikers. It's doable, but steep. Make wise decisions.

PREVIOUS SPREAD: Sunset paints Crater Lake, part of Crater Lake National Park between the Sky Lakes and Mount Thielsen Wildernesses.
ABOVE: Mount Thielsen from nearby Tipsoo Peak in early October, a short side trip from the PCT.
OPPOSITE: The so-called lightning rod of the Cascades and its namesake Thielsen Creek, south of the trail.

Diamond Peak Wilderness

In 1920, within the present boundary of this wilderness, Fred Cleator made the first written record suggesting the PCT. Then he hiked 14 miles up and back from the summit of Diamond Peak—which might tempt you, too. This was once part of a boiling volcanic zone, ground swelling up, rising with the tumultuous activity of forming earth. Receding glaciers carved the mountain. Dozens of small lakes surround the peak as well, providing ample campsites for weekend backpackers and horse packers. Diamond Peak Wilderness covers 52,611 acres. The PCT meanders through it for 15.4 miles, begging hikers to stop and breathe.

OPPOSITE: Moonlit Diamond Peak.

Three Sisters Wilderness

One of the most spectacular places on the PCT, being here really drives home to visitors how volcanic activity shaped the landscape of the Pacific Northwest. The Sisters—South (10,358 feet), Middle (10,087 feet), and North (10,085 feet)—along with Broken Top (9,175 feet) and, outside the wilderness area, Bachelor Butte (9,068 feet) and Three Fingered Jack (7,844 feet), are nearly indescribable in their size and beauty. Snowcapped year-round, you'll feel beckoned ever onward along 53.1 miles of the PCT. Walking the pumice fields of the Wickiup Plains feels like being on a surreal moonscape. The wilderness was designated in 1964 and includes a whopping 283,630 acres, the second largest in the state. The Collier Glacier, between North and Middle Sister, one of 14 glaciers in the wilderness, is the largest in Oregon.

OPPOSITE: The sun rises over Elk Lake with South Sister in the background. ABOVE: Taken from the summit of South Sister, a moderately difficult day trip off the PCT, this photo showcases the views of Middle Sister and North Sister and other Cascade peaks in the distance.

Mount Washington Wilderness

It may be named for George Washington, but that's where the connection ends. The summit of this 7,794-foot volcano with its rock-hard lava core was stripped to a telltale point by glaciers and is surrounded by 75 miles of black lava fields, thick pine and hemlock forests, and a couple dozen lakes. If you are a Pacific Northwest mountaineer, this peak is on your bucket list. If you are a hiker, you might curse under your breath as the PCT traverses miles of ankle-biting lava. Designated as a wilderness area in 1964, its 54,452 acres provide ample cover for deer and other wildlife. For 13.3 miles, the PCT crosses the wilderness beginning at McKenzie Pass in the south. It passes Belknap Crater, a 6,872-foot cinder and ash cone that birthed the immense lava fields, before meandering west of Mount Washington and past several lakes.

PREVIOUS SPREAD: Obsidian Falls thunders its way to low ground northwest of the mountains in the well-used Obsidian Basin (left); Opie Dilldock Pass, another landmark in Obsidian Basin, with views of surrounding peaks (right). OPPOSITE: Mount Washington, another quiet volcano, from the shores of an unnamed lake. ABOVE: The moon rises over the Little Belknap lava flow and the Three Sisters, as seen from Mount Washington Wilderness.

Mount Jefferson Wilderness

Three national forests—the Willamette, Deschutes, and Mount Hood—meet in Mount Jefferson Wilderness, a hugely popular recreation area for nearby Portlanders. The 108,958-acre wilderness, designated in 1968, includes the must-see and high-use Jefferson Park, a lake-strewn plain on the northwest side of this picturesque, glacier-covered peak, which stands 10,497 feet tall. Named by Lewis and Clark in 1806, this peak is a formidable target of local mountaineers. In the south, Three Fingered Jack, a 7,841-foot decomposing volcano, greets PCT hikers as they begin a 37.6-mile trek north through the wilderness. Along the way you'll find alpine meadows, talus slopes, and more than 150 small lakes. The forests include Douglas and silver fir, mountain hemlock, lodgepole and ponderosa pine, and cedar. The wilderness borders the Warm Springs Indian Reservation.

PREVIOUS SPREAD: Two views of the slowly decomposing volcano, Three Fingered Jack, yet another Cascade summit within reach of the PCT. ABOVE AND OPPOSITE: Indian paintbrush carpets the landscape along the trail in Jefferson Park.

Mount Hood Wilderness

Just south of Mount Hood, the highest peak in Oregon at 11,240 feet, you'll feel like you are slogging through the world's longest sand trap. This dormant volcano towers over Portland to the west, providing a recreation beacon for millions of hikers, skiers, horseback riders, cyclists, backpackers, and Sunday drivers. The mountain hosts 11 glaciers and is climbed by more than 10,000 people annually, the most-visited snowcapped peak in the country. The wilderness includes 64,742 acres, and was designated in 1964. The PCT wanders for 17.9 miles through the wilderness past historic Timberline Lodge before circling the western flank toward the Columbia River, jumping in and out of glacier-fed canyons and past spectacular waterfalls and old-growth forests.

PREVIOUS SPREAD: Mount Jefferson reflected in Scout Lake (left); a shallow lake in Hunts Cove, visible from the trail in Mount Jefferson Wilderness (top right); huckleberry bushes turn with the fall in the Jefferson high country (bottom right). OPPOSITE: The PCT passes beneath the canopy of a typically lush and tall Douglas fir forest in Mount Hood Wilderness. ABOVE: Mount Hood rises high from Lolo Pass.

Mark O. Hatfield Wilderness

Named for the venerable former Oregon senator, the Mark O. Hatfield Wilderness butts against the Columbia River Gorge, leading northbound PCT hikers and horseback riders to grand views of the surrounding Cascade volcanoes and the milestone of the mighty river. Elevation changes are major, from 100 feet near the river to 4,900 feet on Mount Defiance. Cascading waterfalls prevail, including several on the popular Eagle Creek, whose accompanying trail is more beautiful, and therefore more popular, than the actual PCT for descending into the gorge. The PCT has nearly 14 miles in the wilderness area, designated by Congress in 1984. It includes 65,537 acres and is a special respite for Portland day hikers and weekend backpackers.

ABOVE AND OPPOSITE: The trail in the Eagle Creek drainage is one of the most popular alternate routes on the PCT because of its sheer beauty, including Tunnel Falls.

WASHINGTON

Glacier Peak
Wilderness

o Stehekin

Lake Chelan

Skykomish

o Seattle

MOUNT RAINIER
NATIONAL PARK

Olympia ★

Goat Rocks
Wilderness

o Trout Lake

Cascade Locks

Mount Hood Wilderness

Portland

—— The Pacific Crest Trail

—— Interstate Highway

—— US Highway

Salem ★

0   50   100   200   300   400

Three Sisters
Wilderness

PREVIOUS SPREAD: The PCT
crosses an elegant bridge
over the Wind River.
OPPOSITE: The PCT loops
through the lush growth
near Panther Creek in Gifford
Pinchot National Forest.

Indian Heaven Wilderness

Welcome to Washington! (And mosquitoes and huckleberries.) In late spring and early summer, the locals like to call this wilderness "mosquito heaven," but that doesn't keep them away. In late summer, ripe huckleberries are the big draw, sweet and abundant enough to stain lips and lengthen what you thought would be a "short break." It's a two-hour drive from Portland to many trailheads. By fall, when cooler nights prevail and the bugs go away, it really is paradise. The PCT crosses a forested plateau dotted with picturesque meadows and ambles past deep blue lakes for 13 miles. Its 20,784 acres were designated as wilderness in 1984. Deer and elk abound, and black bears gorge on summer's berry bounty, once a staple of several local tribes who hunted and gathered in this hospitable haven, or heaven.

OPPOSITE: The trail crosses the Sawtooth Berry Fields in Indian Heaven Wilderness. ABOVE: The route known as the Indian Race Track, where Native Americans met to harvest huckleberries and race their horses.

Mount Adams Wilderness

You'll feel like a giant is always looking over your shoulder as you tread the flanks of this wilderness's namesake volcano, a massive presence at 12,276 feet and the second-highest peak in the state. With 10 glaciers dressing its sides like white fox-fur stoles, it's popular, but it's remote, far enough away from the big cities that it feels like wilderness when one visits its forested slopes. It's a popular summit, with its relatively gentle south slope seeing much climbing and backcountry skiing activity. The Yakama tribe owns the east half of the mountain. The wilderness was designated in 1964 and holds 47,122 acres, including 19.8 miles of the PCT.

ABOVE: Horseback riders take off on the PCT near Mount Adams.
OPPOSITE: In late season, the openings on Mount Adams Glacier are evident from the PCT.

Goat Rocks Wilderness

Only one long trail is featured on a US postage stamp—the PCT. And the area featured is right here in this wilderness, the iconic razor-ridge Goat Rocks. Bookended by Mount Rainier to the north and Mount Adams to the south, the 108,023-acre Goat Rocks Wilderness is in a rare class of special places, even among wilderness areas. Designated in 1964, this place was formed by receding glaciers that scrubbed away an old volcano, leaving behind twisted and rocky terrain that includes pocket lakes and dense forests. Elevations range from 3,000 feet to 8,201 feet at Gilbert Peak. Pikas, marmots, deer, and elk enjoy the varied terrain, and mountain goats, with their wispy white beards, can be spotted up high. There are many trails into the wilderness from all sides, including 34.6 miles of the PCT. Ridgetop views of the Cascades and surrounding landscapes are world class.

OPPOSITE: The famed ridge hike in Goat Rocks Wilderness provides jaw-dropping vistas. ABOVE: A chipmunk sighting is all too common in the north woods.
FOLLOWING SPREAD: A cascading creek at Cispus Pass (left); pasque flower seedpods carpet a slope in Cispus Basin, Goat Rocks Wilderness (right).

William O. Douglas Wilderness

For 36 years, from 1939 to 1975, William O. Douglas was a Supreme Court justice. He also was a conservationist who loved wilderness and made frequent pilgrimages here. His childhood home was in nearby Yakima, Washington. This 168,956-acre wilderness was named as a tribute to his long public service. Congress designated the area in 1984. Old-growth fir, hemlock, and cedar rise to rocky ridges and there are dozens of lakes. Mount Rainier stands guard to the west of the wilderness and you'll have great photo opportunities to catch the peak lording over the treetops. The PCT snakes along the western edge of the wilderness for 23.6 miles, three times briefly straying into adjacent Mount Rainier Wilderness. The area is popular with horseback riders and there are dozens of welcoming trails for riding, one of Douglas's favorite pursuits.

ABOVE: A campsite surrounded by blooming lupine above One Lake in William O. Douglas Wilderness. OPPOSITE: The colorful canvas of Chinook Pass.

Mount Rainier Wilderness

Fifty miles southeast of Seattle and Tacoma, Washington, Mount Rainier National Park is world renowned for its beauty. Designated by the Washington Park Wilderness Act of 1988, its 228,480 acres are shadowed by the grand giant of the Cascades that tops out at 14,410 feet. Its 26 named glaciers are a training ground for mountaineers who aim to tackle the greatest peaks in the world. It's also an active volcano whose last significant eruption is estimated to have occurred in the mid-1800s. While the likelihood of an eruption is low today, scientists say such an event would be devastating because of the proximity of people living near the mountain and the amount of glacial ice trapped in its highest reaches. Regardless, the complex wilderness, with more than 300 lakes, hundreds of plant and animal species, and countless recreational opportunities, offers everything one would expect in pristine northwestern forests and more. The PCT enjoys all of this bounty at three separate points, snippets of the trail that total 3.6 miles.

OPPOSITE: A field of purple lupine guides the eyes to Mount Rainier on the southern edge of the wilderness. ABOVE: A hazy day in Sheep Lake Basin in Mount Rainier National Park.

Norse Peak Wilderness

You'll see firsthand the difference between eastern and western forests here, with the typical western stands of Douglas fir and lush, damp undergrowth giving way to drier larch, spruce, and pine to the east. Just outside the north wilderness boundary is the rarest of PCT trail sights, an actual shelter—named for forester Mike Ulrich, who died in 1957, this snug log cabin is complete with a wood stove, sleeping loft, and hooks to hang your gear away from the nosy mice. In an area of prevalent rain, you may find sleeping indoors a godsend. The American River separates Norse Peak Wilderness from the William O. Douglas Wilderness to the south. Norse Peak stands at 6,856 feet in the southern part of the wilderness, one of many jagged volcanic peaks in the area. Created in 1984 and encompassing 52,297 acres, it includes 13 miles of the PCT with three more that cling just outside.

ABOVE: A hiker climbs the PCT in Norse Peak Wilderness. OPPOSITE: Basin Lake beckons the weary below the PCT. FOLLOWING SPREAD: Fall colors delight through Snoqualmie Pass (left); the trail skirts a forested hillside in Alpine Lakes Wilderness (right).

Alpine Lakes Wilderness

Don't feel bad if you feel dizzy on the Kendall Katwalk. The PCT is a blasted narrow ledge and it has that effect on many after they enter this wilderness from Snoqualmie Pass. For this wilderness as a whole, think amazing, popular, and gorgeous. This area, set aside by the Alpine Lakes Area Management Act of 1976, includes high-alpine lakes and forests. And—some say—all this rivals anything you might find in the Sierra. This is what Congress had in mind when it labeled the PCT a national scenic trail. The terrain was formed by glaciers, which left deep pockets that now are filled with water. More than 700 lakes and ponds exist here. In its western reaches, 180 inches of rain falls annually, leaving hanging moss, mushrooms, and large-tree forests, while at the same time in the east there's a mere 10 inches of annual precipitation, leaving a landscape filled with sparse, dry ponderosa pine. Overuse has meant that a permit is required for visitors in several spots in the wilderness. But PCT thru-hikers with a long-distance permit are welcome for all 65.4 miles of the winding trail.

OPPOSITE: Waptus Lake is a mirror on a bluebird September morning in Alpine Lakes Wilderness.

Henry M. Jackson Wilderness

Together with Mount Shasta and Mount Hood, Glacier Peak is one of the iconic PCT summits, visible for many a trail mile. Entering this wilderness from Stevens Pass you see it for the first time after just 10 miles. This wilderness commemorates the conservation legacy of Washington Senator Henry Jackson. A hawkish democrat, "Scoop" Jackson was a force in wilderness preservation during his time in office (from 1943 to 1951 in the House and from 1953 until his death in 1983 in the Senate). The Cascades crest splits the 102,910 acres designated in 1984. Rocky crags and stone towers of the North Cascades rise from deep glacier-cut valleys, providing an endless playground for climbers and backcountry thrill seekers. For 29.4 miles, the PCT snakes through it all.

OPPOSITE: Lake Valhalla sits below a rocky peak in the North Cascades. ABOVE: Huckleberry plants frame the well-worn trail on the banks of Lake Valhalla.

Glacier Peak Wilderness

Copper mine or wilderness? The decision over this area was a knockdown, drag-out fight. "An Open Pit Visible from the Moon," trumpeted a Sierra Club ad in the 1960s *New York Times*. Kennecott Copper fought back, but in the end it was no match for Senator Henry Jackson's opposition and a protest hike led by Supreme Court Justice William O. Douglas. Today, Glacier Peak remains unmarred, snowcapped, and remote, one of the toughest volcanoes for peak baggers to climb in the Northwest. It stands 10,541 feet high, surrounded by high-alpine lakes and meadows, woodland forests, and icy creeks draining from all sides. The wilderness suffered one recent loss. In the 100-year storm of fall 2003, Kennedy Hot Springs, a must-stop PCT oasis, was destroyed in a mudslide. The PCT winds through the wilderness for 72.9 miles, affording a near 270-degree view of Glacier Peak if the weather stays clear. This huge wilderness was designated in 1964 with the original Wilderness Act and includes 566,050 acres.

ABOVE: A marmot takes a turn at sentry duty as the PCT approaches White Pass.
OPPOSITE: A sunrise lights the sky above Glacier Peak from a perch on Lost Creek Ridge.

Stephen Mather Wilderness

Protected by Congress in 1988, this rugged landscape is named for the conservationist and industrialist who helped lead the charge to create the National Park Service in 1916. In fact, Mather was appointed its first director in 1917 and served until 1929. What a fitting tribute, then, to name the wilderness that includes North Cascades National Park and the Ross Lake and Lake Chelan National Recreation Areas after him. Together, they total 634,614 acres. PCT hikers, as they walk in and out of the eastern corner of this wilderness for 17.2 miles, often are looking forward to or already carrying baked goods from the Stehekin Pastry Company on Lake Chelan, reputed to make the best cinnamon roll for the entire length of the trail. This is a place one could spend a lifetime of campfires getting to know.

PREVIOUS SPREAD: Mica Lake in Glacier Peak Wilderness (top left); a mossy bank of a creek near the Suiattle River (bottom left); expansive views of a long ridge in Glacier Peak Wilderness (right). ABOVE: The PCT rises to Cutthroat Pass in Stephen Mather Wilderness. OPPOSITE: The emerald pool below the crossing at Bridge Creek. FOLLOWING SPREAD: Sunrise highlights fresh snow on Mount Hardy near Methow Pass (top left); lupine at Rock Pass in the North Cascades (bottom left); snow blankets the PCT north of Harts Pass (right).

Pasayten Wilderness

This book's cover features the Pasayten Wilderness, another huge and rugged wilderness tract dedicated by Congress in 1968. It is 531,375 acres and runs along the United States-Canada border for 50 miles. Think peaks, spires, mountains, whatever—there are 150 of them that stretch higher than 7,500 feet. These muscle-cramping pinnacles in the western part of the wilderness "flatten" to forested plateaus in the east, where people can find plenty of solitude if they don't mind communing with deer, moose, mountain goats, bighorn sheep, gray wolves, and grizzly bears, not to mention the largest population of lynx in the Lower 48 states. Yeah, think wild, because it is. The 24.7 miles of the PCT are almost lost in the more than 600 miles of trails that exist here, including 73 miles of the Boundary Trail, part of the much larger Pacific Northwest National Scenic Trail.

OPPOSITE: October colors reign as the PCT skirts Tamarack Peak in Pasayten Wilderness.
ABOVE: A hiker walks on a snow-covered ridge near Three Fools Peak.
FOLLOWING SPREAD: The North Cascades dominate the sky on Lakeview Ridge.

EPILOGUE

IT'S CLEAR THAT THE PACIFIC CREST TRAIL IS THE COLLECTIVE SUM of many parts: beauty, preserving wilderness, and communing with nature among the most important. It's about saving the best landscapes America has to offer so generations to come have a sense of what was there before humans put their indelible stamp on the earth. And it's about searching deep within ourselves to find strength and determination.

But in our effort to tell you even a small part of how the trail came to be, the sacrifice, and, yes, the suffering that went into it, we came to another powerful conclusion: the trail is much more than a scratched-out path in the dirt.

The PCT is about people. It's about our connections to the trail and the land around it and, most importantly, to one another. It's about the very best of the concept of community. And it's there for all of us.

People have made a trail. Each one made a difference. Together, they shaped and changed lives by understanding and investing in the wonder that the trail brings, giving back to their community in immeasurable ways. In that spirit, we'd like to tell you one last story about a father and his remarkable young daughter.

Dave Foscue was a horseback rider who became a PCTA board member and, eventually, its president. His first encounter with the PCT was in 1972. Hiking with a friend in the North Cascades, he came across the PCT and realized he could walk to Canada. But his connection to the trail really began in 1991, when he and his son, Matt, rode their horses from the Columbia River to Mount Adams over a long weekend.

The following year, he and his wife, Ellen, attended the PCT Conference's annual meeting at Oregon's Timberline Lodge on a whim, with little knowledge of the organization or the breadth of the PCT project. He said his biggest impression from the weekend was the hotel hot tub.

Still, he knew, somehow, that he wanted to get involved. Eventually, he'd ride the entire trail. From 1991 to 1998, Foscue rode the PCT in sections with a variety of partners. By 1995, he was asked to join the board and stayed on until 2002. He served as board president for two years during this crucial period. He was there as membership increased, Bob Ballou was hired, and Alan Young's plan to turn the organization around took hold.

"The PCT is just a cool idea," Foscue said. "It's kind of strange that you can have unity around something that's 2,650 miles long."

Foscue spent his career as an attorney and superior court judge in Montesano, Washington, west of Olympia. His PCT rides started as a simple way to bond with his family. He and Ellen did the section from Mount Adams to White Pass. He eventually became one with his horse, Stub, as he rode most of Oregon and Washington alone. The California sections were tougher to conquer logistically speaking, but he made it happen with the help of friends and family.

OPPOSITE: A hiker atop Vasquez Rocks in Southern California.

In 1995, he and his daughter, Jessie, who was 26, did 700 miles in the Sierra, a tough route logistically and one that is also physically demanding. Jessie was born with Down syndrome. On that trip, she saddled her own horse, Dolly, and did almost everything that needed to be done in camp. She was an accomplished rider.

As they traveled north from Donner Pass, the snow became deeper and the animals struggled. Foscue decided to turn around and head back to Truckee, California. Heading south in the snow, Foscue's mount, Stub, stepped off the trail into deep snow and fell over. Foscue was pulling Ernie, a pack mule carrying supplies, and when he hit the ground he let go of the mule's rope. The mule bolted down the trail and Stub followed.

"Jessie rides up from behind and says, 'Don't worry, Daddy. I get 'em,'" said Foscue.

Foscue stood there in disbelief as his daughter took off before he could utter a word. He was responsible for her and the animals. But he didn't let panic get the best of him. He did the only thing he could do. He started walking, eventually reaching a spot on a hill where he could see in the distance.

There was Jessie, about a mile away. She had the mule under control and was grabbing for her father's horse. "That was the most embarrassing and proudest moment of my life," Foscue said.

Stories like this are amazing and limitless, both in quantity and for what they say about us as a community. There are far too many to tell. And they go on, each year building upon the last. Our community, our individual and collective connection to the trail, and our service to the very idea of it and what it provides us as citizens of the world are all the ultimate legacy of the trail.

We are bound to it. We are the Pacific Crest Trail.

Staff and Acknowledgments

PCTA Staff

Liz Bergeron, executive director and CEO; Mike Dawson, director of trail operations; Teresa Fieth, chief financial and administrative officer; Megan Wargo, director of land protection; Angie Williamson, director of philanthropy; Ryan Brizendine, web developer/system administrator; Daniel Carmin-Romack, *Communicator* design/production; Ellen Coyle, volunteer programs assistant; Shari Hansen, annual fund manager; Jack Haskel, trail information specialist; Bill Hawley, regional representative; Dana Hendricks, regional representative; Mark Larabee, managing editor; Anitra Kass, regional representative; Justin Kooyman, regional representative; Tammy Marsh, accounting specialist; Lanz Nalagan, development assistant; Ian Nelson, regional representative; Leslie Sabin, executive assistant; Jennifer Tripp, trail operations manager; and Mark Waters, associate director of philanthropy

PCTA Board of Directors

John Crawford, La Jolla, California, chair; Scott Jacobsmeyer, Round Rock, Texas, vice chair; Denise Gilbert, Portola Valley, California, secretary/treasurer; Priscila Franco, Ashland, Oregon; Chip Herzig, Yerington, Nevada; John Hoffnagle, Portland, Oregon; Barney Mann, San Diego, California; Tim McGuire, Carlsbad, California; Jim Newman, Rancho Santa Fe, California; Don Ralphs, Los Angeles, California; Tom Reveley, Bainbridge Island, Washington; Eric Ryback, St. Louis, Missouri; and Ken Schwarz, Corona del Mar, California

Acknowledgments

The authors would like to profoundly thank the following people for their effort and support in the production of this book: Sam Abell, Marian Alexander, Bob Ballou, Stuart Barker, Kate Beardsley, Tamara Belts, Liz Bergeron, Billy Goat, Beth Boyst, Roslyn Bullas, Deems Burton, Paul Cardinet, Cindy Carroll, Dave Cash, Lon Cooper, Mike Dawson, Monty Dodge, Nancy DuPont, Ralph Elle, Rod Farlee, "Meadow Ed" Faubert, Teresa Fieth, Pete and Joyce Fish, Dave Foscue, William Gray, Shari Hansen, Jack Haskel, Linda Jeffers, Jeff Jewell, Brian King, Justin Kooyman, Ron Krueper, Don Line, John Lyons, Barbara Marquam, Ann Marshall, Jim Miller, Kate Mollan, Marcus Moschetto, June Mulford, Ian and Amy Nelson, Dave Odell, Daniel Ogden, Doris Peddy, Steve Queen, Jim Richter, Bob Riess, Bill Roberts, Don Rogers, Hal Roth, Eric Ryback, Shirley Sargent, Forest Shoemaker, Carl Siechert, Susan Snyder, Joe Sobinovsky, Ruth Steele, Jerry Stone, Janette Storer, Lee Terkelsen, Barry Teschlog, Sam Tharp, Jeff Thomas, Jennifer Tripp, William Tweed, Angie Williamson, Glynn Gary Wolar, Valerie York-Watts, Alan Young, and Darlene Young.

A special thanks to Daniel Carmin-Romack for his tireless help with mapping and photography.

A special thanks also to all the professionals at Rizzoli International Publications for their hard work and support, especially Jim Muschett, Candice Fehrman, Susi Oberhelman, and Jessica Napp.

And especially to our wives, Carol Sim and Sandy Mann, with loving thanks.

PCT Resources

PCT Trail Towns and Other Important Resupply Stops

California
Campo, Lake Morena, Mount Laguna, Julian, Warner Springs, Idyllwild, Cabazon, Big Bear, Wrightwood, Acton, Agua Dulce, Green Valley, Lake Hughes, Tehachapi, Mojave, Onyx, Lake Isabella, Kennedy Meadows, Lone Pine, Independence, Bishop, Muir Trail Ranch, Vermillion Valley Resort, Mammoth Lakes, Tuolumne Meadows, Bridgeport, Kennedy Meadows North, Echo Lake Resort, South Lake Tahoe, Truckee, Soda Springs, Sierra City, Bucks Lake, Quincy, Belden, Chester, Drakesbad, Old Station, Burney, Castella, Dunsmuir, Mount Shasta, Etna, and Seiad Valley

Oregon
Ashland, Callahan's, Green Springs Inn, Hyatt Lake, Fish Lake, Crater Lake, Diamond Lake, Crescent Lake, Elk Lake, Sisters, Bend, Big Lake Youth Camp, Olallie Lake, Government Camp, Timberline Lodge, and Cascade Locks

Washington
Stevenson, Trout Lake, White Pass, Snoqualmie, Stevens Pass, Skykomish, Baring, Leavenworth, Stehekin, Mazama, and Winthrop

Canada
Manning Park

PCTA Regional Groups

Regional trail-maintaining groups are the bedrock of the Pacific Crest Trail Association (PCTA) and the backbone for the trail. These devoted volunteers adopt and regularly work on sections of the trail, keeping it maintained and passable.

When you're ready to volunteer, go to the PCTA website at www.pcta.org/volunteer to find up-to-date contact information and project schedules for the group in your area. The groups hold projects and trainings throughout the year.

Trail Gorillas, Southern California
The Trail Gorillas have adopted the PCT's southern 700 miles between the United States-Mexico border and Kennedy Meadows.

Can Do Crew, Southern Sierra, California
The Can Do Crew works on an approximately 30-mile section of the PCT between Donohue Pass in Yosemite National Park and South Crater Meadow in Ansel Adams Wilderness.

Carsonora Crew, Northern Sierra, California
The Carsonora Crew oversees approximately 84 miles of the PCT between Carson Pass and Sonora Pass.

Will Work for Krumms, Northern Sierra, California
Will Work for Krumms works on sections of the PCT throughout Tahoe National Forest.

Pounder's Promise, Northern Sierra, California
Pounder's Promise works from Tahoe National Forest through Plumas National Forest and into Lassen and Shasta-Trinity National Forests.

Lyons's Pride, Big Bend, Northern California
Lyons's Pride works on sections of the trail throughout Shasta-Trinity and Klamath National Forests.

NorCal Trail Crew, Big Bend, Northern California
The NorCal Trail Crew works on sections of the trail near Redding, California.

Southern Oregon Rockers, Southern Oregon
The Southern Oregon Rockers maintain approximately eight miles of the PCT on Mount Ashland.

Mid-Oregon Volunteers, Columbia Cascades, Central Oregon
The Mid-Oregon Volunteers maintain stewardship over more than 160 miles of the trail between Windigo Pass and Breitenbush Lake.

Mount Hood Chapter, Columbia Cascades, Central Oregon to Southern Washington
The Mount Hood Chapter oversees more than 200 miles of trail between Breitenbush Lake in Oregon and Goat Rocks in Washington.

White Pass Chapter, North Cascades, Central Washington
The White Pass Chapter tends to 70 miles of trail in William O. Douglas and Goat Rocks Wildernesses, which includes White Pass.

North 350 Blades, North Cascades, Central to Northern Washington
The North 350 Blades are charged with the care of the PCT from Chinook Pass to the northern terminus at the Canadian border.

Photography Credits and Sources

Contemporary Photos

The credits below feature some extra information about the photographers, including their favorite place on the Pacific Crest Trail and their current place of residence, formatted like this: name / favorite place on the trail / place of residence.

© **Deems Burton** / Cliff Lake, Marble Mountain Range / Happy Camp, California: front cover, pp. 95, 138, 205, 219 (bottom), 258, 262–263, 270 (bottom), 271, 292–293, 304–305, 322–323 (both), 324 (bottom), and 332.

© **Monte Dodge** / Goat Rocks, Knife's Edge / Manson, Washington: p. 83.

© **Aaron Doss** / Bighorn Plateau, Sierra Nevada Range / Richland, Washington: pp. 9 (left), 44, 81, 98–99, 156, 173, 176, 186–187, 188–189, 196–197, 209, 233 (bottom), and 312–313.

© **Tyson Fisher** / Glacier Peak / Silverton, Oregon: pp. 14–15, 72–73, 97, 103, 118–119, 137, 140–141, 153, 177, 202–203, 208–209, 210 (bottom), 224–225, 246, 254–255, 270 (top), 272–273, 276–277, 279, 285, 289 (both), 318–319, 324 (top), and 328–329.

© **Alasdair Fowler** / Glacier Peak Wilderness / Tulloch, Inverness-shire, Scotland: p. 300.

© **Ethan Gehl** / Kearsarge Pass, Sierra Nevada Range / Durango, Colorado: pp. 200–201 and 286.

© **Brad Goldpaint** / Ansel Adams Wilderness / Mount Shasta, California: pp. 1, 9 (middle), 75, 159, 164–165, 167, 168, 169, 174–175, and 292.

© **Vit Hradrecky** / Northern Washington State / Bishop, California: pp. 30–31, 180–181, 219 (top), 253 (bottom), and 324–325.

© **Paul Loofburrow** / Park Ridge, Mount Jefferson Wilderness / Portland, Oregon: pp. 39 and 275.

© **Barney Scout Mann** / Evolution Valley, Sierra Nevada Range / San Diego, California: endpapers (all photos), pp. 65 (right), 69 (right), 171, 307, and 327.

© **Caitlin Barale Potter** / Evolution Basin, Sierra Nevada Range / Seattle, Washington: p. 172.

© **Linda Rostad** / Fire Creek Pass, Glacier Peak Wilderness / Redmond, Washington: pp. 59, 91, and 122.

© **Brandon Sharpe** / Goat Rocks Wilderness / Chicago, Illinois: pp. 6–7, 163, 210 (top), 214–215, 268–269, 302–303, and 331.

© **Bart Smith** / Harts Pass, North Cascades / Lakewood, Washington: pp. 9 (right), 12, 19, 20, 53, 76, 117, 146, 174 (bottom), 187, 190 (both), 194–195, 199, 206–207 (both), 216–217 (both), 222 (bottom), 222–223, 232, 233 (top), 234–235, 237, 245, 247, 249, 252–253, 253 (top), 254, 260, 263, 264, 267, 274, 282–283 (both), 288–289, 290–291 (both), 296–297, 298–299 (both), 300–301, 308–309, 313, 314–315, 318, 320 (bottom), and 326–327.

© **Eric Valentine** / Goat Rocks / La Grande, Oregon: pp. 33, 92, 114, 278–279, 286–287, 306, and 310–311 (both).

© **Ryan Weidert** / Muir Pass at sunrise, Sierra Nevada Range / Westminster, Colorado: pp. 2–3, 26, 42–43, 60–61, 87, 94, 109 (left), 110, 134 (right), 145, 155, 170–171, 178–179 (both), 182–183, 184–185 (both), 195, 198–199, 211, 212–213 (both), 218–219, 220–221, 230–231 (both), 236–237, 248–249, 250–251 (both), 260–261, 264–265, 269, 284–285, 295, 309, 320 (top), 320–321, and 336.

© **Dean Young** / Mount Baden-Powell, San Gabriel Range / Los Angeles, California: pp. 190–191.

© **Paul Zaretsky** / Ansel Adams Wilderness / Aptos, California: pp. 4–5, 16, 78, 121, 130, 142, 150, 174 (top), 192–193, 222 (top), 226–227 (both), 228–229 (all), 238–239, 240–241, 242–243 (both), 256–257 (all), 259, 280–281 (both), 303, 304, 316, 317, and 335.

Historical Photos

Courtesy of The Bancroft Library, University of California, Berkeley (BANC MSS 71/295c Series 17): pp. 27 and 35 (left).

Courtesy of Roslyn Bullas: p. 65 (left).

Courtesy of Dave Cash: p. 107.

Courtesy of Frederick Cleator Papers, Collection No. Ax013, Box 5, Folder 5b, Special Collections and University Archives, University of Oregon Libraries, Eugene, Oregon: p. 23.

Courtesy of Monte Dodge: p. 82.

Courtesy of Ralph Elle: p. 47 (both).

Courtesy of Doug Gosling: p. 70.

Courtesy of Ron Krueper: p. 109 (right).

Courtesy of the LBJ Library: p. 54.

Courtesy of the Library of Congress: p. 18.

Courtesy of Ann Marshall: p. 100.

Courtesy of Marcus Moschetto: p. 36 (right).

Courtesy of June Mulford: pp. 48 and 51.

Courtesy of Bernadette Murray-Macioce: pp. 40, 57, 66, 67, 104, and 133.

Courtesy of Gordon Petrie: p. 36 (left).

Courtesy of Don Rogers: pp. 32, 35 (right), and 52.

Courtesy of Eric Ryback: p. 62.

Courtesy of the Shirley Sargent Collection, as used in *Solomons of the Sierra* (© 1989 Shirley Sargent): p. 21.

Courtesy of Jerry Stone: p. 134 (left).

Courtesy of *Sunset Magazine* / Sunset Publishing Corporation: p. 28.

Courtesy of United States Forest Service: pp. 38, 69 (left), 88, 113, and 160 (both).

Courtesy of Washington State Parks and Recreation Commission / Federation Forest State Park / No. 35.2010.1.1: p. 25.

Courtesy of Valerie York–Watts: pp. 127 and 128 (both).

Sources

The following people, organizations, and websites were instrumental in helping the authors compile information about the wilderness areas that appear in the gallery section of this book: Lon "Halfmile" Cooper; Friends of the River; National Park Service; Sierrawild.gov; United States Bureau of Land Management; United States Forest Service; Matt Volpert; Wilderness.net; Wilderness Press Pacific Crest Trail guidebooks; and The Wilderness Society.

PACIFIC CREST TRAIL
CANADA 1233 mi →
← MEXICO 1417 mi

P.C.T.
Cajon
Junction
EL 3000

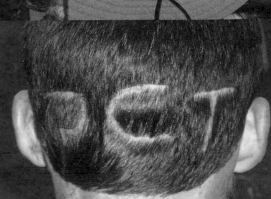